FREUD AND THE IMAGINATIVE WORLD

Harry Trosman, M.D.

FREUD AND THE IMAGINATIVE WORLD

Harry Trosman, M.D.

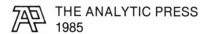 THE ANALYTIC PRESS
1985

Distributed by
LAWRENCE ERLBAUM ASSOCIATES, PUBLISHERS
Hillsdale, New Jersey   London

Distributed solely by

Lawrence Erlbaum Associates, Inc., Publishers
365 Broadway
Hillsdale, New Jersey 07642

Library of Congress Cataloging in Publication Data

Trosman, Harry.
   Freud and the imaginative world.

   Bibliography: p.
   Includes index.
   1. Freud, Sigmund, 1856–1939. 2. Psychoanalysis and
literature. 3. Psychoanalysis and the arts.
4. Humanism. I. Title. [DNLM: 1. Humanities.
2. Psychoanalysis—biography. WZ 100 F889T]
BF173.F85T74   1985   150.19′52   84-21533
ISBN 0-88163-028-4

Printed in the United States of America
10 9 8 7 6 5 4 3 2 1

Contents

List of Illustrations   ix

Preface   xi

Part I
The Claims of Humanism – Influence and Identity

1. Freud and the Formative Culture   3

2. Natural Sciences and Human Concerns   25

3. Modes of Influence on Freud's Creativity   50

4. Artistic and Neurotic Fantasy   70

5. A Claim Avowed: Freud's Jewish Identity   89

Part II
Psychoanalysis and the Arts

6. Freud's Style and the Matter of Style   111

7. The Psychoanalysis of Aesthetic Response   132

8. Comparative Views of Leonardo da Vinci
   and Psychoanalytic Biography   148

9. Psychoanalysis and Literary Criticism:
   Hamlet as Prototype   173

10. Psychoanalytic Views of Creativity   192

     Conclusion   211

     References   213

     Index   225

List of Illustrations

8.1 Jean Auguste Dominique Ingres,
   The Death of Leonardo da Vinci   150

8.2 Andrea del Verrocchio, *Baptism of Christ* 152

8.3 Leonardo da Vinci, *Mona Lisa*   156

8.4 Leonardo da Vinci, *Madonna and
   Child with St. Anne*   162

10.1 Michelangelo, *Tomb of Pope Julius II,*
   detail of *Moses*   194

10.2 Sigmund Freud, Drawings after
   Michelangelo's *Moses*   196

For Mardi
and the "Who's there" Cry of Players,
Elizabeth, Michael, and David

Preface

I have always found most stimulating the Freud who was primarily a clinician—but a clinician enlivened by the imagination of a creative writer. When Freud wrote about scientific matters, literary models guided his pen. He labored as a scientist, empirically forming and testing hypotheses, but he lived near Mount Parnassus, and he was refreshed by the Castalian spring. Steeped in the humanist tradition, he considered art a fundamental human activity. I am convinced he could not have given shape to psychoanalysis without capitalizing on his artistic leanings.

And yet Freud was not really "artistic." However great his literary skill, only for a brief period in his adolescence did he seriously consider a career as a creative writer. He was preoccupied with scientific and material truth. Although he found much to learn from poetic illusion, this illusion was distinct from the reality in which the conventional scientist was interested. The artist and the psychoanalyst worked with the same subject matter. But the commitment to imagination had to be limited, the artistic demon held in check.

This book is about Freud's link with the humanities. It rests on the assumptions that psychoanalysis is the product of a humanist tradition and that Freud's work extends and illuminates that tradition. In examining Freud's major theoretical and clinical writings, I look to their literary yield rather than their primary scientific contribution. His literary writings, on the other hand, are scanned for their clinical or theoretical formulations and their contributions to psychoanalysis as a science. Although I highlight Freud the humanist, it is my conviction that his work forms an integrated whole, bridging the distinction between art and science.

The sheer frequency and range of Freud's literary allusions emphasize the relevance of humanistic sources for the creation of psychoanalysis. Examples from literature, comments on art, literary quotations and citations are found in almost all of his writings, regardless of their subject matter or their direct link with literature. Indeed, Freud is unique as a scientist for the profusion of his literary references, and their range provides a valuable insight into the culture available to him. Although he had the highest regard for science, he also learned from novelists, dramatists, and poets. The transmission of ideas from the arts to science, and from psychoanalysis to art and literary criticism, the psychological processes mediating this transfer, and the effect of tradition on originality and creativity are the abiding interests of this study.

Freud's writings on art, literature, history, and aesthetic theory extended over the entire course of his psychoanalytic career. The correspondence from his pre-psychoanalytic days provides insight into the nature of his aesthetic preferences; his predilection toward humanist concerns appears even during the periods of neuroanatomical and physiological research. With the shift of his interest toward psychology in the 1890s, his published writings acquired a definitive literary stamp. The discussion of *Oedipus Rex* and *Hamlet* in *The Interpretation of Dreams* inaugurated a tendency that became characteristic of his writing style. Freud turned to literary allusions to buttress his scientific work, for he regarded the great themes of literature as valid data of universal accessibility, as valid indeed as actual case material. He was convinced that in the works of imaginative literature, as in case studies, one could uncover a repository of profound insights into human motives.

At first glance an examination of Freud's literary interests and writings may seem to concentrate on a secondary characteristic of his work. Freud saw himself as a scientist trained within a biological tradition and committed to observation as a methodological prerequisite. Yet it is no simple matter to tease out the sources of Freud's observations or the raw material for his theoretical constructions. In some instances, he used literature to substantiate his clinical material; in other cases, the literary sources take a position of priority; in still other cases, his own literary writings offer the best exposition of a psychological formulation.

It is particularly important to consider Freud's literary writings in the context of his simultaneous scientific preoccupations. At times he dealt with similar issues in a variety of genres. His monograph on Leonardo da Vinci, for instance, presented some of his earliest thoughts on the psychology of narcissism and homosexuality as he prepared to deal more extensively with these topics in the Schreber case. Here the literary work displays an insight in advance of his theory. In other instances, the literary piece is an "application" of discoveries from the clinical arena, as in the *Hamlet* section of *The Interpretation of Dreams*.

It is my belief that insufficient emphasis has been given to Freud's literary writings and interests. Only two works in German (Muschg, 1930; Schönau, 1968) and two in English (Hyman, 1962; Mahony, 1982) deal extensively with Freud's literary style. None has attempted a synthesis of the literary and the clinical, the artistic and the scientific. To reflect on the totality of Freud's work is to comprehend its organic unity.

My study is based on Freud's published writings in the *Gesammelte Werke* and *The Standard Edition*, various collections of his letters, Jones' biography, and other historical and biographical works. In addition, I have examined the Freud Library in London, which contains those books that accompanied him from Vienna to London in 1938 (Trosman and Simon, 1973). This collection by no means delimits the extent of Freud's reading. He was an omnivorous reader with wide interests, and his familiarity with many works cited in his published writings attests to a wider range than the contents of his library. Particularly under the circumstances of Freud's departure from Vienna, the current London collection cannot be considered to offer a comprehensive view of Freud's reading. Nevertheless, the library, with its many volumes on art, literature, history, archaeology, and anthropology, documents the breadth of

Freud's readings.[1] Even more, it provides insight into the intensity with which certain works were pursued. Although he was not a habitual annotator, Freud occasionally made selective markings in his books, especially if he intended to quote a passage in one of his own writings.

The influences on any writer are invariably subtle and not always understandable in concrete, measurable terms. There is little doubt that Freud was influenced by ideational currents, social and political factors, teachers and associates, the writings of others, his own life experience, work with patients, and a casual word here and there. To comprehend the impact of such influences on Freud, one must also consider the psychological experience of being influenced. How, for instance, did this affect his conviction about the importance of sexuality in the neuroses?

The second half of my study concerns the value and risks of applying Freud's views to our understanding of the arts. I am convinced that the benefits are great in the psychological study of aesthetics, biography, analysis of literary and visual works of art, and approaches to creativity. But I also believe that the psychoanalyst must refrain from wild speculation and become an expert in the artistic field being studied. Only then can the insights gleaned from clinical work be usefully applied, and only then will the two intellectual currents move closer together.

A work of such scope as the present study could not have been completed, let alone undertaken, without the support of others. The University of Chicago and its unique climate provided the set-

---

[1]Less informative, in terms of Freud's literary interests, is the Freud Library at the New York Psychiatric Institute. It consists of the remnants of the library left behind in Vienna in 1938, as well as a number of other volumes from other collections, which were added later. Often it is difficult to tell which books actually belonged to Freud. In contrast to the London collection, where many of the books are signed by Freud on the cover or flyleaf, only a few in the New York collection bear Freud's signature. In any case, none of the books in the New York collection that are clearly Freud's deal with art, literature, or the humanities in general; they are psychiatric, neurological, or psychological.

ting that allowed me to follow paths not well trodden by others. The Chicago Institute for Psychoanalysis was equally tolerant of interests that were not conventional and mainline. I am grateful to the Institute for permission to include material in Chapter 1 that originally appeared in the first volume of *The Annual of Psychoanalysis.* My colleagues at the Center for Advanced Psychoanalytic Studies, in Princeton and Aspen, were a continuous source of stimulation and intellectual camaraderie.

Anna Freud allowed me to study the Freud Library and art collection; I thus could literally see the extent of Freud's interest in literature and the arts. Ernest S. Wolf was helpful with translations, and I benefited greatly from our work together. Francis D. Baudry, John E. Gedo, Robert S. Liebert, and George H. Pollock read sections of the manuscript and made valuable suggestions. My editor, Paul E. Stepansky, was more than an editor. His knowledge of the field I was covering and his high standards have been a spur, and I owe him for many helpful suggestions. Lastly, Genevieve Curley has done an excellent job of transcribing the manuscript, and has quietly added her improvements as well.

PART I

The Claims of Humanism — Influence and Identity

1

Freud and the Formative Culture

It may be no exaggeration to claim that psychoanalysis "has detonated throughout the intellectual, social, artistic and ordinary life of our century as no cultural force . . . since Christianity" (Malcolm, 1981, p. 22) – a comparison Freud might well have found apt. If, indeed, psychoanalysis has had such an impact, it must have been seeded in rich soil, whose varied nutriments were remarkably energizing. This was the case. Although psychoanalysis was shaped primarily by one man and is even today best understood through his writings, Freud drew on a cultural background of great breadth and complexity. He managed to integrate a diversity of intellectual influences, and his work bears witness to his antecedents.

Attempts at a retrospective examination have already begun. Choosing to highlight the scientific nature of psychoanalysis, some have focused on how Freud's thought derived from the biological thought of the nineteenth century. Particular emphasis has been placed on what is loosely called "the Helmholtz School," the group that highlighted mechanical forces as expressed through physical and chemico-physiological processes (Bernfeld, 1949a, 1949b; Sulloway, 1979). Other investigations have traced the origins of Freud's thinking in the psychological thought of the day, specifically that of Herbart, Fechner, and Brentano (Dorer, 1932, Merlan, 1945; Jones, 1953; Barclay, 1959a, 1959b; Fancher, 1977). I propose to add components of the cultural and humanist tradition to which Freud was indebted.

Already in his pre-scientific days Freud was exposed to a broad
cultural and humanist tradition. His classical education provided a
complex substratum upon which universals concerning the human
mind could be tested. Through his interest in German literature
and particularly the writings of Goethe, he became conversant with
the romantic tradition and its regard for the irrational and unconscious. Although intrigued by the romantic concern with the powers of nature, he responded, not philosophically, but with an interest in observation. Vienna, his native city, provided an environment that did not interfere with this interest in observation and
even encouraged an openness and acceptance of learning and innovation. On a different note, from his early political aspirations, he
gained an attitude of independence and an unwillingness to bow to
authority, supplemented by the strength to tolerate prejudice and
opposition, as well as a tenacity that he associated with the Jewish
tradition.

These influences on Freud occasionally emerge as deliberately intended autobiographical remarks; more often they are revealed in a
context other than conscious self-disclosure. Indeed, such
unintended autobiographical fragments are more likely to divulge
humanist than scientific influences. As he considered the clinical
situation and examined his own psychological experineces, the literary tradition came readily to mind. His own work thus provides access to the intermingling of the personally significant and the imaginative world of the arts. The roots of this humanist influence lie
early in Freud's life, before he immersed himself in the scientific
work of Brücke's physiological laboratory during his early twenties.

The Impact of Romanticism

In the late eighteenth century, finding a universe increasingly
emptied of God, men of thought tried to fill the conceptual void.
They required some manner of accounting for order and energy, a
regulatory agency — preferably impersonalized and inoffensive to
empiricism. With the passing of a theological point of view and the

coming of romanticism at the beginning of the nineteenth century, Nature was credited with the power previously attributed to a deity.

As an adolescent, Freud showed an early interest in the study of nature. Yet this interest vied with another derivative of the romantic movement—the pull of revolutionary politics. The revolutions of 1848, the subsequent concessions to bourgeois demands, the tottering monarchies and stirring nationalist movements made a political career a promising choice for young men in the early 1870s. Nature and politics—the first a field for learning something of the world, the second a means for changing it—became the twin enthusiasms of the young Freud. In this, we see the impact of romanticism. Indeed, Trilling (1950) goes so far as to state: "Psychoanalysis is one of the culminations of the Romanticist literature of the nineteenth century" (p. 44). Beres (1965), too, points to common elements in the romantic tradition and psychoanalysis.

Romanticism as a current of thought stresses spontaneity and emotional expressiveness. As a stylistic movement in the history of literature and art, it can be viewed as a revolt against the neoclassicism of the late eighteenth century. Increasing concern was shown for ordinary people and everyday speech. Forms became more experimental, previously taboo themes were taken up, Nature and the individual were glorified, and a heightened emphasis was placed on passion and sensibility—as we find in Goethe's *The Sorrows of Young Werther*. A positive value was attached to the irrational; unconscious psychological processes were regarded as routes to higher truths. Man was seen as complex; his nature as conflicted and ambivalent. An appreciation for the value of early childhood experience and the conception of an unconscious, hidden nature were accompanied by a focus on imaginative over logical mental processes.

Historically, the romantic movement is associated with the political upheavals at the end of the eighteenth century. Both the American War of Independence and the French Revolution produced declarations of the rights of man. Concerned with human dignity, literary figures supported movements of national and personal liberation. The exploration of private mental states encouraged an interest in introspection, the dream, the uncanny, and the supernatural. "Feeling is all," stated Goethe. In its more extreme forms, romanticism led to suspicion and depreciation of reason, knowledge, and rationality.

The romantic movement gained impetus from German writers of the early nineteenth century, with whom Freud was quite familiar. The influence of the lyric poetry of Goethe and Heine, the writings of Jean Paul Richter and E. T. A. Hoffmann, of Herder and other folklorists, spread throughout Europe. Their view of Nature is expressed in a theme from Wordsworth (1798, p. 377):

> One impulse from a vernal wood
> >   May teach you more of man,
> Of moral evil and of good,
> >   Than all the sages can.

Although it is not my intent to highlight the romantic influence at the expense of the positivist and rationalist side of Freud's heritage, it can hardly be minimized. Freud encountered this literary and philosophic tradition not only in writings of German origin but generally in the half-dozen languages he read. The influence is clear with Goethe's German translation of Diderot's work, *The Nephew of Rameau*, which contains an explicit and unambiguous statement of the Oedipus complex. Freud quoted the passage several times: "If the little savage were left to himself, preserving all his foolishness and adding to the small sense of a child in the cradle the violent passions of a man of thirty, he would strangle his father and lie with his mother " (1916–1917, p. 338). Diderot's suggestion of a hidden element in human nature and the dangers in blunting the emotional life are also prominent in the writings of Byron—another author Freud read (Jones, 1953, pp. 55–56; Reik, 1968, p. 648).

The romantic influence even permeated the psychiatric writings of the nineteenth century (Ellenberger, 1970a, pp. 210–215). Indeed, it was in part as a counterromantic reaction against over reliance on poorly conceptualized and vaguely understood subjective states that psychiatry moved into a more organic and objectively descriptive phase in the second half of the century (Zilboorg and Henry, 1941).

In its excesses, romanticism tended toward one-sided repudiation of rationality and reason, a rejection of all artistic norms, a glorification of force, and a revival of pantheism. The latter became identified with *Naturphilosophie* and the German philosopher Schelling. But most significantly, the romantic movement produced an essential shift in the mentality of the nineteenth century by changing previously held views of nature.

On Nature

What is nature? Nature may be characterized as anything that exists, anything apprehended by the senses but not created by man. In its simplest sense (omitting capitalization), nature refers to landscape and the world of growing things—to mountains and valleys, trees, grass, flora and fauna. Nature (often capitalized) also denotes the creative and controlling force of the universe. Nature is distinct from culture and society, if not opposed to both. It may be benign or indifferent to man, but also cruel and attacking. Occasionally, man-made artifacts such as castles and cathedrals, which have some initial charm or beauty and show the ravages of time, are considered a part of nature. The ruins of Tintern Abbey in the eyes of Wordsworth became transformed into a natural object.

To the romantics, the natural state was simultaneously primordial and the fullest expression of man's being; a growing person's subsequent involvements with the world were anticlimatic, if not corrupting. Civilized man could only strive for the reattainment of original unity with natural forces. The *Naturphilosophie* promulgated by Schelling supported a belief in the indissoluble unity of natural and spiritual forces. Nature, it was suggested, could not be understood in terms of mechanical or physical concepts. The visible, organic world arose from a common spiritual principle, a world soul, which produced matter, living nature, and the human mind.

At the risk of casting too wide a net, one may note links between the ideas of the romantic philosophers and more abstract theorizing in psychoanalysis. *Naturphilosophie* affirms a law of polarities, stipulating a dynamic interplay between the antagonistic forces that govern natural phenomena. This dualistic principle finds an echo in the bipartite instinct theory of psychoanalysis.[1] The notion of a primordial state followed by a series of metamorphoses evokes the genetic and developmental approaches. To the romantic philosopher, the unconscious is a true bond linking man with nature and permitting an understanding of the universe through mystical ecstasy or dreams.

A romantic interest in Nature appears early in Freud's development. He stated that his choice of a career as a natural scientist was decided at seventeen, after he heard Goethe's essay on Nature read at a public lecture.[2]

> Nature! [exclaimed Goethe]. We are surrounded by her and locked in her clasp: powerless to leave her, and powerless to come closer to her. Unasked and unwarned she takes us up into the whirl of her dance, and hurries on with us till we are weary and fall from her arms. . .
>
> She has thought, and she ponders unceasingly. . . . The meaning of the whole she keeps to herself, and no one can learn it of her. . . .
>
> She has placed me in this world; she will also lead me out of it. I trust myself to her. She may do with me as she pleases. She will not hate her work. I did not speak of her. No! what is true and what is false, she has spoken it all. Everything is her fault, everything is her merit [1782, pp. 207–213].

---

[1]Bernfeld (1944) and Jones (1953) regard "the solemn oath" sworn by du Bois-Reymond and Brücke when they embarked on their scientific careers as prototypical for the mechanistic school in which the young Freud learned the rudiments of science. Yet even this program pledges scientists to investigate "matter, reducible to the force of attraction and repulsion," thus recalling the duality of *Naturphilosophie* (Jones, 1953, pp. 40–41). Cranefield (1966) has called attention to the romantic underpinnings of Brücke's teachings.

[2]Or at least it was assumed by many that Goethe had written the essay. In actuality, the ideas were Goethe's but were recorded by a Swiss theologian, Tobler, in a conversation with Goethe. Years later, Goethe incorporated Tobler's essay into his collected works, believing it was his, since the ideas were so consistent with his own line of thought (see Freud, 1925a, pp. 8–9, n. 4).

The essay is a challenge to uncover the hidden secrets of Nature, to find knowledge through a pantheistic mysticism. Man is powerless and submissive. Nature is pictured as an omnipotent mother — unfathomable, creating and destroying, changing and eternal. No one can comprehend her fully, and love is the only means of even partially understanding her.

Although Freud's initial enthusiasm for science soon suffered because he felt he could not find an arena in which to use his natural gifts (1925a, p. 9), he never lost his enthusiasm for the Goethe essay. More than twenty-five years after first hearing it, he referred to it as *unvergleichlich schön* (incomparably beautiful) (1900b, p. 443).[3] By this time, however, he had begun to see additional meanings in the Nature of the essay. He cited a patient whose mental illness was attributed to the reading of Goethe's essay. The young man, who cried "Nature! Nature!" and later castrated himself, was referring, stated Freud, to the sexual sense of the word.

Freud's references to Nature are extensive. Echoing Goethe, he wrote of the secrecy of Nature. Discovering the sexual etiology of neuroses, he told Fliess: "I have the distinct feeling that I have touched one of the great secrets of Nature" (1887–1902b, p. 83). Elsewhere, he announced that it is one of the "constraints of Nature to which mankind is subject," in that procreation is entangled with the satisfaction of the sexual need (1898, p. 277). Leonardo da Vinci's interest in Nature was viewed as a sublimation for the kindly mother who nourished him (1910b, pp. 122–123). In another context, Nature was credited with keeping love fresh and guarding it against hate (1915, p. 299). Further, Freud combined Nature with the power of Eros, the power to create and multiply life. Our bodily organism thus becomes a minute part of the superior power of Nature. "Oh, inch of nature," he quoted without recalling the source, in reference to the helpless infant at birth (1930a, pp. 86, 91, 121; Reik, 1968, p. 648).

---

[3]Poorly translated as "striking" in the *Standard Edition* (1900a, p. 440). Kaufmann (1980) suggests that Freud might well have been put off by the effusive style had it not been for the content of the essay.

But Nature, for Freud, was also cruel and terrorizing. The task of civilization was to defend us against Nature, which brought earth-quakes, floods, storm, diseases, and death. Man first responded to the inexorable power of Nature by humanizing what he had little control over. When he found, however, that the natural forces con-formed to independent and autonomous law, these forces lost their human traits. They were the Moira (Fates) above the gods (1927, pp. 15–19).

Perhaps one of the most revealing references to Nature occurs in a repeated misquotation. Commenting on the advisability of not deceiving patients about their terminal illnesses, Freud stated, "Shakespeare says: 'Thou owest Nature a death'" (1887–1902b, p. 276), counseling submission to the inevitable. The quotation, a remark of Prince Hal's to Falstaff from *Henry IV, Part I*, actually reads: "Thou owest God a death." Freud made the same error on two subseqent occasions, once in association to a dream, later referring to the belief that death is the necessary outcome of life (1900a, p. 205; 1915, p. 289). He thus partially impersonalized and deanimated those forces to which man must submit, deprived the powers of their masculine identity, and removed the conception from a religious framework.

The idea of God was too close to a conception of a regulatory agency – tied in Freud's mind to obedience to authority and adher-ence to the will of an arbitrary father. A deity was not observable and thus not subject to examination and study. Nature, on the other hand, was eminently observable, feminine, and thus less threatening. In addition, there was the hope that an immersion in the world of Nature would increase man's storehouse of truth.

Thoughts concerning Nature accounted for the immutable in the human condition. Nature might be a source of endless fascination, a font of wisdom and creativity; still, man could do little but submit to its inexorable laws or fend off its destructive effects. Politics, on the other hand, dealt more with the man-made and so held out the promise, at least during Freud's adolescence, of bringing about inci-sive changes. As a boy of six, Freud recalled, his mother rubbed her hands together to show him we are made of earth. When he saw the blackish scales of epidermis, he acquiesced in the belief of our inevitable return to Nature (1900a, p. 205). But as a boy of eleven or twelve, he shared in the hope of social reform promised by the first bourgeois ministry formed after the ratification of the new Austrian constitution in 1867. Indeed, until a few months before entering the university in 1873, he aspired to a political career, and even after matriculation he maintained his political interests.

On Politics

In the latter half of the nineteenth century, Vienna was the capital of a quasi-feudal state. The Austro-Hungarian empire was a polyglot collection of Czechs, Magyars, Germans, Croatians, and Slovaks; few of its inhabitants thought of themselves as distinctively Austrian. But the "German spirit" of high culture and social humanism was admired by the German-speaking intelligentsia, and the monarchy felt threatened by political movements that promoted closer ties with Germany.

It is interesting to consider Freud's choice of career as a reaction to the bankrupt Liberal political culture of nineteenth-century Vienna. For a time, the Liberal middle class—devoted to the values of advanced German thought but not to a German nationalist ideal—was dominant. Several of the Liberal cabinet ministers in the government of 1867 were Jews who, by and large, adhered to the values of the progressive German-speaking bourgeoisie (Freud, 1900a, p. 193). One of their number, admired by Jakob Freud and the eleven-year-old Sigmund, was J. N. Berger. He contended that "the Germans in Austria should strive not for political hegemony but for cultural hegemony among the peoples of Austria." They should "carry culture to the East, transmit the propaganda of German intellection, German science, German humanism" (Schorske, 1967, p. 343).

Although the bourgeois ministry of the 1860s urged a program of liberal reform and attempted to mitigate the power of the upper classes, the net result was failure. It did not succeed in unifying the divergent national elements within the Austro-Hungarian empire, nor could it control the explosive lower classes. Instead, claims Schorske, "the liberals unwittingly summoned from the social depths the forces of a general disintegration" (1967, p. 344). New anti-liberal and anti-monarchial mass movements, including Czech nationalism, Pan-Germanism, Christian Socialism, Social Democracy, and later, Zionism, stood ready to replace an ineffectual and short-lived spirit of moderate liberalism. Although morally committed to supporting the rights of minority groups within the empire, the German-speaking middle class realized that any concessions to Bohemia and Moravia would weaken their own power and create disorganization. By the mid-1870s, the academic intellectuals – both students and faculty – were prepared to give up imperial stability and middle-class oligarchy for the promise of unifying German nationalism. But under the influence and eventual leadership of Georg von Schönerer, a racial ideologue, the German nationalist movement in Austria became progressively illiberal and totalitarian. In 1878 Schönerer declared in the Austrian Reichsrat: "If only we belonged to the German Empire!" The next year he began to show his anti-Semitic leanings and railed against "the Semitic rulers of money and the world." In 1882 Schönerer raged at the "sucking vampire . . . that knocks . . . at the house of the German farmer and craftsman" – the Jew (Schorske, 1967, pp. 351–352).

Schönerer's anti-Semitic appeals held a strong attraction for the Austrian lower classes, who were inclined to blame their economic ills on Jewish capitalists and their more proximate representatives, Jewish peddlers. The artisan, who had previously made and sold his product in his own home, was now replaced by the itinerant peddler, who went from house to house developing his own clientele. Schönerer's anti-Semitism, however, was largely motivated by internal needs; it was one manifestation of an intrapsychic disturbance that culminated in social ostracism and a jail sentence when he physically attacked a political opponent. But the advantages of using prejudice to organize latent social discontent were not lost on others.

A few years later Karl Lueger made use of the anti-Semitic feelings of the lower classes for opportunistic political purposes. Unlike Schönerer, he was a man of some culture and charm, and he was less swayed by intense psychopathology. Five years after Schönerer's introduction of anti-Semitic sentiment into the German nationalist movement, Lueger began to use it as a focus to organize the Christian Socialist party. Pan-Germanism became of less interest to Lueger when he had collected a sufficient majority of Viennese artisans to lead him to political victory as mayor of Vienna in 1895. Schorske (1967) states that the last stronghold of Austrian liberalism may well have been the emperor's refusal to ratify Lueger as mayor on two occasions before he was finally forced to do so in 1897. The Fliess correspondence informs us that Freud broke a temporary smoking fast to celebrate this autocratic action of the emperor against Lueger on the first occasion in 1895 (1887–1902b, p. 133). Lueger's anti-Semitism lacked the rancor of Schönerer's, and he apparently modulated it by treating some Jews with favor. "Der schöne Karl," as Lueger was known, became famous for his statement of flexible anti-Semitism. "I will decide who is a Jew," he asserted.

But let us return to an earlier phase of Freud's life. From 1873 to 1877, during his early university days, he belonged to a German nationalist group, the *Leseverein der deutschen Studenten* (which, after several years, was disbanded through governmental pressure because of its anti-Austrian leanings). The association attracted young Viennese such as Freud who were interested in political change and who were Germanic in sympathy. Germany was regarded not only as the seat of an advanced nationalism but also as a haven from an oppressive and outdated oligarchy (McGrath, 1967).

While still at the Gymnasium, Freud seriously considered a political career, and until the spring of 1873 he planned to study law as a preparatory step. Much later, he stated that Heinrich Braun, his inseparable friend of the time, had awakened in him a host of "revolutionary feelings" (1873–1939a, p. 379). During his early adolescence, these competed with his budding scientific interests.[4]

---

[4]Freud eventually lost touch with Braun, though Braun is referred to in the associations to the "Count Thun" dream as one of his school fellows who "seemed to have taken Henry VIII of England as his model" (1900a, pp. 211–212). Braun married four times and later had a distinguished political career. It is noteworthy that the dream association concerns a revolt against an unpopular schoolmaster. Although Braun was the moving spirit in planning the revolt, the leadership in the assault was left to Freud.

It is ironic that the political movement of German nationalism, which was originally associated with freedom from the Austrian yoke, shortly became repressive and baldly anti-Semitic. In the 1870s it had represented the highest aspirations of students like Freud, who saw in the movement toward Pan-Germanism closer links with the culture of Goethe as well as a more genuine expression of their political identity. Indeed, the adherents, many of whom were young Jews, saw alliance with Germany as a socialist goal. The students of Freud's generation, in contrast to their fathers (for whom German nationalism was no positive objective), were radicalized through their pride in German culture. In the *Leseverein*, the subject of student discussion frequently revolved about the manner in which the "stable bourgeois world of their liberal fathers could best be overturned" (McGrath, 1967, p. 185).

Bismarck's creation of a united German empire in 1870 had given a sense of reality to the aspirations of the German-speaking students at the University of Vienna. Freud's *Leseverein* took Schopenhauer, Wagner, and Nietzsche as ideational leaders. It was believed that a new and artistically vital culture, opposed to the excessive rationalism of the past, had to be created. Political activity was to appeal to the integrated man and not regard his rational aspect as more important than his emotional side. Freud's friend Braun was elected to office in the *Leseverein* and participated actively over several years. In 1877 Braun was one of the joint signers of a letter to Nietzsche declaring devotion to his outlook and offering to follow in the wake of his criticism of liberal society. Yet it is doubtful whether Freud's own active interest continued much beyond his first years at the university. Even in an early heated discussion with Viktor Adler, the subsequent leader of the Austrian Socialist party—which probably occurred at a meeting of the *Leseverein*—he was already nonpolitical, "full of materialistic theories" (Freud, 1900a, p. 212). Soon he was to become totally immersed in scientific activity.[5]

---

[5]Of interest, however, is the fact that Freud's subsequent teacher, Theodor Meynert, whom he initially followed with "deep veneration," was an active participant in the *Leseverein* and frequently lectured to the membership on psychiatry (Freud, 1900a, p. 437; McGrath, 1967).

By the 1880s, when anti-Semitism had become an ingredient of German nationalism, Freud had disassociated himself from political goals. His membership in the *Leseverein* terminated in 1877, a few years before it was prohibited by government edict. But it is likely that his interest had already waned the previous year when he entered Brücke's laboratory and for the first time felt that he had found his niche (Freud, 1925a, p. 9).

Interestingly enough, we hear of an appeal to the remnants of Freud's nationalistic interests several years later. In 1885, Freud had come to Paris to study with Charcot at the Salpêtrière. One evening at a gathering at the home of Charcot, the French neurologist Gilles de la Tourette baited Freud by predicting a ferocious war between France and Germany. Freud promptly countered that he was a Jew and aligned himself with neither Germany nor Austria. That evening he wrote Martha that he found such conversations very embarrassing for he felt something German stirring within him. However, he immediately added, he had long ago decided to crush such stirrings (1873–1939a, p. 203).

Life in Vienna

In spite of the political ferment, several observers are united in the belief that the vitality of Vienna in the last half of the nineteenth century fostered a spirit of creativity (Zweig, 1943; Sachs, 1944; Barea, 1966; Schick, 1968–1969). On the other hand, Gay (1978) and Kaufmann (1980) are inclined to minimize the importance of Vienna per se as an influence on Freud, pointing out that Freud identified with a broadly based German culture, of which Vienna was only an outpost. Nevertheless, the city had a character all its own. Intellectual values were highly prized; learning was treasured; art and science were idealized. "There is hardly a city in Europe where the drive toward cultural ideals was as passionate as it was in Vienna," affirms Stefan Zweig (1943, p. 12). A country that for centuries had been politically expansionist now found itself unsuccessful as a military power and looked for supremacy on artistic levels.

This striving for excellence was not, however, characteristic of the totality of the educated classes. The Austrian ruling class, the old aristocracy of the emperor's court, the seat of German Catholicism, had settled for the status quo. They were content to practice their casual refinements and enjoy their intellectual sluggishness. Instead, the drive toward scientific and artistic supremacy took hold in the flourishing middle class, and it was fostered by the city's assimilation of divergent people and cultures. Jews who had lived peacefully in Vienna for two hundred years – although without full civil rights until 1867 – took on the sponsorship of art supported by the aristocracy in earlier generations. "Nine-tenths of what the world celebrated as Viennese culture in the nineteenth century was promoted, nourished or even created by Viennese Jewry," claims Zweig (1943, p. 22). Nor did these Viennese Jews see their artistic production as specifically Jewish. Mahler and Schönberg in music; Hofmannsthal, Schnitzler, and Beer-Hofmann in literature; Max Reinhardt in theater – all saw themselves as European or Viennese rather than Jewish.

"What spirit engendered such a concentration of creative powers in Vienna?" asks Schick (1968–1969, p. 531). He inventories the surrounding idyllic landscape, the well-planned educational system, the profundity of wit, the peculiar Viennese vacillation in prizing both reality and fantasy, and the simultaneous enjoyment and cynical disparagement of the creature comforts. But to catalog such factors and attempt to apply them to Freud leaves a sense of dissatisfaction, particularly when we consider the lack in Freud's basic outlook of any fin-de-siècle world-weariness. Antithetical to Freud's sense of the tragedy of the human condition is the well-known Viennese epigram: "the situation is hopeless but not serious."

Perhaps we do best if we consider creative activity operating in opposition to ongoing ideational currents. Freud had something like this in mind when he discussed the influence of his native city on his thought. He ridiculed the belief that psychoanalysis owed its character to the alleged sexual looseness of Vienna. What he suggested was that the crucial factor regarding locality might well be the degree of openness with which observations were permitted. Here

Freud, who generally was disparaging of Vienna, pointed with favor to his milieu. The Viennese, he believed, were less embarrassed and less prudish regarding sexual relationships than Northern or Western European city dwellers (Freud, 1914b, p. 40). Cultural life was not characterized by hypocrisy; there was little dissembling for its own sake or in the interest of so-called higher cultural aims. Indeed, Hanns Sachs, also no great lover of Vienna, made a similar observation, although he remained firm in the conviction that "the allegation that Vienna had put her stamp of origin on Freud's work is a hollow pretense" (1944, p. 19).

The Jewish Tradition

A more vital matter concerns Freud's link with the Jewish tradition. Although he discarded any adherence to religious belief or ritual, he never repudiated his Jewish identity. In later life he acknowledged that his early familiarity with the Bible had had "an enduring effect" (Freud, 1900a, p. 97, p. 334; 1925a, p. 8). In his early attempts to find Semitic military heroes for idealization, he freely and incorrectly attributed a Jewish identity to Napoleon's general, Masséna, and valued the link with the Carthaginian Hannibal as a fellow member of an alien race (Freud, 1900a, pp. 196–198). He believed it unworthy and senseless to deny one's Jewish identity at a time when baptism to Christianity was by no means uncommon (Bakan, 1965, p. 46). Being a Jew, he believed, prepared him to take a position of solitary opposition against a compact majority (Freud, 1925a, p. 222); it enabled him to be free of prejudices, repudiate arbitrary authority (Freud, 1926a, p. 274), and respect intellectual values (Bakan, 1965, pp. 48–49; Freud, 1934–1938b, p. 115).

The experiences of Freud's family of origin were typical of the lot of the Central European Jew. Toward the middle of the nineteenth century, with the new freedom permitted in traveling, Jews in search of economic opportunity began to infiltrate the Central European cities from the eastern countryside. The first-known traces of the Freud family were in Lithuania; the family then moved to

Galicia. Freud's father and mother were both born in Galicia and had moved to Přibor in Moravia by the time Sigmund was born. When he was three they moved to Leipzig for a year before settling in Vienna.

In the towns of Central Europe the ancient laboring guilds were inadequate to cope with the needs of expanding populations. Hence Jews with commercial experience drifted from region to region as needs arose for the transmission of goods and services. "Many remained petty tradesmen looking for opportunity, always hopefully expecting something to turn up but rarely finding security," indicates Handlin (1967, p. 165). Freud in later life described his father in similar terms.

In view of the uncertainty of the political and economic situation, and in response to emancipation, a secular education became an enthusiastically sought-after prize. Handlin points out that Jews who emigrated to America before 1900 showed no such eagerness for schooling. "In Austria and Germany, by contrast, the university became the object of young people's ambition. . . . In this society *Bildung*—the possession of defined cultural symbols—carried with it a status that could partially compensate for the disadvantages of affiliation with a minority discriminated against for centuries" (1967, p. 165). Suddenly, the generation of Jews of which Freud was a member was precipipated into Western society and modern life. The attempt to wrestle with the problems of their new secular lives at times led to great feats of creativity and innovation.

Commenting on the mode of thought transmitted through the Jewish tradition, Handlin states:

> The insistent confidence that an orderly arrangement of the universe made all phenomena susceptible to rational comprehension was characteristic of a people whose culture, for centuries, had stressed the need for interpreting every particular action and event in the light of the Divine purpose of creation. The sense of divinity was no longer immediate for those whose outlook was increasingly secular; but the sense of purpose and meaningfulness remained even for those who had moved away from traditional modes of thought [1967, p. 168].

In assessing the significance of his Jewish background, Freud tended to designate a broad cultural attitude rather than systematic Judaic knowledge or specific content. Although Abraham pointed out to him the "Talmudic" nature of his thought, nowhere do we see any real familiarity with the Talmud or any citations from it (Freud, 1873–1939a, p. 153; Freud and Abraham, 1907–1926, p. 36). Freud was of course deeply interested in Moses and particularly identified with the Jewish military leader. But specific Jewish sources for his thought do not stand out.

Although Freud did receive some religious instruction in his boyhood, his liberal teachers attached no great value to knowing the Hebrew language and literature (Freud, 1925b, p. 291). What he acquired in childhood, he soon lost, describing himself as "ignorant of the language of holy writ" in his Preface to the Hebrew translation of *Totem and Taboo* (1930c, p. xv).

Bakan (1965) bases his supposition that Freud was influenced by the Jewish mystical tradition on similarities between psychoanalysis and the Kabbala, citing particularly the similarity in techniques of interpretation and the importance both attach to sexuality. He also points to Freud's interest in numerological discussions and his concern with discovering hidden meanings in "trivialities." Further, he proposes that Freud's interest in law was related to his interest in becoming a rabbi, and quotes from a Jewish scholar who claimed that he had discovered the Zohar and other books on Kabbala in Freud's library in Vienna. As if to minimize disagreement, Bakan suggests that Freud was interested in dissembling the mystical influence and took steps to cover his tracks so that this would not be discovered.

Bakan's evidence is not impressive. He fails to distinguish the Jewish mystical tradition in terms of its unique attributes, and he acknowledges that there are many similarities between Jewish mysticism and other cultural movements of the time, such as romanticism. His interpretations are poorly supported, as, for example, when he suggests that the pseudonym "Dora" for one of Freud's patients is a cover for the word "Torah"! We have far greater evidence that Freud was interested in the law as preparation for a political career rather than the rabbinate. The argument that Freud was interested in hiding such mystical influence because he feared rejection by the scientific community is contradicted by Freud's openness on his Jewish identity throughout his writings and the pride he took in establishing links with his past. Moreover, in my perusal of the Freud libraries in London and New York, I found no literature dealing with the Kabbala or any significant collection of Judaica.

Nevertheless, in attempting to evaluate factors in Freud's cultural background, it is best not to dismiss readily a possible source of influence. Freud himself came to believe that his interest in the significance of numbers was related to an unconscious incorporation of Jewish mysticism. In a letter to Jung of 1909, he remarked:

> Some years ago, I discovered that I had the conviction I would die between the ages of 61–62. . . . It all began in the year 1899, when two events occurred simultaneously; first I wrote *The Interpretation of Dreams*, and second, I was assigned a new telephone number – 14362. A connection between the two could easily be established; in the year 1899, when I wrote *The Interpretation of Dreams*, I was 43 years old. What more natural, then, that the other numbers should refer to the end of my life, namely, 61 or 62. Suddenly, there was method in the madness. The superstition that I would die between 61 and 62 showed itself to be the equivalent of a conviction that I had fulfilled my life's work with *The Interpretation of Dreams*, didn't have to produce anything further, and could die in peace. You will admit that with this knowledge the thing no longer sounds absurd. . . . You will find confirmation here, once again, of the specifically Jewish nature of my mysticism [Jung, 1961, pp. 361–363].

Reference has already been made to the affinity between the Jews and the Germans in the nineteenth century. German culture in its universalist form, as exemplified by Goethe and Schiller, provided emancipated Jews with a ready source for involvement in the Western ideal. A Jewish writer of the 1880s wrote:

> To no other people have the Jews grown so close as they have to the Germans. They are Germanized not only on German soil, but far be-

yond the German boundaries. . . . There must be correspondence in the basic disposition of the two people which made Germany and all things German particularly attractive for the Jews, and the Jews an especially useful complement to the German character [Kahler, 1967, p. 24].

The special attraction of the Jews for "all things German," their love for the language, the literature, and the land, is illustrated by an anecdote years later. In the 1930s, after the German writer Erich Maria Remarque had emigrated, a Nazi official tried to woo him with the promise of much honor if he would return to Germany. When he refused, the Nazi said, "Are you not a bit homesick?" "Homesick?" Remarque replied. "No. I am not Jewish" (Kahler, 1967, p. 33).

Freud responded to German culture, and he even admitted, in his letter to Martha from Paris, he felt the Teutonic tug. But he was not submerged by the attractions of national identity. His identity as a Jew kept him from a narrow chauvinistic allegiance. By his mid-twenties, anti-Semitism had clearly cast its shadow over nationalist aspirations and Freud was fully taken up with his scientific life.

Freud's Classical Education

If romanticism led Freud in the direction of nature and politics, and the Jewish tradition prepared him for opposition, his classical education exposed him to universals in the Western tradition. By "classicism" we denote certain values characteristically revealed in the literature and art of Greece and Rome. The essential elements were filtered through the neoclassical revival of the eighteenth century; subsequently the emphasis was placed on restraint, order, serenity, and repose. Classicism has come to stand for the ideal over the real, the abstract over the concrete, reason and intellect over the emotions. But, in actuality, the affective part of life was not neglected by the ancients.

Sterba (1969) has pointed out the intense humanistic bent in the classicism of antiquity. Although order and integration were valued, there was no slighting of instinctual life and the pleasure-seeking components of the personality. Freud wrote of the glorification of instinct among the ancients in contrast to the modern idealization of the object (1905b, p. 149, n. 1). Commenting on the importance the Greeks assigned to the dream, he intimated that he was following in the footsteps of the dream interpreters of antiquity (1916–1917, pp. 86–87). Generally, Freud, whose knowledge of classical writings and art was extensive, turned to classical antiquity to illustrate the power of irrational instinctual forces more than qualities of order, control, and integration.

Freud's secondary school education took place in the classical Gymnasium with its heavy emphasis on Greek and Latin (Sterba, 1969; Knoepfmacher, 1979). Under the influence of educators and humanists such as Alexander and Wilhelm von Humboldt, European education had rediscovered classical antiquity at the beginning of the nineteenth century. The humanistic tradition, developed during the European Renaissance, found its contemporaneous form in the university preparatory schools of the nineteenth century. Universalism, order, and harmony were to be arrived at through exposure to the highest levels of Western thought, as exemplified by the classical ideal. The formal discipline acquired by the mind in the mastery of the rudiments of the literature and languages of Greece and Rome would carry into other modes of thinking and provide a basis for an educated outlook.

Along with reverence for the classical ideal were other side effects from the Gymnasium experience. The teachers were usually ambitious men of learning and ability who saw themselves advancing in scholarly careers. It was not unusual for universities to recruit their faculty from the classical Gymnasium, and many scholarly papers were the products of teacher and pupil collaboration in the secondary school. The classical Gymnasium became the prestige school, identified with the attainments of the "educated man." The author who wrote for readers educated in the classical Gymnasium could leave Latin and Greek quotations untranslated. Robert Waelder described the culture shock following his arrival in the United States when he discovered that educated men could not be relied upon to understand Greek and Latin quotations (Sterba, 1969, p. 437).

The curriculum of the classical Gymnasium called for hard work and skill in languages. After a two-year preparatory period in Latin, which Freud began at nine, he was assigned Livy's *History of Rome*. Freud also read much of Ovid's *Metamorphoses*, with its poetic rendering of many of the Greek myths. The writings of Sallust, the Roman historian; Cicero's *Orations*; Virgil's *The Aeneid*; Horace's poems; and Tacitus' *History* rounded out a rather full exposure to Latin. In Greek, Xenophon's *Anabasis* and *Cyropaedia* familiarized Freud with the Greek struggle with the Persians. In Herodotus he read of the death of Darius, Xerxes' invasion of Greece, and the Battle of Thermopylae. Demosthenes' orations, Sophocles' *Ajax* and *Antigone*, Homer's *Iliad* and *Odyssey*, and Plato's *Apology* and *Crito* were read in the original Greek over a period of almost six years.

Did these readings leave an impression? Freud refers on several occasions to *The Aeneid*. Not only does he use a quotation from it as the motto for *The Interpretation of Dreams*, he recalls with ease Dido's curse on Aeneas when it is forgotten by a young man described in *The Psychopathology of Everyday Life* (1901, pp. 8–11). In contrasting the classical reverence for instinct with the modern repudiation of instinctual life, he doubtless falls back on Plato, Ovid, and perhaps Catullus. Freud first read of the favorite hero of his youth, Hannibal, in the pages of Livy. The assigned portion of the *History of Rome* covers the Second Punic War, the character of Hannibal, and the campaign against Rome. A line from a Horatian ode read in 1873 is quoted as a memorial to Karl Abraham in 1926. The use of Greek names for crucial psychological concepts (Oedipus, Eros, Thanatos, Narcissus), the frequent references to classical myth, the shared values regarding morality and aesthetics, the fascination with Greek and Roman sculpture and archaeology – all attest to the indelible impression of the classical Gymnasium.

How did Freud react to his secondary school curriculum? Darwin, similarly educated, stated that the classical curriculum had stultified his mind. The general negative reaction to the classical influence is highlighted in Butler's book *The Tyranny of Greece over Germany* (1935). In Freud's case, we hear of only one episode of direct rebellion against his teachers. Once, when he was fifteen, he recollects,

"We had hatched a conspiracy against an unpopular and ignorant master. . . . The leadership in the chief assault was allotted to me" (1900a, pp. 211–212). We hear of no reprisal for this confrontation, nor did his conduct interfere with making the honor roll that year (as in every other year of his Gymnasium career). Freud wrote of his teachers with affection when his secondary school asked its distinguished graduates to comment in a *Festschrift* celebrating its fiftieth anniversary. In Freud's words, it was his classical education that provided his "first glimpse of an extinct civilization which . . . was to bring me as much consolation as anything else in the struggles of life" (1914b, p. 241).

Freud's library, now in London, documents his fascination with Greek and Roman culture. He had an extensive collection of art and archaeological objects, subscribed to archaeological journals, and had more than an amateur's knowledge of the field. It is not surprising that the founder of psychoanalysis should be intrigued by glimpses of an extinct civilization: both archaeology and psychoanalysis value the understanding of the past through present-day remnants (Bernfeld, 1951). It is likely that an additional factor in Freud's love for the literature of antiquity was the opportunity it provided for authenticating the universal nature of psychoanalytic findings. He was sustained by the awareness that discoveries made in a specific clinical situation had a general applicability, already hinted at in cultures centuries old. Classical antiquity gave surety to the findings clinical experience first revealed.

In the final analysis, the young Freud chose from the past what was useful; he did not restrain himself by adhering to a unilateral tradition. From what we may loosely call romanticism, he derived a high regard for emotion, but he also believed that the irrational must be studied rationally. From classicism, he derived a notion of balance and order as regulatory principles, but he was also aware that the tradition of antiquity treasured expressions of desire. As Freud moved into an immersion in biological science, he carried with him a powerful and sustaining humanist tradition.

2

Natural Sciences and
Human Concerns

In 1926, looking back over a career of forty-one years as a practicing physician, Freud wrote, "I have never been a doctor in the proper sense. I became a doctor through being compelled to deviate from my original purpose; and the triumph of my life lies in my having, after a long and roundabout journey, found my way back to my earliest path" (1926d, p. 253). Clearly, the "original purpose" referred to his intense interest in the humanities and the rich cultural tradition to which he was attached. In his autobiography he stated that from early life he had been "moved . . . by a sort of curiosity which was, however, directed more toward human concerns than toward material objects" (1925a, p. 8).

At first glance Freud's immersion in biological research appears as a shift away from the rich cultural climate by which he had been stirred in adolescence. I propose, however, that even during his intense anatomical and physiological studies, Freud was exposed, through his teachers, to broadminded and cultured sensibilities. Indirectly, his seemingly materialist and positivist mentors provided channels for Freud's return to a humanist psychology. When Freud gave up his work in the physiological laboratory, he did so not only for practical economic considerations but also because he was ready to start the return back to his original humanist concerns.

The Prelude to Science

In view of his remarkable skill as a writer and as a master of language, a literary career could have been considered an appropriate choice of a profession for Freud. In later life, when critics alleged that psychoanalysis was artistic rather than scientific, he disclaimed that he was essentially an artist. Indeed, Freud maintained that such an allegation was a form of resistance to the painful truths of psychoanalysis. If his creative work were fundamentally "artistic," then it might be relegated to fantasy and simply dismissed (Freud, 1920b, p. 263).

Nonetheless, even Freud saw his immersion in science as a deviation from his true path. His strong interest in the humanities, his love of literature and the arts, and the bond he felt with cultural figures of the past easily lead an interpretative biographer to believe that a career in the world of arts would have been most logical. Looking at Freud's life in midadolescence, one would assume that "a promising literary career awaited him" (Eissler, 1978, p. 464), that he would become a novelist or at least a professor of German literature. That such an eventuality did not take place and that even the aim of studying law to prepare for a political career was aborted and replaced by a turn toward natural science calls for an explanation.

Eissler writes that Freud "threw his treasure of innate talents to the winds by choosing to study medicine" (1978, p. 465). In his opinion, Freud's claim that he was motivated to turn to natural science because of Goethe's essay on nature is suspect, perhaps a rationalization. Feeling uneasy and even guilty about the choice, he could maintain he was still being true to his intellectual father, Goethe.

Instead, Eissler offers the intriguing suggestion that Freud was motivated to turn away from the humanities toward the rigors of science by the traumatic impact of an adolescent love affair. He defended against the onslaught of his feelings by choosing a field concerned with externals, which would help to discipline his unruly passions and enable him to avoid the turmoil of direct emotional involvement. The humanities were repudiated because they were connected with freedom of emotional expression, affective intensity, and drive gratification.

Freud's adolescent love for Gisela Fluss is described in a paper he wrote in 1899 on screen memories. The episode is recounted as if it had happened to someone else, but it is now established that the disguise conceals an autobiographical event (Bernfeld, 1947; Jones, 1953; Eissler, 1978).

In the summer of 1872, when he was sixteen, about six months before he wrote his friend, Emil Fluss, about his choice of a profession, he visited the town of his birth, Freiberg, and fell in love with Gisela, Emil's fifteen-year-old sister. Claiming that he was reporting from the account of a patient, he wrote that she "excited me powerfully. . . . It was my first calf-love and sufficiently intense, but I kept it completely secret. After a few days the girl went off to her school . . . and it was this separation that brought my longings to a really high pitch. I passed many hours in solitary walks through the lonely woods" (1899, p. 313). Freud felt utterly helpless against the sudden onslaught of passion (Eissler, 1978, p. 468); the power of the excitement he experienced at the time was to exert its effect for years.

Shortly after his return to Vienna from Freiberg, he wrote to his friend, Silberstein: "This sentiment for Gisela appeared like a nice day in spring, but my nonsensical 'Hamlethood,' my shyness, prevented me from conversing with . . . the girl. . . . I am unable to make fun of Gisela" (Letter of September 4, 1872, Stanescu, 1971, p. 202; R. W. Clark, 1980, p. 14). With time, however, ridicule became important as a regulatory device, bolstering his defenses. He referred to Gisela in correspondence as "Ichthyosaura"—an aquatic dinosaurian reptile. On occasion he described her with mordant wit; on other occasions, with ironic Horatian detachment. In his correspondence with Silberstein she was "torn to shreds" (Letter of September 28, 1872, Freud, 1969, p. 421). When Gisela married, three years later, Freud claimed that he was now indifferent to her; yet he wrote a scornful and derisive wedding poem, making fun of her rotund proportions and visualizing the wedding night (Gedo and Wolf, 1970; Rogawski, 1970). For years thereafter, references to

her continued to arouse his feelings. In 1907, when a patient mentioned the name "Gisela Fluss" during an analytic session, Freud
added three exclamation marks after it in his notes (1909, p. 280).
And years later, he tried to disguise further the autobiographical episode he reported in the paper on screen memories (Jones, 1953,
p. 24).

In all, it is clear that he was greatly affected by the adolescent love
affair. As far as we know, he had no emotionally meaningful heterosexual relations for the next ten years. Instead, he became intensely
preoccupied with rigorous scientific research. "The adolescent who
had found delight in Virgil, Sophocles, and Goethe narrowed his
principal interest to the choking confines of a static visual field that
imposed maximal constraint on fantasy and power of imagination"
(Eissler, 1978, p. 486). He was not prepared psychologically to
emerge from this moratorium until he was twenty-six years old.
Nevertheless, as he worked productively in Brücke's physiological
laboratory, he continued to be stimulated by the humanistic tradition that surrounded him. These years enabled him to fuse successfully the artistic and scientific sides of his interests; in this he was
helped by the cultural breadth of his medical and scientific teachers.

At the University of Vienna

The period in Freud's life from his entry into the University of
Vienna in 1873 until his trip to Paris to study with Charcot in 1885
was a time of rigorous preoccupation with biological research and
training for a career in neurological medicine. A few months before
his matriculation, he wrote, "I am neither this nor that, not really
anything completely" (1873–1939a, p. 4). Within three years, he enthusiastically embraced his scientific studies and felt that he had
found his niche. Although six years later he would write that he
could let his "arms droop for sheer lack of desire to live" and knew no
joy of living (1873–1939a, pp. 28, 113), in the intervening years he
was sustained by his investigative interest in biological science,
which he hoped would lead to his life work.

During the first year (1873–1874) at the university, Freud's basic science curriculum consisted of anatomy, chemistry, general biology and Darwinism, botany, mineralogy, and a course with Ernst von Brücke on the physiology of voice and speech (Bernfeld, 1951). The next year (1874–1875), he added zoology, two more courses in physiology with Brücke, two courses in physics, and a reading seminar on philosophy with Franz Brentano. For the first two years he followed the regular medical school program in the basic sciences. By the summer of 1875, however, he had made a detour from the prescribed route of the usual medical student and registered for another course in zoology — one for biology rather than medical students. He also took several course in physics and continued with his seminar in philosophy, even adding a course on Aristotle. During the first three years he felt that he was ranging around from science to science until, in 1876, he found "rest and full satisfaction" in Brücke's Institute of Physiology (Freud, 1925a, p. 9).

His physiological research enabled him to pursue his medical career. In the winter semester (1876–1877), Freud began pathology, clinical work in medicine and surgery, and two specialized courses, on poisons and higher mathematics for medical students. He continued with the standard medical school curriculum until 1879, although his enthusiasm continued to be directed toward histological research. He postponed taking his medical examination for his degree until 1881, apparently expecting that he would obtain a post in Brücke's Institute when one became vacant (Freud, 1925d, p. 10). The year after his graduation, in the summer of 1882, he left Brücke's Institute when it became clear to him that a position was not available. He decided to renounce a career in laboratory research and began to prepare for the practice of medicine.

Once Freud embarked on his medical school training, he came in contact with a number of men who were not only distinguished in science but also familiar with the humanities. The broad range of his cultural exposure may be blurred for us by his intense dedication to science. Yet his scientifically oriented curriculum did not preclude extensive cultural influence.

Theodor Gomperz

One of the leading philosophers at the university, Franz Brentano, recommended Freud to the prominent classical scholar, Theodor Gomperz (1832–1912), who was looking for a translator for
one of the volumes of the German edition of the collected works of
John Stuart Mill. Thus in 1880, during the period of his military
service (which mainly involved standing about in hospitals while he
continued to live at home), Freud occupied his time with translating
four of Mill's essays. These dealt with the labor question, the enfran-
chisement of women, socialism, and an analysis of the work of
George Grote, the English historian, on Plato (Jones, 1953).

Gomperz was the brother of Josephine Wertheimstein, the leader
of a highly influential and cultivated salon in Vienna during the last
quarter of the nineteenth century where Jew and Gentile mixed
freely. Indeed, the existence of this salon may explain how Brentano, a former Catholic priest and a frequent visitor, came to recommend his apt student to his friend Gomperz, an emancipated
Jew, when the former translator of Mill, a tutor in the Wertheimstein home, suddenly died (Barea, 1966, p. 307).

Freud continued to have contact with the Gomperz family over
many years. The Gomperz name appears several times in Freud's biography. At the time of the publication of *The Interpretation of
Dreams* (1900a), Freud agreed to meet regularly with Gomperz's
son, Heinrich, in order to interpret his dreams. Gomperz's wife,
Elise, was a patient of Freud's at about the same time, and it was she
who was instrumental in influencing the minister of education to
grant Freud his long-delayed professorship in 1901. The closeness of
their relationship is indicated by Freud's letters to her with their hu-
morous salutations: "Your Highness" and "Protectrix." Freud also
credited Theodor Gomperz with having stirred his interest soon
after their meeting in dreams of primitive man (1873–1939a, Letters 115, 117, 118, 165). And he recommended Gomperz's *Greek
Thinkers* as one of his ten favorite books (Freud, 1907a).

Franz Brentano

Brentano's intercession on Freud's behalf suggests that the medical student had made a special impression on the philosopher. Freud's attendance at Brentano's lectures was completely voluntary. By 1873 medical students no longer had to study philosophy, although this was required until the year before Freud's admission to the university. In spite of his later negative statements about philosophy, Freud maintained an interest in philosophy during the three years of his medical student career, attending a total of five courses with Brentano from 1874 to 1876 (Freud, 1914b, p. 15). He even enrolled in a private seminar offered by Brentano (Gedo and Pollock, 1976).

Franz Brentano (1838–1917) had arrived in Vienna the same year Freud began to attend his lectures. His reputation as a brilliant lecturer had preceded him, and "half of Vienna" soon came to listen (Barea, 1966). The son of a liberal, literary Catholic family, Brentano was ordained as a priest in 1864 at twenty-six and then pursued an academic career. Impatient with the authoritarian church and opposed to the doctrine of papal infallibility, he resigned his professorship at Wurzburg and seceded from the priesthood the year before his appointment at the University of Vienna.

Brentano had aligned himself with the liberal Catholic theologian Johann Dollinger, a former teacher. During the 1860s there was much discussion over the doctrine of the infallibility of the Pope. Brentano published a refutation of the doctrine in 1869. When the Vatican Council accepted the doctrine of infallibility the next year, Brentano's faith in the church crumbled. Although he gave up the priesthood, he continued to think of himself as a Catholic and a believer throughout the rest of his life.

In 1880 Brentano again felt forced to leave his academic post. He wished to marry a Catholic, but under Austrian law such a step was not permitted to a former priest. Thus Brentano again resigned his professorship, took citizenship in Saxony, married, and later returned to the University of Vienna, this time as a lecturer.

Brentano had an influential position in Vienna during the first six years of his professorship. He moved in a liberal, intellectual circle, and was described by a contemporary observer as a sparkling debater, often engaged in animated discussion with Freud's professor of psychiatry, Theodor Meynert, and Brücke's assistant, Ernst von Fleischl-Marxow (Barea, 1966, p. 307).

Freud's thorough exposure to Brentano's teachings was likely to have made a deep impression on him. The courses covered a broad philosophical tradition stemming from Aristotle through the Scholastic philosophers of the Middle Ages to Kant.[1] Thus Freud encountered the major philosophical disputes of the Western tradition. Although Brentano was highly critical of *Naturphilosophie* and particularly of its proponent, Schelling, he was careful to provide a balanced viewpoint in his teaching, with a fair assessment of the position he opposed.

Freud also became acquainted with contemporary thought in psychology through Brentano. Coincident with his arrival in Vienna in 1874, Brentano had completed his magnum opus, *Psychologie vom Empirischen Standpunkt*. In opposition to Kant, Brentano proposed that psychology be considered as basic to philosophy and other fields of study. Unlike Wundt, he stressed observation over experiment. Moreover, he defined psychology as the science of psychic phenomena, thus counteracting the heavy physicalistic emphasis psychology had received from the Helmholtz group and its representative, Freud's other influential teacher, Ernst von Brücke.

To Brentano, psychology was a study of acts rather than states of mind. Intentionality was a central concept. Psychic phenomena were recognized by their directional quality—as acts (ideating, judging, emoting), requiring an object in order to be carried out. Overall, his was a psychology that emphasized personal experience in a somewhat dynamic fashion, a psychology that took account of

---

[1]There are two books by Kant in Freud's London Library. The *Critique of Pure Reason* has several marked passages (Trosman and Simon, 1973).

the affects of love and hate and interpersonal relations as pleasurable or unsatisfying. Intention was immanent, and psychological phenomena were distinguishable from physical ones by their motivated nature (Barclay, 1959a, 1959b; Fancher, 1977).

Freud probably first came in contact with the notion of the unconscious in Brentano's lecture halls. Although Brentano was opposed to a concept of the unconscious, he discussed the variety of arguments others had presented in its support, to conclude with his own refutation. On the other hand, Brentano advocated a notion of instinct as instrumental in psychic development, and he recommended an investigation of psychic phenomena such as somnambulism and dreams.

In spite of presumptive evidence of Brentano's influence on Freud, only one direct reference to Brentano appears in Freud's writings, and there is only one book by Brentano in the remains of Freud's London Library. In 1879 Brentano, under the pseudonym "Aenigmatias," published a book of riddles, *Neue Räthsel*. The book illustrated various specimens of riddles, including a new type recently introduced to Vienna from the Main region of Germany. These Brentano described as "fill-up riddles." A name is used twice; when it is used the second time, it is broken into syllables and thus a new meaning is added. As an example, Freud, in his monograph on jokes (1905b), offered a riddle devised to poke fun at the "elderly" philosopher's engagement (he was 42). Brentano's name is used twice: "Brentano brennt-a-no?" (meaning "Does he still burn?").[2]

For the ten years following Freud's philosophical courses, he displayed little interest in philosophy or psychology. His total immersion in the view through the microscope and clinical neurological studies left no room for the views of the teacher who had early noted

---

[2]Merlan (1945, 1949), Jones (1953), Barclay (1959a), Rancurello (1968), and Fancher (1977)—all of whom have examined Freud's link with Brentano—have neglected this residuum of Freud's contact with the philosopher. The work was published three years after Freud discontinued Brentano's classes, but the memory of a lecturer who frequently added spontaneous jokes and witticisms to his material doubtless persisted.

his ability. By the time Freud was ready to return to psychology, he came by an altogether different route—the route of hypnosis and psychopathology. Yet it is not unlikely that Brentano's ideas served as stimuli, encouraging his observation of psychological events; of dreams, representations, and affects, early stages of development, and the importance of experience as subject matter. There is more than a hint of Brentano's "intentionality" when Freud writes as late as 1937 that the ego may after all be "endowed from the first with individual dispositions and trends," i.e., an intention to act (p. 240; see also Rancurello, 1968, p. 128).

Ernst von Brücke

In spite of Freud's recognition by Brentano and Gomperz, his first years at the university were disappointing. He felt that he had not been fully accepted within the academic community; he was to explain his exclusion on grounds of anti-Semitism. Equally dissatisfying was his initial experience with scientific work. He found himself dipping into one field of science after another without any success or sense of achievement. Not until he had completed three years of study did he discover his métier working in Brücke's laboratory (Freud, 1914b).

Ernst von Brücke (1819–1892), Freud's venerated teacher, was a distinguished physiologist and a man of high cultural attainments. Brücke studied in Berlin, where he was assistant to Johannes Müller, professor of anatomy and physiology. In 1849 he joined the faculty of the University of Vienna, where he remained an outsider because of his Prussian origins; his Berlin colleagues even called him "our Ambassador in the Far East" (Jones, 1953, p. 41).

Freud regarded Brücke as the authority who had the most effect on him, and he always spoke of him with respect (1925a, p. 9; 1926d, p. 253). Brücke took the position that biological processes were to be understood in terms of strict physiochemical forces. He wrote on cell theory and development, the physiology of the senses and of speech, color theory, and optics. Clearly, his influence on Freud was in the direction of hardheaded materialism and empirical observation. But this influence was more extensive.

Not only was Brücke a scientist, he has also been described as one of the most versatile scholars of the nineteenth century (Johnston, 1972, p. 230). At times he related his physiological findings to the arts (Eissler, 1978), as in *Die Physiologischen Grundlagen der neuhochdeutschen Verskunst* ("The Physiological Principles of Modern High German Verse") and *Physiologie der Farben fur die Zwecke des Kunstgewerbes* ("The Physiology of Colors with a View toward the Applied Arts"). He also authored a book entitled *The Human Form: Its Beauty and Imperfections*, addressed to artists and amateur painters. Here he dealt with aesthetic appreciation of the human figure—a surprising subject for a leading physiologist, but more understandable when we learn that Brücke's father was a distinguished painter of portraits and historical events. The book offered a conception of ideal proportions based on principles of anatomy and the nudes of Greek antiquity. The decline of contemporary art, Brücke believed, was due to a disregard of the classical ideal of beauty. The Baroque style, with its emphasis on sensuous form, received his special disapprobrium. How Brücke felt toward a city renowned for its Baroque architecture can only be guessed (Jones, 1953, p. 43). He was a shy, stern man with terrifying eyes. On one occasion Freud recalled how these eyes had "reduced him to nothing" when Brücke reprimanded him for arriving late in the morning at the students' laboratory (1900a, p. 422). On the other hand, Brücke could reduce the austerity of the Physiological Laboratory and Institute with the Renaissance paintings he brought back from his trips to Italy, where he vacationed every summer to paint (Brücke, 1928; Johnston, 1972).

In 1847, together with Carl Ludwig, Emil du Bois-Reymond, and Hermann von Helmholtz, Brücke formed a group known as the *Berliner Physikalische Gesellschaft*, loosely designated as the "School of Helmholtz" by Bernfeld (1944).[3] The group was principally

---

[3]Cranefield (1957) has been justly critical of this label.

pledged to reducing physiology to physics and chemistry. Ludwig stated: "We four imagined that we should constitute physiology on a chemicophysical foundation and give it equal scientific rank with physics" (Cranefield, 1957, p. 407). The group was intensely anti-vitalistic in its attempts to account for phenomena on the basis of an intelligible causality, advocating observation and experiment rather than speculation.

In spite of the mechanistic appeal of physics and chemistry, the group soon found that it could not adhere to such a rigid program. Workers in physiology who were strongly oriented toward a physical approach in 1850 had, by the 1870s, turned to other methods of study. Brücke himself ranged far afield, and certainly did not confine himself to a biophysical orientation. Although du Bois-Reymond, looking back at his career in 1884, confessed himself a failure in that the strict physical and chemical approach did not carry the day, Brücke had no such regrets.

The success of the 1847 group was in its promotion of the scientific method. Its emphasis was on exact observation. Such strict positivism did not, however, remove all remnants of the old-style *Naturphilosophie*. Meynert, a latter-day product of the mechanist school, was addicted to "brain mythology." He explained the origin of ideas of grandeur and persecution, for instance, in terms of the reactivation of phylogenetically older centers of the brain (Cranefield, 1957; Ellenberger, 1970a).

Hermann von Helmholtz (1821–11894), the most brilliant of the original foursome, gave up biophysics and physiology altogether to become a leading physicist, laying the foundations for modern thermodynamics and physical chemistry. Freud had an intense admiration for Helmholtz all his life. When Helmholtz visited Vienna in 1883, Freud regretted that he did not catch sight of him. "He is one of my idols," wrote Freud to Martha at the time (Jones, 1953, p. 41). The Freud Library in London contains the two-volume set of Helmholtz's lectures presented to Freud by Fliess in 1898 as well as a photograph of Helmholtz. Kris believes that the later importance of Fliess to Freud was in part related to the fact that Fliess was a representative of the Helmholtz group (see Freud, 1887–1902b, pp. 22–23).

Histological and Anatomical Research

Freud's first research project, assigned to him by the anatomist Carl Claus, was an examination of an organ in eels believed to be the gonad. After entering Brücke's laboratory, he described the pathway of the posterior nerve-roots, spinal ganglia, and spinal cord of the Petromyzon (brook lamprey). He assumed that he was the first to discover the roots of the posterior nerves in a large cell of the spinal cord, the Reissner cell. (His next paper, a more thorough discussion of the same subject, with a bibliography, included an apology for having claimed the discovery, which was actually made by a previous investigator.) Freud proposed that the ganglia cells had migrated from the spinal cord along the roots of the nerves and that the pathway of migration was apparent by noting the cells that had remained behind. Many years later he used this early work as an analogy for fixation and regression, pointing out that "the lagging behind of a part at an earlier stage is called a fixation" (1916–1917, pp. 339–340). Here the emphasis is Darwinian; evolutionary processes are understood as a result of an investigation of structure and its variations. Analogies from the cultural history of peoples who migrate from one land to another are linked with the migration of testicles from the abdominal cavity to the scrotum.[4]

Other papers stemming from Brücke's laboratory include the presentation of a staining method for anatomical preparations of the nervous system, a study of the structure of nerve fibers and nerve cells in the crayfish, and a more general work on the nervous system suggestive of the neuron theory. These papers reveal an in-

---

[4]Freud's ability to discover a link between psychological processes and highly specialized neuroanatomical research calls to mind Greenacre's (1957) emphasis on the characteristic tendency of the creative mind to find common factors among varying, seemingly disparate forms.

terest in method and technique consistent with the type of research encouraged by Brücke, as well as an ability to use observations on structure for productive speculation. Later, Freud complained that, during his Brücke period, physiology was too narrowly restricted to histology (1925a, p. 253). Bernfeld (1949a) believes this reproach is unjustified; certainly Brücke's own work was functional in emphasis. Bernfeld suggests that a strict experimental approach did not fit in with the particular qualities of Freud's mind; his attempts in this mode turned out to be rather poor efforts.

It is likely that the sense of fulfillment Freud initially experienced when he began working under Brücke in 1876 permitted him to settle down sufficiently to complete the medical curriculum. When he graduated on March 31, 1881, he made no attempt to do clinical work, but continued to work in Brücke's laboratory for another fifteen months. During the last year, however, he worked primarily as a demonstrator and apparently did no physiological research (although he attempted some research on the analysis of gases in Ludwig's Chemical Institute). Later, he stated that it was humiliating for him to recall this work and he considered 1882 "the gloomiest and least successful year of my professional life" (1900a, p. 476).

Jones, Bernfeld, and other biographers have tended to accept that Freud gave up a career in basic science because he was determined to marry, and thus for the first time became concerned with financial security. Yet other factors were also instrumental in this change of direction. The choice of a career concerned him as early as August 1878, when he wrote a friend that he still had not decided between "flaying of animals" and "torturing of human beings" (1873–1939a, p. 7). And in the midst of his physiological endeavors, he never gave up on medical practice and human concerns. In view of his lack of productivity during the last year of his work with both Brücke and Ludwig in chemistry, it is likely that he had come to appreciate that a career in the scientific research of the day did not suit his temperament. When he had mastered the skills for biological research, he was ready to move on. His meeting with Martha Bernays simply catalyzed the shift in his goals. He followed Brücke's advice to give up his work at the Physiological Institute, decided to prepare for practice, and in the summer of 1882 began to do serious clinical work.

The Choice of Medicine

Ironically, the fulfillment of Freud's anatomical work probably served a purpose he could not have anticipated at the time. This was not to be the route for him. Hindsight suggests that he was moving toward a more humanistic arena, wherein his natural capabilities would find their proper métier. One is reminded here of one of his favorite anecdotes. He wrote Fliess, several years later, that he felt like Itzig, the Sunday rider. When asked, "Itzig, where are you going?" he replied, "Don't ask me, ask the horse!" The horse seemed to know (1887–1902b, p. 258).

Nevertheless, it is surprising how late in Freud's medical school training his vacillation regarding the choice of a career continued. The "flaying of animals" was still favored over the "torturing of human beings" in 1878, the year Freud was in the midst of his clinical work in surgery, dermatology, obstetrics, syphilis, pathology of the nervous system, and physical examination. Simply to qualify for a medical degree did not denote an interest in the practice of medicine. Medicine was also considered a route toward a nonclinical academic career. For Forel, Brücke, and Helmholtz, a medical degree was seen as an appropriate step toward a career in the natural sciences (Ellenberger, 1970a, p. 430).

The University of Vienna encouraged a leisurely progression and made it possible for medical students to follow up areas of study or research that stirred their enthusiasm. There was flexibility regarding the timing of courses; few courses were compulsory; and—as in Freud's case—one could postpone sitting for the medical qualifying examination until one felt ready.

By the time of Freud's graduation in 1881, basic science research was seen as a necessary step toward the further advance of clinical medicine. Indeed, an atmosphere of therapeutic nihilism enveloped the Vienna General Hospital (Johnston, 1972; Lesky, 1965). The medical leaders had begun to doubt the effectiveness of the program of therapeutics laid down by the previous generation (Bernfeld, 1951, p. 211). More basic science knowledge was considered mandatory for further progress to be made. Bright young men were encouraged to follow research careers. In this light it is understandable that Freud, even after taking his examinations and graduating in March 1881, continued to work in Brücke's laboratory for another fifteen months. Yet his sense of failure and depression following his graduation from medical school stands in striking contrast to the fulfillment he had experienced six years earlier (Freud, 1900a, p. 476; 1925a, p. 9).

How are we to understand this period in Freud's life? Erikson (1958, 1968) points out that, during late adolescence or early adulthood, gifted individuals may go through a period of marking time "as if driven by mere circumstance" to engage in activities that appear unrelated to later adult commitments. Such a period, however, may be necessary to subsequent development in allowing for consolidation of the personality and resynthesis of early identifications. It is a phase characterized by self-concern and inner scrutiny as well as a sense of wasting valued time and energy. Interestingly, in *The Interpretation of Dreams* Freud relates a dream that evoked a memory of Brücke chastizing him for neglecting his responsibilities. He felt himself to be a "young sinner" — ostensibly for coming late to the laboratory, but perhaps also for being unproductive and purposeless (1900a, p. 422).

In July 1882, Freud began his clinical training at the Vienna General Hospital in preparation for a career as a practicing physician. His training was broad and, until 1885, not oriented toward any particular speciality. He worked on the surgical wards in August and September 1882 and on the medical wards from October 1882 to April 1883, under Hermann Nothnagel (1841–1905), professor of medicine. Freud described Nothnagel as "no great beauty, a Germanic caveman with two enormous warts," but the embodiment of the "good physician." At the same time Freud could not avoid indicating Nothnagel's academic pretentiousness, as revealed by his concern with the number of Freud's publications rather than their quality (Letters of October 5, 1882, and January 16, 1885, in 1873–1939a; see also Bernfeld, 1951, p. 210).

In 1882, Freud began to work in Meynert's Laboratory for Cerebral Anatomy and continued to do so until October 1885. In 1883, he began an extensive study of the medulla oblongata. He thus passed from the study of the spinal cord of fish to the central nervous system of humans. As he slowly moved toward psychology, his interest in neurological techniques continued. He began, for instance, to use a method of embryonic dissection suggested by Meynert's rival, Flechsig, later to appear in the psychoanalytic literature as the physician of Schreber (Jones, 1953, pp. 202–203).

From March to September 1883, Freud worked in psychiatry under Meynert. This five-month period of exposure to psychiatry was probably rather intensive, for he left home and moved into the hospital in order to follow changes in his patients at close quarters. He read for the first time the works of two prominent clinical psychiatrists of the nineteenth century, Esquirol and Morel.[5] In October 1883, he began work in dermatology and neurolaryngology. For all of 1884, he worked on the ward for patients with nervous diseases under Scholz, whom he described as a "fossil" and "feebleminded" (Letter of August 4, 1884, in 1873–1939a).

In January 1885, Freud applied for the prestigious position of *Privatdozent* in neuropathology (the equivalent of a specialty board certification). A *Privatdozent* could teach small classes on topics of his own choosing. Although the position carried no salary and did not permit attendance at faculty meetings, it was seen as a step toward academic advancement. Meynert, Brücke, and Nothnagel were appointed to a committee to evaluate Freud's application. They recommended acceptance, and Freud then went on to the next two obligatory steps: he underwent an oral examination on June 13 and gave a trial lecture on June 27. The Ministry for Public

---

[5]It is of interest that during the summer of 1883, while on the psychiatry service, he also read *Don Quixote* for the second time (Grinberg and Rodriguez, 1983).

Instruction confirmed Freud's appointment as *Privatdozent* in neuropathology on September 5, 1885.[6]

Meynert and Neurology

Freud's relationship with Theodor Meynert (1833–1892), a transitional figure in the shift from Brücke to Charcot, proved highly difficult. Meynert, the son of a writer and a singer at the Court Opera, was born in Dresden (Lesky, 1965). He joined the faculty of the University of Vienna in 1865, and became professor and chief of psychiatry in 1875. Euphemistically described as having "a problematic nature" (in that he formed violent enmities), he supported a huge head on a short body, with "disheveled locks that had an annoying habit of falling down over the forehead and had to be pushed back every so often" (Ellenberger, 1970a, p. 434). In his youth Meynert was a radical who wanted to fight on the barricades and was only restrained from doing so by a dominant maternal grandmother. He remained interested in social action and spoke frequently at Freud's revolutionary *Leseverein*, expressing admiration for Viktor Adler, the leader of the Austrian Socialist Party. He was also a poet (his poems were published posthumously in 1905), a connoisseur of music and art, and a member of the intellectual elite of Vienna.

Meynert and Flechsig were considered the greatest brain anatomists in Europe. Although many of Meyner's scientific concepts found a place in later psychoanalytic formulations, as noted earlier, he fell prey to "brain mythology," giving in to the popular tendency

---

[6]The dispatch with which the appointment to *Privatdozent* was carried out contrasts with the desultory manner with which Freud's appointment as Professor Extraordinarius was handled more than ten years later. Some have tried to explain the later delay as a natural one, not atypical. Gicklhorn and Gicklhorn (1960), for instance, contend that Freud waited no longer than his contemporaries and that he himself was not sufficiently diligent in fulfilling his university responsibilities; Eissler (1965) has suggested, surprisingly, that there was little anti-Semitism involved in the delay. These arguments, however, are not convincing. Although we are not certain of the reasons for the delay, there is little doubt that by the late 1890s, after the introduction of psychoanalysis, there were negative reactions to Freud's work, which doubtless interfered with his appointment.

to relate psychological experience directly to hypothetical brain anatomy, and even occasionally inventing brain tracts to account for behavior. His principle works were *Psychiatrie* (published in 1884 and immediately made available to English readers the following year) and *Klinische Vorlesungen über Psychiatrie* (published in 1890). Freud retained five of Meynert's works in his library.

Meynert, in considering the whole spectrum of nervous and psychological phenomena, assumed that one type of excitation was transmitted throughout the nervous system—a functional energy responsive to stimuli he labeled "sensitiveness." In Meynert's view, cortical processes were determined by the inflow of excitation. Association psychology was used to explain central processes in terms of connections established among sensations. Although he advanced a concept of *individuality* and a notion of *primary* or *body ego*, he did not have a conception of the unconscious or of instinct. All nervous activity was considered to be either innate and mediated subcortically or determined by experience and mediated cortically. In contrast to Darwin, Meynert believed that ideas were not inherited but the result of perception and association (Amacher, 1965).

Initially attracted to the neurological emphasis on brain localization, Freud had to break free of this tendency before he could deal with psychological factors in their own right. He offered an amusing instance of a group of American physicians walking out of one of his early lectures when he diagnosed a neurotic patient with persistent headaches as a case of chronic localized meningitis (Freud, 1925a).

If Freud read Meynert's *Psychiatrie* (the publication coincided with Freud's active work with Meynert), there is no indication that Freud responded to the minimal psychological conceptions in it at the time. Indeed, Freud did not return to it until he began to think in terms of general psychological theory many years later (Riese, 1958). Only then did Freud reveal his conceptual debt to Meynert—for instance, in his discussion of the ego and elaboration on the reflex arc model. Meynert's distinction between primary and secondary ego is echoed in Freud's *Project for a Scientific Psychology* (1895, in 1887–1902b). And Meynert's notion of endogenous stimulation may have been an antecedent for instinct theory. Other psychoanalytic notions, such as loss of ego defenses, wish fulfillment, primary and secondary processes, reality testing, cathexis, and repression can also be considered as fruits of Meynert's primitive theory of the mind (Priest, 1970). More directly, Freud made use of Meynert's conception of amentia (Freud, 1917a, p. 230). Hallucinations were recognized by Meynert as regressive reactions, based on percepts before the formation of an ego. In other words, the hallucinatory experiences were ancillary percepts, present at the time of the need but not organized as leading to a goal. Meynert called this early state of development "confusedness."

It is of interst to consider the personal relationship of Meynert and Freud since Freud refers to him several times in a variety of ways. Initially, Freud was quite attracted to Meynert; he enjoyed his instruction and respected his mind. Freud referred to him as "the great Meynert" and confessed to following in his footsteps with "deep veneration" (1900a, p. 437). Moreover, Meynert was instrumental in advancing Freud's career, helping him to become a *Privatdozent* and to obtain a traveling grant to study in Paris with Charcot. Yet after Freud's return from Paris, Meynert's attitude toward Freud changed. Meynert appeared hostile to the ideas about male hysteria Freud brought back from Charcot. In turn, Freud was disappointed by Meynert's dismissal of hypnotism before learning something about it from personal experience. It appeared to Freud (1889) that Meynert used his great authority to damn challenging ideas with which he was not familiar.

It has been generally accepted that Meynert's criticism of Freud's lecture on his return to Vienna from Paris was due to their disagreement over male hysteria, an illness from which Meynert himself suffered. Ellenberger (1970a) disputes this notion, contending instead that male hysteria was well recognized in Vienna at the time. However, patients so diagnosed did not receive disability compensation in the absence of somatic findings on physical examination. The presence of somatic signs, to the Viennese, implied a diagnosis of a traumatic neurosis and thus made a patient eligible to receive payment. Viennese physicians were therefore cautious in diagnosing hysteria in males, in order not to deprive them of compensation. Ellenberger suggests that the basis for the controversy was not understood by Freud, who reacted as if he were being challenged to turn from the depravity and wickedness he had been exposed to in Paris (see Freud, 1889, p. 96; Ellenberger, 1970a, pp. 437–443).[7]

In any case, Freud's subsequent reaction to Meynert was critical, if not indiscreet. He condemned Meynert for demonstrating the "intolerance of great men" in his opposition to hypnosis (1889, p. 95). By referring to hypnosis as "artificial insanity," quipped Freud, Meynert could no more interfere with its efficacy than vegetarians could lower the good taste or nutritive value of meat by denouncing it as "carrion." In *The Interpretation of Dreams*, he mentioned that Meynert had been a chloroform addict as a youth and had to be institutionalized. Freud added that, during his fatal illness, Meynert confessed to having opposed Freud because he, Meynert, had always been "one of the clearest cases of male hysteria" (1900a, pp. 437–438). Here the discussion with Meynert may have supplied Freud with an early example of resistance in the form of denial (Ellenberger, 1970a, p. 556, n. 151).

In passing, one is impressed with Freud's dramatic mode of presentation in writing about Meynert in *The Interpretation of Dreams*. Ellenberger (1970a) notes Freud's Dantesque technique in relegating the people in his life to various levels of purgatory. Meynert's alleged terminal confession evokes memories of Sophoclean scenes of tragic recognition, an aspect of dramatic resolution subsequently echoes in reports of the clinical psychoanalytic situation.

Neurological Research

While Freud worked under Franz Scholz in the Department for Nervous Diseases of the Vienna General Hospital in 1884, he wrote three case studies in clinical neurology. He described an acute cere-

---

[7]Sulloway (1979) has argued that Freud grossly exaggerated the negative response he received in general and particularly when he lectured on male hysteria on his return from Paris. Sulloway sees this hypersensitivity on Freud's part as an interest in mythologizing the origins of psychoanalysis and an attempt to present himself as an isolated hero fighting against great odds. Yet Sulloway has been faulted for overlooking documents that support the view that Freud's early work was indeed subject to much hostility (Masson, 1983).

bral hemorrhage with basal symptoms secondary to scurvy (1884), a case of polyneuritis, the first such case successfully diagnosed before autopsy (1885); and a case of syringomyelia with bilateral muscular atrophy (1886a). In the laboratory he studied human fetuses in which myelinization of the medullary tracts was incomplete, and he traced the course of fibers entering the medulla from the auditory nerve and cerebellum by way of the cerebellar peduncle (Bernfeld, 1951, pp. 211–213). He also did electrophysiological experiments on transmission in nerve preparations (Jones, 1953, p. 201).

The culmination of Freud's neurological work was his monograph *On Aphasia*, published in 1891 (see Stengel, 1954; Marx, 1967). It refuted the presence of minute cerebral localization schemata and proposed that subvarieties of aphasia were to be explained functionally. Specifically, Freud refuted Meynert's beliefs that the cortex contained a projection of the various parts of the body and that ideas could be localized in nervous elements, with word concepts in cells and sensory perceptions in the cortex. "The psychic is a process," declared Freud, "parallel to the physiological" (1891, p. 55).

In his discussion Freud was the first on the Continent to cite Hughlings Jackson's theory of "dis-involution," suggesting that more recently acquired capacities of the nervous system, like "naming," were the first to lose their functional capacity. Further, Freud distinguished "naming" from "recognizing objects," and coined the term "agnosia" for a defect in the latter. In many ways this early conception of aphasia as a regression to an earlier state of mental functioning heralds his later discussion of regression in psychopathology.

Even in presenting neurological research, Freud's literary interests come through. The writing style in the aphasia monograph is lively, engaging the reader in an imaginary dialogue or debate — an expository technique Freud later used extensively. He compares theorizing to erecting a building and suggests that nerve tracts contain the body periphery the way a poem contains the alphabet. Similar analogies abound in his later psychoanalytic writings.

Although Freud continued to write on neurological topics until 1897, by the mid-1890s his interest had waned. For a twenty-year period he had worked diligently in a variety of areas in the biological sciences. He was proficient in macroscopic and microscopic neuro-anatomy and histology, neuropathology, clinical neurology, and theoretical neurology. Several ideas incorporated into psychoana-lytic theory were initially shaped in this neurological matrix. For in-stance, the hydraulic reflex model, with the notion of a flow of exci-tation and conceptions of energy under pressure stimulated at sense organs, owes something to the neurological model. The view that the total quantity of energy remained constant and the idea that motor activity was proportional to the amount of sensory stimula-tion also provided a framework for later theorizing.

But neurology was not satisfying to Freud. It failed to gratify the humanist side of his nature. In later life Freud described neurology as "a silly game of permutations" (Bernfeld, 1951, p. 214). There was little he could do in the way of treatment, nor was there much op-portunity for the fulfillment of what he later came to express as "an overpowering need to understand something of the riddles of the world in which we live" (Freud, 1926d, p. 253). He passed from neu-rology to the neuroses "prompted by fresh influences" (pp. 253–254). A crucial fresh influence was Charcot, with whom Freud stud-ied in Paris.

Charcot and Paris

During the last two decades of his life, Jean-Martin Charcot (1835–1893) was generally accepted as Europe's leading clinical neu-rologist. A dramatic, austere, and impressive man, he was fre-quently compared to Caesar and Napoleon (Guillain, 1959; Ellen-berger, 1965). In 1862 he became chief physician at the Salpêtrière, and he converted the institution—previously used as a depository for beggars, insane, and demented women—into a clinical labora-tory for the study of neurological illnesses. In 1882 he was appointed professor of clinical diseases of the nervous system, a new chair cre-ated at the time by the Chamber of Deputies. He attempted to dis-tinguish epilepsy from hysteria, describing differences between or-ganic and hysterical paralysis, as well as various stages of the hypnotic trance. His case demonstrations with hysterical patients (which were often rehearsed by his students and patients) attracted large crowds of onlookers. Indeed, his remarkable hypnotic results evoked skepticism in scientific circles because of their theatrical quality.

Charcot was an exceptionally learned man, fluent in German, English, and Italian. He was a gifted sketcher, well read in Shakespeare and Dante, and a master of French prose. His house was like a museum, filled with period furniture, ancient Greek sculpture, Italian Renaissance art, Flemish and Dutch paintings, stained glass windows, tapestries, and rare books. Beyond his numerous neurological articles, he wrote and collaborated on books dealing with the demonic in visual art and the deformed and diseased in plastic art of the past. His home became a gathering place for the leading scientists, politicians, artists, and writers of the day.

In a period of tension between Germany and France, Charcot and Pasteur were regarded as proof of French scientific genius—a challenge to alleged German scientific superiority. Freud spoke several times, rather favorably, of the peculiarly "French" nature of Charcot's world. By this he meant that clinical observation took precedence over abstract theorizing, an emphasis he gladly accepted (Freud, 1892–1894, pp. 134–135).

All in all, Charcot made an intense impression on the young Freud (Anderson, 1962; Miller et al., 1969). In contrast to Meynert, who was often confusing and exhausting in lectures, Charcot was exhilarating. The vibrant qualities of his personality, the breadth of his culture, the novelty and excitement of his ideas about hypnosis and hysteria, and his inroads toward a psychology of the neuroses made Freud write to Martha that no other human being had ever affected him in the same way: "Charcot, who is one of the greatest of physicians and a man whose common sense borders on genius, is simply wrecking all my aims and opinions" (Letter of October 21, 1885, in 1873–1939a, p. 175). He contrasted Charcot with "our great men [the Viennese] with their veneer of distinguished superficiality." Being with Charcot was like spending an evening in the theater; his lectures were like Notre Dame (see Letter of November 24, 1885, in 1873–1939a, pp. 184–185).

The psychological importance of Charcot in Freud's life cannot be overestimated. Charcot combined an artistically endowed nature with the keen observation of a scientist; he was a visionary (*"un visuel"*) who used his intuitive capacity for ordering the chaos found in the clinic (Freud, 1893, pp. 12–13). When Freud left Paris to return to Vienna in March 1886, he had passed from neuropathology to psychology, and he had learned from Charcot that it was possible to integrate his imaginative inclinations with an identity as a scientific investigator.

Looking back at Freud's early career, one has a sense of inevitability regarding its progression. After a long and roundabout journey, Freud did indeed return to his original path. As we have seen, even during the period of his immersion in the hard sciences, his humanist concerns were kept alive by the rich cultural interests of the scientists whom he idealized. Following his intense exposure to biological research, he began to move more and more toward clinical medicine, work with patients, and human concerns. By the time he returned from Charcot's clinic in 1886, he was ready to embark on the study of hysteria.

3

Modes of Influence on Freud's Creativity

A wide variety of sources and influences have been cited as instrumental in the development of psychoanalysis. Freud himself, in his autobiography (1925a), reviewed some of the influences. Looking at his own development, he considered the interplay between external factors and originality, the effect of significant intellectual currents and individuals on the potential for creativity. The problem is one expressed by Cardinal Ippolito d'Este. Awed by the prodigious output of the Italian Renaissance writer Ariosto, he wondered, "Where did you find so many stories, Lodovico?" (Freud, 1908, p. 143).

What is the nature of influence and, how is it experienced? Clearly, individuals may be influential even though their impact may not be acknowledged and may even be repudiated. The experience of being influenced can be viewed on a continuum from the markedly pathological to the highly adaptive and as an aspect of the process of creativity. External influences vary in their connections to previously warded-off components of the personality. Some are indifferent to the contents of the repressed; others serve as convenient expressions for available unconscious contents and help provide an outlet for their expression. Receptivity to influence from significant others is fundamental to creative activity; the specific manner in which the influence occurs may be hidden or only visible retrospectively.

The theories of Darwin, Goethe's essay on nature, the scientific models of Brücke, Exner, and Fleischl von Marxow, the stimulation by Charcot, Breuer, and Bernheim – all these are considered by Freud (1925a) as factors in the development of his thought. In 1935, for the second edition of his autobiography, he added his deep interest in the Bible, which he read from early childhood, and the influence of his friend Heinrich Braun (see Chapter 1).

Other psychoanalytic writers, particularly Jones (1953, 1955, 1957), Shakow and Rapaport (1964), Eissler (1965), Ellenberger (1970a, 1970b), Ritvo (1970), and Sulloway (1979), have shared Freud's interest in tracing sources, and they have added to the factors Freud discerned. Yet in listing selected factors to be emphasized, they have not evaluated how such influences acquired their effect. Broadly speaking, the influences on Freud can be viewed as cultural or personal; that is, the influence may derive from the historical period (an impersonal factor), or it may lie in the specific effect of someone with whom Freud came into direct contact. Admittedly, it is difficult to consider an influence crucial unless it is personal, either transmitted by a specific person in the form of an attitude, value, or idea, or demonstrated through direct experience in a face-to-face encounter. Nevertheless, the broad cultural background, the Zeitgeist, deserves some attention.

The Zeitgeist

The Zeitgeist, the intellectual and cultural spirit of an era, is generally recognized as pertinent in evaluating the birth of a set of ideas (Ross, 1969). The prevailing opinions, basic philosophical precepts, and sanctioned values form an amalgam so that it becomes possible to speak, for example, of the Age of the Enlightenment or the Age of Romanticism. These broad cultural outlooks affect the content of creative works even when the contact between the representative, individual artists may be quite indirect. Wordsworth and Delacroix, for instance, reflect a basic romantic attitude. We speak of Voltaire and Adam Smith as children of the Enlightenment. In Freud's case, the classical tradition, passed down from antiquity and reactivated by Winckelmann and Mengs in the neoclassical revival, as well as the romantic tradition brought forward by *Naturphilosophie*, had an affect on the Zeitgeist of the second half of the nineteenth century. In addition, the interest in evolutionary ideas and the high regard for the biological sciences molded the temper of the time. Again, as we saw in Chapter 1, the tradition of imaginative literature with its wealth of psychological insights, as well as the political residues from the French Revolution and the rise of the bourgeoisie, contributed to the soil in which the radical findings of psychoanalysis took root and flourished.

There are, however, major difficulties in weighting the Zeitgeist as an explanatory concept. The concept is limited to general and nonspecific features of an influence. Because the notion refers to the broad tradition and the spirit of the times, one cannot always investigate the unique impact on the creative individual. Nor does the concept account for the mode in which influence is experienced by an individual. Moreover, the issue of Zeitgeist is often discussed in terms of the generally accepted belief that there is a unity to the spirit of the time and that this unity exists at that time. But does this unity lie in the eyes of the historian, who unites the disparities within the panoramic view that temporal distance provides? Although we may have a fairly clear notion of what we mean by romanticism[1] and be able to identify readily typical figures of that era, witness the difficulty we have in understanding what we mean by modernity—the spirit presumed to be characteristic of our own time.

The Zeitgeist for Freud's historical period may be blurred by the lack of distance, which hampers the clarity of our observation. It is significant that when Freud came to write of *Weltanschauung*, as late as 1932, he did not include contemporary preoccupation with the alienation of self and dehumanization but returned instead to a Vic-

---

[1]Lovejoy (1923) questions whether even "romanticism" is clear, for he emphasizes the varied and contradictory meanings associated with the term.

torian belief in progress as a result of immersion in science – the ideology of a Zeitgeist seriously questioned and found insufficient by many today. Was that Freud's Zeitgeist? In any case, the Zeitgeist notion is always prone to the fallacy of circular reasoning. A highly creative individual may, in fact, determine the Zeitgeist, with the era defined by what this individual has found in it for his or her own creative purposes.

Awareness of Influence

Putting to one side the effects of the Zeitgeist, let us take a more individualized approach to the sources of influence. Clearly, the influences on Freud varied in terms of their subjective impact, Freud's awareness of their effects on him, and their ultimate significance. Ellenberger (1970b) has addressed himself to the problem of awareness.

There are, to begin with, sources of influence that Freud readily recognized and clearly described. Brücke, Breuer, and Charcot fall within this category. As we have seen, Freud always held Brücke in the highest esteem. On one occasion, Freud described being "reduced to nothing" by Brücke when he was lacking in diligence (1900a, p. 422). On another occasion, he allowed an original discovery to lie fallow until Brücke energetically drove him into publishing it (p. 454). Brücke was a model of scientific integrity. He influenced Freud to adopt a rigorous scientific attitude and an evolutionary approach. His views on the interaction of forces within natural phenomena find a place in the dynamic point of view in psychoanalytic thinking. (A similar sketch might be drawn for Freud's acknowledged debt to Charcot.)

Beyond such clear sources are those that may be only casually mentioned but to whom a significant link can nonetheless be established. Moritz Benedikt (1835–1920), whom Freud rarely referred to, falls into this category (Ellenberger, 1970a, 1970b). Benedikt, a Viennese psychiatrist twenty years older than Freud, emphasized the importance of fantasy life in the normal and neurotic, as well as the frequency of sexual trauma in the childhood of hysterics.

Other sources may not be mentioned but can still be traced with certainty. Although Freud never directly acknowledges a debt to the German philosopher and psychologist Johann Friedrich Herbart (1776–1841), his ideas were the basis of Lindner's *Lehrbuch der empirischen Psychologie nach genetischer Methode*, the required textbook in Freud's Gymnasium during his last year. Freud claimed that the theory of repression came to him independent of external influence and that he knew of no outside source, but repression is clearly referred to by both Herbart and Lindner. Indeed, Lindner stated that "ideas which were once in consciousness and for any reason have been repressed (*verdrängt*) out of it are not lost, but in certain circumstances may return" (Jones, 1953, p. 374).

There are also sources not mentioned by Freud that can be presumed to have exerted an influence because of both similarities of content and evidence for direct personal contact. As was noted in Chapter 2, Brentano's ideas are never credited by Freud, but the similarities are striking, and we know of their direct contact in the lecture halls at the University of Vienna.

Still another source that must be evaluated is one that is expressly denied. Ellenberger suggests that Freud avoided reading Nietzsche "in order not to be influenced by him" (1970b, p. 37). He then questions whether it was possible not to be influenced since Nietzsche's ideas permeated the intellectual atmosphere of the time and were likely to have been absorbed unawares.[2] Yet Ellenberger may be misleading here, for Freud did not state that he avoided Nietzsche's influence, but that he did not read Nietzsche in order to avoid "being hampered in working out the impressions received in psychoanalysis by any sort of anticipatory ideas" (1914b, pp. 15–16). Freud appears to be making a point about the manner in which he chose to internalize Nietzsche's pervasive influence. Some forms of influence may be most effective while one is in the midst of creative work rather than serving as an impetus to the beginning phases. It is unlikely that Nietzsche's ideas were best incorporated while Freud felt

---

[2]Kaufmann (1980) and Holmes (1983) also point out the ubiquity and dominance of Nietzsche's ideas.

himself swayed by impressions derived from the clinical context; earlier exposure to the weight of Nietzsche's authority might have curtailed rather than fostered Freud's observational powers.

An Example of Influence

To examine in greater detail the effect of external influence on Freud's creativity, we may look at a particular instance for which the data are relatively good—namely, the development of the theory that sexual factors are responsible for neuroses. Freud described three separate occasions early in his career when the importance of sexuality as an etiological agent was revealed to him. We are informed about who influenced him, the circumstances in which the knowledge was given, and his emotional reactions to the information. He later came to write that in exchange for having to give up the belief that he had come up with a new and original idea, he had "a valuable insight into the processes of human creative activity and the nature of human knowledge" (1914b, p. 13).

The argument may be made that, because the incidents of influence I have selected are culled from Freud's "On the History of the Psycho-Analytic Movement" (1914b), they are suspect. The intent of the book was decidedly polemic. Freud was responding to the dissidents who had broken with him; he was concerned with what was psychoanalysis and what was not; and his use of the incidents was an "oblique strategy" to strengthen his case (Skinner, 1969). He clearly wished to establish that psychoanalysis was his brainchild and that he was in a better position to know what it was than others. Thus he may have been inclined to color the past in the interest of contemporary tendentious considerations.

Nevertheless, I do not believe that such an objection to my approach is warranted. Had Freud been interested in establishing priority for political or narcissistic reasons, it would have been more appropriate for him to ignore that he had been influenced by others and to claim that the discovery of the sexual etiology of the neuroses was his own creation. Instead, he maintained that others under-

stood the impact of sexuality before he did. Furthermore – and this I
believe is most telling – Freud arrived at the knowledge of having
been influenced as a result of a period of self-examination and introspection. The incidents had been repressed and were recovered
later. He stood to gain little from such revelations aside from docu-
menting that it was as true for him as for others that we do not like
to grasp fully facts which are objectionable.

The first incident occurred one day in the early 1880s, while
Freud was walking with Breuer on the streets of Vienna. The husband of a patient of Breuer's approached Breuer, and with some ur-
gency asked to speak with him. Freud politely moved out of earshot.
When the distressed man left, Breuer explained to the young Freud
that the wife, whose symptoms consisted of behaving in a peculiar
way in society, was actually a case of "secrets of the alcove." Aston-
ished, Freud asked for clarification. Breuer explained that he was
referring to the "marriage bed." Breuer did not realize how strange
this unheard-of (*unerhört*) matter appeared to Freud (1914a, p. 51).

The next incident occurred in 1885 or 1886 while Freud was in
Paris. One evening, at a reception at the home of Charcot, Freud
overheard Charcot describing an interesting clinical situation to a
colleague. The case concerned a young married couple; the woman
was in misery, the man was either impotent or a bungler. Charcot,
very animated, exclaimed, "In such cases, it is always something gen-
ital, always . . . always . . . always!" Freud recalled Charcot crossing
his arms over his abdomen, hugging himself, and jumping up and
down several times in an apparently characteristic manner. Again,
Freud was surprised; in fact, he "was almost paralyzed with amazement" (1914b, p. 14). His reaction was immediate: if Charcot knew
this, why did he never say so? Soon, however, Freud forgot the incident and continued his absorption in neuroanatomy and experimental induction of hysterical paralysis.

The third incident occurred a year later. Chrobak, the professor
of gynecology at the University of Vienna, referred a woman patient with attacks of nonspecific anxiety. Her symptoms were only
alleviated if she knew the exact presence of her doctor at every moment of the day. In making the referral, Chrobak told Freud that,

although the woman had been married for eighteen years, she was still a virgin; her husband was completely impotent. The only remedy for her misfortune was one the doctor was powerless to prescribe: repeated doses of normal penis (*penis normalis dosim repetatur*). Again, Freud reacted as if he had never heard of such a thing and registered disbelief.

Reflecting back on these incidents as he attempted to reconstruct the development of his ideas, he saw a sizable difference between his informants' attitude and his own toward the idea of a sexual etiology for the neuroses. After all, they had uttered a passing *aperçu*; their comments did not involve them in a serious commitment. He, on the other hand, had taken up the idea and pursued it in the face of all obstacles. They were merely carrying on a casual flirtation; he had *espoused* the idea, embarking on a legal marriage with all its attendant difficulties and responsibilities. (Freud, 1914b, p. 15).

Although there is little question that Freud's commitment to the sexual theory was solidified by his clinical experience, the three incidents suggest a germinal, catalytic force. Like the day residue, which serves as a focus for transference derivatives in the formation of a dream, the incidents served as points of crystallization for a host of related clinical observations. In reexamining the incidents, one is struck by a number of similar facets. To begin with, each incident involved a respected, older colleague and teacher in a context that hardly seemed appropriate for the communication of such a choice piece of insight. In each incident there was a sense in which Freud was being let in on a secret. The matter was communicated to him as a shrewd insight, with conviction—as if it were absolutely established, despite later denial by his informants. Freud's reaction was intensely emotional; he was even shocked to the point of disbelief. Even after Breuer told him that nervous conditions were always related to the secrets of the marriage bed, he reacted to both Charcot and Chrobak as if he had never heard of the idea before. The presumption is that, in each instance, Freud repressed the uncomfortable idea because of its sexual content. The idea continued to remain active in its repressed state, perhaps even directing and influencing the quality of his observations, but did not become integrated into an acceptable theory of neurosogenesis until it became free of conflictual connections or until his ego was capable of tolerating the anxiety connected with it. Both these steps had to be taken before Freud could make the move toward asking patients about their sexual lives or even hearing their unsolicited associations.

Interestingly, Freud's initial view of the sexual etiology of neuroses is closer to these incidents than his later formulation. The initial emphasis was on sexuality as a physical act, whether it was performed satisfactorily or at all; the later view had more to do with the psychological meaning of sexuality. The Breuer incident hints at secret dysfunctions; Charcot and Chrobak clearly point to sexual abstinence. As Freud came to appreciate the intrapsychic, conflictual basis for sexuality, his theories of neurosogenesis became less linear and more complex.

It is also worth considering an element of possible misunderstanding in each of the incidents. Freud later believed that he had been informed about etiological agents in the neuroses, but was this, in fact, true? Although Breuer himself wrote that "the great majority of severe neuroses in women have their *origin* in the marriage bed" (Breuer and Freud, 1893–1895b, p. 246; my italics), he made a later disclaimer, suggesting that he had been too readily caught up in Freud's enthusiasm. Charcot and Chrobak explicitly denied imparting such knowledge to Freud; they claimed they did not comment on etiology, merely on linkage. To the contrary, they may well have believed that some patients have sexual difficulties because of underlying factors rather than considering that sexual problems cause the neurotic disturbance. In terms of Freud's own work, however, primary significance was attached to the sexual disturbance at this point in his thinking. Indeed, much of his creative achievement stemmed from his fastening passionately upon an idea and exploring its multiple ramifications in order to see where it might lead. Through exploring this possible etiology, he arrived at a conception of the meaning of sexuality and intrapsychic conflict as agents in the psychoneuroses.

It is likely that Freud was thrown into considerable conflict by the incidents, and his initial need was to repudiate the importance of sexuality by disavowal and partial repression. The idea stirred him sufficiently to produce an intense emotional reaction, but it was not sufficiently traumatic to invoke total repudiation. The fact that the idea bore the authoritative stamp of a venerated teacher, that he was being let in on something secret, that the secret was not even understood by the informant, and that he was permitted, as it were, to take up the unpopular idea and find a legitimate place for it in the established world of intellectual thought – all these factors contributed to the value Freud attached to the influence.

Freud's sense that he was participating in the transmission of a tradition recalls his adolescent wish that his father had resembled Hamilcar, who made his son Hannibal "swear before the household altar to take vengeance on the Romans" (Freud, 1900a, p. 197) The failure of authority figures to appreciate the true worth of the idea also contributed to Freud's sense that it was his own. He felt that, although the idea had not originated with him, he had made it his own because he appreciated its value. Unlike his predecessors, he had struggled with it; and like Hannibal, he was willing to fight for it.

To reiterate, the entire episode was retrospectively important to him because it gave him "a valuable insight into the processes of human creative activity and the nature of human knowledge" (Freud, 1914b, p. 13). When Freud stated that his informants denied or would have denied their statements, perhaps he was not only referring to their unconscious resistance but also to his own. He himself came to appreciate the limitations of his earlier views in assessing the causes of the neuroses, and he expanded the conception of sexuality to refer to more than the presence of dysfunction or the absence of the physical sexual act. Here a fruitful error was of more use than a dull truth. Through his early concern with interferences with orgasmic discharge, he arrived at his psychological understanding of the meaning of sexual experience. Although the sexual etiology of neuroses was given lip service by Freud's forerunners, in some vital sense the importance of this knowledge was not accepted and was never put to use. Freud's creative activity did not consist in the discovery of the information but in the seriousness with which he responded to the knowledge. Here Freud was pointing out that creative activity often implies the overcoming of resistance, in this instance, the resistance of treating a serious matter as frivolous.

Fears of Influence

Freud's response to influence was not always acknowledged retrospectively, nor was it invariably receptive. In fact, two of his biographers claim that a degree of unsusceptibility was more characteristic. According to Wittels (1924), "He [Freud] finds it a nuisance when lights other than his own are thrown athwart his path, or when others try to push him forward or to divert him from his chosen course. Whenever necessary, he erects outworks to cut off inconvenient crosslights" (p. 150). Jones (1955) points to Freud's imperviousness to other people's opinions: "Freud had inherently a plastic and mobile mind, one given to the freest speculations and open to new and even highly improbable ideas. But it worked this way only on condition that the ideas came from himself; to those from outside he could be very resistant and they had little power in getting him to change his mind" (p. 429).

Freud himself complained bitterly of having to review the literature for *The Interpretation of Dreams*. In a letter to Fliess, he grumbled, "The literature [on dreams] which I am now reading is reducing me to idiocy. Reading is a terrible infliction imposed upon all who write. In the process, everything of one's own drains away" (1887–1902b, p. 270). We have seen how he avoided reading Nietzsche so as not to be "hampered in working out [his] impressions" (1914b, pp. 15–16). As Freud wrote Abraham, "I do not find it easy to feel my way into unfamiliar trains of thought, and generally have to wait until I have found a point of contact with them, by way of my own complicated paths" (Freud and Abraham, 1907–1926, p. 345).

In one sense, Freud's reluctance to be influenced by others is readily understandable. The Nietzsche remark underlines his wish to be influenced by observations derived from the clinical phenomena of the analytic situation rather than *a priori* conceptions, predisposing him to see things in a particular light. Yet Freud did understand that such uncontamination was virtually impossible. He realized that observations are guided by antecedent conceptions. He believed that originality is often only "apparent" and that influences of which an observer is often unaware determine modes of thought (Freud, 1920b; Trosman, 1969). As much as he could, he tried to eliminate the effect of conscious influences while permitting himself to be exposed to a wealth of stimuli through which he might be influenced by indirection.

On a deeper level, psychologically, the experience of being influenced was linked with conflicts and developmental difficulties that were reactivated by Freud's creative work. In the three incidents described earlier, the oedipal implication of Freud's reaction is clear. He felt that sexual knowledge, the true meaning of which was not recognized by a paternal authority, was imparted to him unwittingly. A secret was being shared, but the sharer did not appreciate the significance of the secret. The metaphor about flirtation and legal marriage further documents the sense of oedipal avoidance and triumph that Freud experienced (1914b, p. 15).

The literary critic Harold Bloom (1973) has put forward a theory of poetry based on the poet's relations with literary ancestors. Although his concern is with literature, his approach is psychological, and he offers a number of insights applicable to the general problem of influence. According to Bloom, creative poets are threatened by their predecessors, fearing that their voices will merely echo the master who influenced them most. Here Bloom draws on the remarks of various literary figures on the vicissitudes of influence from the point of view of both the one who influences and the one who is influenced. According to Oscar Wilde, for instance, "Influence is . . . a mode of giving away what is most precious to one's self and its exercise produces a sense, and it may be, a reality, of loss. Every disciple takes away something from his master" (quoted in Bloom, 1973, p. 6). Wilde continues, "To influence a person is to give him one's own soul. He does not think his natural thoughts or burn with his natural passions. . . . He becomes an echo of someone else's music" (p. 6). The repudiation of influence is illustrated in the comments of Wallace Stevens. He asserted, "While, of course, I come down from the past, the past is my own . . . I know of no one who has been particularly important to me" (p. 6). Stevens wrote to Richard Eberhart, a younger poet who was alleged to have been influenced by him:

> I sympathize with your denial of any influence on my part. This sort of thing always jars me because, in my own case, I am not conscious of having been influenced by anybody and have purposely held off from reading highly mannered people like Eliot and Pound so that I should not absorb anything, even unconsciously. But there is a kind of critic who spends his time dissecting what he reads for echoes, imitations, influences, as if no one was ever simply himself, but is always compounded of a lot of other people [p. 7].

Note that Stevens stated, "I am not conscious of having been influenced by anybody," not "I have not been influenced by anybody."

A comparison with Freud is of interest in this context. Stevens' avoidance of potential influence recalls Freud's reluctance to read Nietzsche; however, where Freud feared interference with the clarity of his observations, Stevens saw the experience of being influenced as taking something away from the individuality of his achievement. Again, Stevens, in stating, "I am not conscious of having been influenced by anybody," is quite unlike Freud, who stated that he was willing to grant that all his apparently original findings had been anticipated by others (1914b, 1920b).

Influence may be feared for a variety of reasons. The power of the predecessor may be experienced as an interference with one's own sense of achievement and uniqueness, as in Stevens' case. Or one may feel such an indebtedness to another that a sense of obligation and gratitude obsessively interferes with the freedom creative work needs. The idealized achievement of the predecessor may also be experienced as a seduction, stirring passive homosexual wishes and castration fears. The temptation to submerge one's own personality in the greatness of the other and the fears associated with such passive wishes were well appreciated by Freud. In discussing the terminal phase of analysis, he noted how difficult it frequently proved to be to persuade a man that a passive attitude toward other men does not always imply castration; he indicated that recovery from psychological illness may frequently be interfered with because success implies subjection to a father-surrogate (1937, p. 252).

Bloom states, "The anxiety of influence is an anxiety of expectation of being flooded" (1973, p. 57). Not only are fears of castration aroused by the passive position, but Bloom implies that the ego must deal with an intense and overwhelming, quantitative traumatic factor as well. The increase in excitation in response to intense stimulation may interfere with judicious and clear-minded assessment. Something of this intensity is suggested by Freud's early remark in response to Charcot:

> Charcot . . . is simply wrecking all my aims and opinions. I sometimes come out of his lectures as from out of Notre Dame, with an entirely new idea about perfection. But he exhausts me; when I come away from him I no longer have any desire to work at my own silly things. . . . My brain is sated as after an evening in the theatre. Whether the seed will ever bear any fruit, I don't know; but what I do know is that no other human being has ever affected me in the same way [Letter of November 24, 1885, in 1873–1939a, p. 185].

Although Freud continued to admire Charcot and considered him one of the greatest men with whom he had ever had direct contact, it soon became clear that the intensity of his admiration did not interfere with his ability to make independent judgments about Charcot's work. Only three years after the above-quoted remarks, he criticized Charcot for "unconsciously" suggesting intention to hypnotic subjects (Freud, 1888b, p. 78). By 1892, when he translated Charcot's *Leçons du mardi de la Salpêtrière* into German, he appended a number of footnotes that were further critical of Charcot's ideas (Freud, 1892–1894).

Still, Freud's initial reaction was one of being overwhelmed, similar to the astonishment and amazement he felt when informed of the sexual etiology of the neuroses by Breuer and Chrobak. But there is a difference between being intensely affected by someone and feeling a loss of self or ego boundaries in response to such influence. Freud did not lose himself in response to Charcot and become, in Wilde's sense, an echo. Rather, he gained a new concept of the ideal and a content for his ambition. It would appear that he had an immediate awareness of the significance Charcot's work was to have for him. The intensity of his reaction indicates the germinal quality of the influence and the likelihood that, after integrating Charcot's ideas, he would move further from those stepping stones.

It is also noteworthy that Freud showed little hesitation in exposing himself to Charcot's influence. Nor, for that matter, did he shun direct contact with others, such as Brücke, Meynert, or Breuer, who could guide his clinical interests. He did, however, avoid other opportunities of influence, such as philosophical systems and psychological viewpoints that would be likely to interfere with direct clinical observation. His avoidance of Nietzsche and Schopenhauer is to be understood not only on the basis of the "constitutional incapacity" he claimed (1925a, p. 59). He feared that philosophical influence might color the impartiality necessary if novel and perhaps unpopular observations were to be made. Instead of seeing something new, one might conveniently fit it into a heretofore accepted system. Freud wanted to erect his own conceptual scaffolding.

The Psychology of Influence

The intellectual historian concerned with the effect of influence on innovation may frequently arrive at conclusions for which there are no subjective referents. For instance, as we have seen, Freud did not implicate Brentano as instrumental in the development of psychoanalysis; yet there is no reason to deny his role since we have objective data of Freud's contact with him. One might even speculate that Brentano's influence on Freud took place in a manner that was barely discernible as a conscious subjective experience. Freud may have responded to a variety of external factors—such as the philosophical lectures of Brentano, the psychology of Herbart, or the psychiatry of Moritz Benedikt – as if these were acceptable views of reality. The influence, then, may have seemed no more significant than that of a Gymnasium instructor who taught him the rudiments of Greek grammar.

It may be that someone is significantly influenced by another and yet this influence leaves no apparent trace. The problem here is similar to the difficulty in attempting to group the psychological qualities at "the core of our ego" (Kohut, 1966, p. 251). Binswanger (1956) told Freud that he believed that Freud had "an enormous will to power . . . to dominate." Freud responded that, although he was unaware of such a tendency in himself, he could not contradict Binswanger's claim. He was prepared to accept not only that repressed content of the psyche was unconscious but that the core of the ego was also unconscious. Critial influences may, in a similar fashion, exert their effect on core qualities through means that are unconscious but not repressed. The earliest identifications the young child acquires as a result of direct contact with the parents fit into this group of influences.

We shall be on safer heuristic ground, however, if we examine influences that are acknowledged or are accepted after the overcoming of resistance – that is, influences that were suppressed or repressed in the first instance. Initially such influences – defined as acts or forces that attain perceptual quality and produce a discernible effect – may be either consciously or unconsciously experienced. They may affect components of the psyche such as a mode of cognition, a method of observation, an ideational or behavioral pattern, or a mode of integration. Influential ideas or attitudes may be experienced as fitting in with a line of thought already present or as a foreign element, which becomes integrated only with time.

Through looking at the phenomenon of influence as a psychological experience in the clinical psychoanalytic situation, we gain additional insight into the manner in which influence is brought about, how it is disregarded or disclaimed, and how it is integrated into adaptive and autonomous activity. On one end, there is the pathology of influence, which covers a wide range of psychological states. The schizophrenic patient's delusion of the influencing machine is an example of the projection of regulatory factors, separated off from the self and attributed to external reality (Tausk, 1919). The self feels powerless in the face of such forces and can only weakly, if at all, resist their dictatorial rule. There is a regressive return to an archaic ego state where control and regulation are primarily external; the feeling of being influenced overrides the capacity to experience volition or choice. Similarly, the "as if" personality is guided by an intense wish to submerge the self in the beliefs, values, and lifestyle of another in order to compensate for an inner sense of emptiness and lifelessness (Deutsch, 1942). Being influenced and merging become synonymous.

In hypnosis we observe a relatively clear instance of influence brought about through the establishment of a regressed ego state; suggestion is responded to as if it were equivalent to the will of the subject. There is an absence of criticism and initiative as the hypnotist takes on the role of a powerful ego ideal (Freud, 1921). The factor of idealization is also evident in the state of sexual bondage, in which an individual develops an intense dependency upon someone with whom there has been a satisfying sexual relationship. Although Freud pointed out that this state of bondage is more common in women than in men, it may occur in men as a result of overcoming physical impotence with a particular woman, who then remains the object of permanent sexual attachment (Freud, 1918b). A crucial factor is the amount of sexual resistance overcome by the man and the concentrated nature of the experience.

Similarities between influence and the biological phenemenon of imprinting described by ethologists also come to mind. Although ethologists emphasize the developmental and phase-specific aspects of the imprinting event, the stability of the attachment is reminiscent of the bondage described by Freud. (In the latter case, the impact of the influence is increased by the fact that the influential person provides a channel for the satisfaction of a pressing drive, which had heretofore found no adequate means for discharge.) Moreover, the phase-specific nature of influence cannot be discounted. Particular critical phases and traumatic states heighten susceptibility. As one matures, or at least grows older, susceptibility to new ideas decreases. We speak of youth as impressionable, and we say that you can't teach an old dog new tricks.

The influences brought to bear upon the patient in the psychoanalytic situation also throw light on the influences on creativity. The establishment of a therapeutic alliance, the patient's expectations of receiving help, and the analyst's benign and concerned attitude serve as a favorable matrix for change. The additional contributions of a positive, erotic or a negative transference—the investment of the analyst with the attributes of powerful parental images—heighten the impact of the analyst's interventions. Interpretations and working through, which establish a connection between previously warded-off unconscious content and preconscious forms of expression, influence the patient to find ego-dominated modes for the discharge of id derivatives.

Some forms of influence are immediately apparent and are the direct result of identification processes with the analyst. The analysand who begins to dress like the analyst or the analytic candidate who tries out an interpretation he received on his next patient exemplifies such manifest forms of influence. Yet the analytic situation also exerts influence in subtler ways. The stability and regularity of the analytic session, the emphasis on understanding as a response to emotional tension rather than direct discharge, the high regard for truth, and a caring attitude are attributes of the situation that become internalized as components of the patient's ego.

The influence of both the analytic relationship and interpretation rests on economic factors. The salutary effect is gradual; it depends on the weakening of resistance and defensiveness, permitting drive derivatives to surface in the transference. Influence works by indirection. Perhaps, as in the situations with which Freud was confronted, it is most effective when it is least deliberate and consciously planned. Psychoanalysts' generally critical attitude toward a consciously planned corrective emotional experience takes this factor of indirection into account.

Also of value in clarifying the dynamics of influence is our understanding of the dream process. In dream formation, a particular day residue serves as the nidus for the latent dream thoughts and their unconscious roots. In itself the link between the day residue and the unconscious content may be emotionally insignificant; the link may depend on other factors—for example, linguistic similarity or temporal continuity. In Freud's dream of the botanical monograph, for instance, the fact that he had seen a monograph in a bookshop window entitled *The Genus Cyclamen* served as a recent but indifferent influence (Freud, 1900a, pp. 169–176). What this stimulus allowed was a clustering of ideas, linked primarily by verbal association. In this case, the lack of psychic intensity permitted the transfer of unconscious content. Thus, one may speak of a stimulus or influence that is weakly cathected initially but has capacity for further evocation of associationally meaningful links.

Another form of influence may be responded to because its ideational content is lined with conflict, which is activated or partially surmounted. In his gradual move toward free association as the psychoanalytic method, Freud was influenced by a number of patients who demonstrated the usefulness of unimpeded access to preconscious mental contents. He mentions incorporating several suggestions from patients, which encouraged him to turn from hypnosis toward a concentration on free association. The radical implications of these suggestions were responded to because of an intimate connection with a similar idea Freud had encountered at the age of fourteen and subsequently forgotten (Freud, 1920a). He had read about the technique of free association in an essay by Ludwig Börne and had probably tried it as an introspective method. In this instance, the influence of his patients and the clinical situation was attended to because of a similarity to previously warded-off material. What had been excessively traumatic at fourteen, (when the ego was in a relatively weakened state) either continued to undergo modification or became utilized in carrying out an appropriate adaptive task once the ego was no longer threatened. A potential influence can thus be strengthened by its similarity to an unconscious idea, which then finds an available route for expression (Trosman, 1969).

The fear of being influenced may be considered in terms of either the content of the transmitted idea or the act of transmission and the attendant meaning of the act. In Freud's case, when told of the crucial importance of sexuality in neuroses, he doubtless reacted to both factors. He was overwhelmed by what he had been told by Breuer, Charcot, and Chrobak; at the same time he needed special conditions for an influence to affect him. As Freud grew older, not only did he overcome his fears of being influenced, he began to welcome evidence that his ideas were linked with a lengthy and profound intellectual tradition. Witness his satisfaction in pointing out the link between his ideas and that of the pre-Socratic philosopher Empedocles (Freud, 1937). If abstract influencing agents such as the link with antiquity or "The Muse" or "one's demon" or "inspiration" can be credited with motivational force, the fear of personal influence is mitigated. A misreading of the influencing agent or the direction of attention toward peripheral findings or minor errors may also serve to authenticate autonomy and originality. A bad memory helps. As Hart Crane wrote, "I can remember much forgetfulness" (quoted in Bloom, 1975, p. 199).

If influence is not resisted but integrated, one may feel that one is developing and completing the work of a predecessor or, as in Freud's case, that a predecessor has unwittingly passed on an essential idea, the true value of which he was unaware. It must have appealed to Freud's sense of irony to believe that he was partly directed by those who would have disclaimed their influence, who would indeed have preferred to dissociate themselves from his ideas and their subsequent unpopularity.

Finally, how much importance are we to attach to the incidents with Breuer, Charcot, and Chrobak? In the long run they do not seem as influential, for example, as Freud's hearing about the case of Anna O. or noting in psychoanalytic sessions the preoccupations of his patients with sexual matters. But some predilection in the personality must be ready to resonate with what is directly presented, as in the clinical context. A piece of knowledge initially warded off and then accepted may add a clarifying charge of intensity to an understanding of what a patient's preoccupations really are.

4

Artistic and Neurotic Fantasy

As Freud began to work with neurotic patients and attempted to formulate a theory to organize his clinical findings, he turned to art as an aid. From the very beginning of his work in psychoanalysis, he was struck with the link between hysterical symptoms and creative writing. As early as May 1897 he recognized the existence of similar mechanisms in both (1887–1902b, p. 256). To illustrate this connection, he cited an episode surrounding the writing of Goethe's *The Sorrows of Young Werther*.[1]

The twenty-three-year-old Goethe had fallen in love with a young woman, Charlotte Buff, who was already engaged to his friend Georg Kestner. When Lotte spurned his love, or perhaps when Goethe was threatened that Lotte might respond, he suddenly departed. Less than two months later, Goethe heard that a mutual friend, Wilhelm Jerusalem, had committed suicide. Jerusalem had loved the wife of a friend and had borrowed Kestner's pistol to kill himself. All at once, when Goethe heard the news of

---

[1]It is no accident that Freud turned to Goethe, a hallowed member of the humanist pantheon. Freud quoted from Goethe's work more often than from any other writer. He later wrote that Goethe "approached [psychoanalysis] at a number of points" and "recognized much through his own insight that we have since been able to confirm" (1930b, p. 208). Goethe indicated the importance of early familial ties in accounting for mature object relations, as well as the importance of mental life in the understanding of dreams; he had even evolved a cathartic form of psychotherapy in helping a friend burdened by irrational guilt.

Jerusalem's death, the plan of *Werther* was formed; the plot for the novel began to take shape.

Freud suggested that Goethe himself had toyed with the idea of suicide and thus found a point of contact between his own fantasies and the suicide of Jerusalem. Goethe could attribute to Jerusalem motives similar to his own. Yet by creating the fantasy and elaborating it in the novel, Goethe could avoid suicide. The fantasy served a protective function and preserved the intactness of the ego while permitting gratification for the vengeful and aggressive drives stirred up by Lotte's rebuff. Freud concluded that "Shakespeare was right in his juxtaposition of poetry and madness (the fine frenzy)" (1887–1902b, p. 208).

In this instance, two links between hysterical fantasy and creative writing are highlighted. First, there is a similarity in the construction of the fantasy and the creative work. A displacement must be brought about through "a point of contact," which permits an accessible substitution. Once Goethe could substitute Jerusalem for himself in fantasy, it was but another step to create Werther, who was a compromise for both. In *The Sorrows of Young Werther,* Goethe uses Lotte's actual name and gives Werther his own birthday, April 28. Just as Jerusalem borrowed Kestner's pistol, Werther borrows the pistol from Lotte's fiancé. And Werther dies, like Jerusalem, with Lessing's *Emilia Galotti* on his desk.

Second, through the route of creative fantasy, Goethe's ego could overcome his suicidal wish. In this instance, literary creation could shore up a partially fragmented psyche and prove a useful buffer against further disorganization. In his autobiographical writings, Goethe himself indicated how the suicidal wish was dissipated:

> Among a considerable collection of weapons, I possessed a handsome, well-polished dagger. This I laid every night by my bed, and before I extinguished the candle, I tried whether I could succeed in plunging the sharp point a couple of inches deep into my heart. Since I could never succeed in this, I at last laughed myself out of the notion, threw off all hypochondriacal fancies, and resolved to live. But to be able to do this with serenity, I was obliged to translate into

literary form and to clothe in words all that I had felt, thought, and fancied on this important point. With this object in view, I collected the scattered elements which had been at work in me the last few years; I called back to mind the cases which had most afflicted and tormented me; but failed in attaining any definite conception: I lacked an event, a plot in which to embody them [1811–1822, pp. 126–127].

The suicide of Jerusalem was the event.

Eissler (1967) has suggested that not only was the creation of the novel a hedge against suicidal wishes but the toying with suicide was a necessary contributant to the power of *Werther*. He argues that in order to evoke in the reader the appropriate mood of grief and despair, the author had to experience it in reality. In Eissler's words: "This ability to evoke a cataclysmic reality in the reader was, in short, made possible by the fact that, for a while, Goethe tried every night to stab himself—in all seriousness, it seems—and repeatedly went through the throes of despair that frequently take possession of the suicide shortly before he executes the deed" (p. 56).

For Freud, the issue at hand had little to do with the indisputable power of *Werther* as a work of art. His interest was in the protective function of fantasy. Goethe could live because he had found a way of discharging his suicidal impulses through fantasy. Displacement could occur because of an opportunity to connect what was heard and what was experienced. The poet's use of fantasy and the mechanism of displacement suggested a similarity between the poet and the neurotic. It also underlined a psychological function in creative fantasy.

Freud's Early Interest in Art and Literature

Freud's application of artistic creation to the understanding of neurosis was anticipated by a wealth of literary observations and enthusiasms which appear in his youthful letters. As a boy of eight, he started to read Shakespeare. At sixteen, he was versed in Goethe and recommended Sophocles' *Oedipus Rex* to a correspondent.

From his reading of Horatian odes, he found he could easily adopt a Horatian tone of ironic detachment (Freud, 1969). And he wrote a parody of a wedding poem in a mock-Homeric style (Rogawski, 1970). At eighteen, in a letter to a friend, Eduard Silberstein, he offered a critique of Thomas Carlyle's *Sartor Resartus:*

> The book is introduced in the manner of Jean Paul [the German novelist] and at times shows Jean Paul's spirit. However, on the whole, it is definitely English and derides us brooding Germans. A German professor, Diogenes Teufelsdroeckh, at the University of Don't-Know-Where, Professor of the science of things in general, has written a "Philosophy of Clothes." This is sent to the author (Carlyle) with the request to publish an English translation thereof. The latter complies with the demand insofar as he translates at least some of the extracts of this peculiar literary effort. . . . There is great wisdom [in the book] and the multi-colored scraps of folly cover the open wounds of humanity and of the hero [in Stanescu, 1971, pp. 200–201].

Freud apparently enjoyed the fun poked at the turgid German philosophical tradition, of which his teacher, Brentano, was a disciple. He also commented on Alexandre Dumas' *Dame aux Camelias*, Georg Lichtenberg's satirical essays, Gottfried's *Tristan and Isolde*, and the plays of Frederich Hebbel.

Freud continued to write extensively of literature and the arts in his correspondence with his fiancée from 1883 to 1886. Goethe, Shakespeare, and Cervantes were referred to several times (Freud, 1873–1939a), with quotations from *Faust* (p. 50), *Twelfth Night* (p. 5), and *Hamlet* (p. 19). Freud also quoted from Milton's *Paradise Lost*, and referred to him as "an even greater poet" than his revered Goethe. When discouraged, he found strength in Milton's lines; as he wrote Martha:

> Let us consult
> What reinforcement we may gain from hope;
> If not, what resolution from despair
> [*Paradise Lost*, Book 7, ll.190–191; quoted in Freud, 1873–1939a, p. 48].

Don Quixote was a source of great pleasure and perhaps an antidote against his own grandiose and unrealistic ambitions. He particularly enjoyed Gustave Doré's illustrations—"a splendid contribution toward dispelling all the romantic nonsense about chivalry" (p. 46).

Freud was familiar with the English novelists. He recommended Charles Dickens' "The Chimes" and "The Battle of Life" (p. 88), and he read and gave as gifts the novels of George Eliot (pp. 131, 168). He suggested Victor Hugo's *The Hunchback of Notre Dame* to Martha as a way of understanding Paris. "Although everything in it is fiction," he remarked, "one is convinced of its truth" (p. 188). In addition, he made several observations on the style of John Stuart Mill, whom he found "lifeless" on the first reading, but later "witty, epigrammatically apt and lively" (p. 75).

In the literature of his native language, he had a wide acquaintance with eighteenth- and nineteenth-century German poetry. He quoted from Gottfried Bürger (p. 37), Frederich von Schiller (p. 214), Ludwig Uhland (p. 17), Johann Herder, (p. 4), and Heinrich Heine (p. 51). He referred to characters in poems by J. B. Hebel (p. 94), Christian Gellert (p. 12), and Anton Auersperg (p. 61). He also knew the novels of Josef Victor von Scheffel (p. 68) and Frederich Theodor Vischer (p. 133) and the plays of Gotthold Ephraim Lessing (p. 17).

While in Paris working with Charcot, from 1885 to 1886, he enjoyed the writings of the Viennese Daniel Spitzer, published in the *Neue Freie Presse* (p. 182). He delighted in the French theater, enthusing about the plays of Beaumarchais (p. 192), but criticizing those of Victorien Sardou (p. 179). Sarah Bernhardt enchanted him (p. 180), as did the brothers Coquelin, playing Molière (p. 172).

Freud made fewer references to musical performances; indeed, music does not seem to have played much of a role in his life. His sister recalled that she was prohibited from practicing the piano because it interfered with his studies (Bernays, 1940; Jones, 1953, pp. 17–18). At seventeen, offered a choice between Schiller's *Die Rauber* and Mozart's *The Magic Flute*, he could still opt for *The Magic Flute* (Freud, 1969). But eleven years later, his attitude toward music had shifted. He related that in 1885, while in Paris, he paid a call on the wife of the Freud family's physician. The doctor's wife was living in Paris next to the Conservatoire with her ten-year-old son, who had won a prize at the Vienna Conservatorium and was said to be highly gifted. Freud wrote Martha that, "instead of secretly throttling the prodigy, the wretched father . . . has sent the boy with his mother to Paris to study at the Conservatoire and try for another prize. Just imagine the expense, the separation, the dispersal of the household. . . . Little wonder that parents grow vain about their children, and even less that such children grow vain themselves" (1873–1939a, p. 186). Freud resolved that he would visit the family weekly, and added that "the prodigy is pale, plain, but looks pretty intelligent." The prodigy of such questionable value was Fritz Kreisler.

In spite of his lack of response to music, Freud drew on a performance of *Carmen* to speculate how "the mob gives vent to its appetites and we deprive ourselves" (1873–1939a, p. 50). Fifteen years later, he could still hum the tune to "Se vuol ballare" from *The Marriage of Figaro* when he was feeling combative and in high spirits (1900a, p. 208). Perhaps the world of music was less of a closed book than he acknowledged.

On a trip to Dresden with his two half-brothers in 1883, Freud had an opportunity to visit the art museum. Previously he had believed that people who praised masterpieces were not genuine in their appreciation. In Dresden, however, he "rid himself of this barbaric notion and began to admire" (1873–1939a, p. 81). He described Van Dyck's portrait of the children of Charles I of England, a Veronese painting, and Holbein's *Madonna with the Meyer Family* (actually a copy of the original in Darmstadt). Although he was enthralled with Raphael's *Sistine Madonna*, he had a serious objection to this Madonna: she looked more like a sixteen-year-old, sympathetic, charming nursemaid from this world than from heaven.[2]

---

[2]Further references to the "nursemaid quality" he saw in Raphael's *Sistine Madonna* occur in later writings (Freud, 1910b). Griggs (1973) and Vitz (1983) point out that Freud's sensitivity to the "nursemaid" quality in the Madonnas of Raphael and Leonardo may have derived from his childhood attachment to a Catholic nanny, who frequently took him to church, where he was enthralled by the services.

But the picture that really captivated him was Titian's *Tribute Money.* The head of Christ he found so convincing he was prepared to accept the eminence of the man. "A noble human countenance," he exclaimed, "far from beautiful, yet full of seriousness, intensity, profound thought, and deep inner passion; if these qualities do not exist in this picture, then there is no such thing as physiognomy" (p. 82).

Initially Freud responded primarily to the figures in paintings. The formal components of an art work—matters of composition, color, line, light, form, foreground-background relationships, handling of space, brushwork—did not interest him until several years later. At this time he was more concerned with the "spiritual content" of a work and the way the artist had chosen to depict sacred figures (Gombrich, 1966). Only later, urged on by Wilhelm Fliess, did he look at Italian art "not for what is of cultural-historical interest, but for absolute beauty clothed in forms and ideas and in fundamentally pleasing sensations of space and color" (1887–1902b, p. 214).[3]

Art and Clinical Work

An examination of the affinity between literature and psychoanalysis might begin with an examination of Freud's early case histories and the unfolding of his self-analysis. "A single case . . . might teach us everything," wrote Freud (1918a, p. 10), thus highlighting the importance he attached to the clinical account.[4] From a different angle, reflecting on the overall effect of his case reports, he commented:

> It still strikes me myself as strange that the case histories I write should read like short stories and that, as one might say, they lack

---

[3]Thus Fliess did more than serve as a scientific mentor; he also appealed to Freud's aesthetic and humanistic side.

[4]On the other hand, he stated "A single case history, even if it were complete and open to doubt, cannot provide an answer to all the questions arising out of the problems of hysteria" (1905a, p. 13).

the serious stamp of science. . . . The fact is that the local diagnosis and electrical reactions lead nowhere in the study of hysteria, whereas a detailed description of mental processes such as we are accustomed to find in the works of imaginative writers enables me, with the use of a few psychological formulas, to obtain at least some kind of insight into the course of that affection. [Breuer and Freud, 1893–1895b, pp. 160–161].

A review of case reports from the time of his return from Paris in 1886 to the publication of *Studies on Hysteria* in 1895 provides evidence of his increasing reliance on the methods of the creative writer. Specifically, one might compare his first case report, on August P. (1886b), and a second report on a mother who was unable to nurse her newborn (1892–1893) to the descriptions in *Studies on Hysteria* (Breuer and Freud, 1893–1895b).

Challenged by Meynert to demonstrate hysteria in a male, Freud presented the case of August P. in front of the Vienna *Gesellschaft der Aerzte* (Society of Medicine). His description of the patient (who attended the presentation) concentrated on the physical examination to the almost total neglect of mental processes (1886b, pp. 25–31). In commenting on the onset of his symptoms, however, Freud did mention that the patient had fallen into a dispute with his dissolute brother, and when the brother threatened him with a knife, the patient felt "indescribable fear." The patient then suffered an exacerbation of his symptoms when he was accused by a woman of theft (pp. 26–27).

The second account, describing the unnamed woman who could not nurse her baby, is more lively and rounded (1892–1893, pp. 117–128). Freud saw this woman, whose communications were restricted to "odourless eructations," about four years after treating August P. He cured her aversion to breast feeding by hypnotic suggestion. In his report Freud offered no explanation for the patient's symptoms, aside from the deduction that the "fortuitous cause was the patient's excited state before her first confinement or her exhaustion after it. A first confinement is, after all, the greatest shock to which the female organism is subject, and as a result of it, a woman will, as a rule, produce any neurotic symptoms that may be latent in her disposition" (p. 123). When he first visited the patient, he indicated, "far from being welcomed as a saviour in her hour of need, I was obviously being received with a bad grace and I could not count on the patient's having much confidence in me" (p. 119). Even when the patient recovered she was still ungrateful. For Freud, it was "hard to understand . . . as well as annoying that no reference was ever made to my remarkable achievement [cure by hypnotic suggestion]" (p. 120) – an achievement he was soon to raise serious questions about himself. Here, although Freud does not tell us much about the patient's experience, he does at least share his own feelings and expectations.

By the time he completed his part of the *Studies on Hysteria*, it was clear to Freud that in order to describe the clinical method, he had to appropriate the technique of the imaginative writer. In the years between his writings for the *Studies on Hysteria* and his initial composition of the Dora case history in 1901 (published in 1905), Freud attained a blend of scientific and literary skill sufficient to warrant the claim that he was "a great writer" and that "one of his major case histories is a great work of literature" (Marcus, 1974, p. 12). Indeed, it has become common for even critics who are not persuaded by the findings of psychoanalysis to praise Freud for his literary skill in the case histories (Burnham, 1967; Ellenberger, 1970a). His *Fragment of an Analysis of a Case of Hysteria* (1905a) has been compared to "a classical Victorian domestic drama" with "novelistic framing action," and described as "Nabokovian," "Ibsenian," and "Proustian" (Marcus, 1974, pp. 15, 20, 89, 94). Freud's 1896 address to the Society of Psychiatry and Neurology in Vienna has been analyzed for its literary skill (Wolf, 1971). And, despite Freud's own reservations about its literary style, *The Interpretation of Dreams* (1900a) has been praised as the work of a great writer who emerged contemporaneously with the psychoanalyst from 1895 to 1900 (Schwaber, 1976).

During this time Freud was not only increasing his literary skills in a stylistic sense; he simultaneously began to use the content of literature as an important adjunct to his clinical findings. His readings of imaginative literature offered support for the knowledge gained through his self-analysis. On June 12, 1897, Freud told Fliess that he was passing "through some kind of neurotic experience, with odd states of mind not intelligible to consciousness—cloudy thoughts and veiled doubts with barely here and there a ray of light. . . . I believe I am in a cocoon, and heaven knows what sort of creature will emerge from it" (1887–1902b, pp. 210–211). When his father had died the previous October, his reaction had been intense; he was left feeling as if he had been "torn up by the roots" (p. 170). He had hoped for relief on his summer vacation at Anssee in 1897, but after an initial period of feeling well, he once more fell into gloom. "The chief patient I am busy with is myself," he wrote on August 14 (p. 213). After returning from a further holiday trip to Italy, his self-analysis began in earnest.

In October 1897, in the midst of his self-analytic work, Freud offered his analysis of *Oedipus Rex*. It is striking that Freud returned to a play he first referred to at age sixteen, as if its availability were never far distant (see Freud, 1969). He pointed out that he had discovered love for his mother and jealousy of his father in himself just as he had in his patients. Indeed, he was prepared to accept that the complex was a universal phenomenon of early childhood. It was the ubiquity of this complex that accounted for the power of the drama *Oedipus Rex*, overriding rational objections to the theme of an inexorable fate. To the contrary, Freud noted that plays in which the fate seems arbitrary are less appealing, for they fail to stir the intrapsychic conflict. "Every member of the audience was once a budding Oedipus in fantasy" (1887–1902b, p. 224). In watching the dramatic reenactment of their repressed wishes, the members of the audience recoil in horror.

In focusing on the reaction of the audience rather than the meaning of the play itself, Freud's comment is in fact compatible with the Aristotelian notion that great tragedy evokes and discharges feelings like pity and terror. His interpretation highlights intrapsychic conflict over a conception of events instigated by external factors such as seducing fathers or inexorable fate. The audience's horror stems from the anxiety attached to the fulfillment of primitive, unacceptable wishes. The power of the play lies in the tension between the wishes that are aroused and the means the dramatist uses to reveal them. *Oedipus Rex* grounds the complex Freud had uncovered within himself and his patients in the origins of the Western literary tradition.

A year or two later, Freud elaborated on these views in *The Interpretation of Dreams*. He discussed the play under the section on typical dreams — dreams that almost everyone has had, with similar content and meanings and arising from similar sources. Not only is the play like a typical dream; it even includes within itself a typical dream. Jocasta consoles Oedipus by telling him that the common dream of a man having intercourse with his mother is best ignored. But this fantasy is the key to the tragedy. The attempt to impose a philosophical and theological meaning on the play, such as man's need to submit to divine will, is a form of secondary revision.

According to Freud, the legend and the play "confirm" the universal nature of oedipal longings. Sophocles' play is like a psychoanalysis because its action is concerned with revelation. As in a psychoanalysis, the major events of the story have all occurred before the play begins; the play itself is concerned with removing obstacles to acknowledging the truth. Further, the play is not just a tragedy of destiny, unless one conceives of destiny as the fate of each member of the audience to experience the oedipal drama. We are compelled "to recognize our own inner minds"; yet after the revelation of the drama, we once more "close our eyes" to the childhood wishes and are blinded like Oedipus (Freud, 1900a, pp. 261–264).

In Freud's view, then, the playwright and the hero of the drama are prototypical psychoanalyst and analysand. The dramatist's skill emerges in the pacing of the revelations. The content of the wishes does not change over time; dramatic artistry is responsible for our tolerance of the repressed content. The "poet [who is] compelling us to recognize our own inner minds" is like the psychoanalyst who unravels the resistance to the analytic work (1900a, p. 263). The hero is fated by his own nature to live out and make conscious the oedipal tragedy. The Greek version of fate as ordered and remorseless resembles the modern view of the inexorable laws of nature — a view to which Freud responded when, in deciding to study nature, he stated that "he would eavesdrop on her eternal process" (1969, p. 424).

Freud, like Oedipus, felt an unrestrained need to follow through the process his investigations had instigated regardless of the painful consequences.

From *Oedipus Rex* Freud moved to *Hamlet*, and he suggested that Hamlet's wish to kill his father because of passion for his mother was at the heart of Shakespeare's play as well. According to Freud (1887–1902b), Shakespeare's unconscious understood Hamlet's, perhaps because he had been motivated to write *Hamlet* by a real event. Hamlet is guilt-ridden because of his deeply repressed incestuous longings for his mother and murderous wishes toward his father. Although he moves with dispatch against Rosencrantz, Guildenstern, and Laertes, he cannot murder his uncle, who has acted out his own wishes. In a typically hysterical fashion, substituting one person for another, Hamlet turns his rage for his father against Ophelia. And by unconscious identification with his father, he finally suffers the fate of his father: his murder is brought about by the same man who killed his father.

In *The Interpretation of Dreams* (1900a), Freud elaborates his commentary on *Hamlet*, in comparison with *Oedipus Rex*. Both plays deal with similar material — guilt for murderous wishes toward the father because of love for the mother. Yet the treatment differs due to the increased repression in the later historical period. *Oedipus Rex* is more like a typical dream, in which a fantasy is openly fulfilled; in *Hamlet*, the wish is repressed. The response of the audience to Shakespeare's play does not depend on a growing conscious awareness of Hamlet's unconscious fantasy, as in the case of *Oedipus Rex*. Instead, Shakespeare focuses on the reactions against the unconscious wishes. The play is structured by Hamlet's attempt to overcome his hesitations. He is not absolutely irresolute; his indecision centers on carrying out the task imposed by his father. He cannot murder the man who has fulfilled his own repressed wishes; he castigates himself not only for his delays but also for his wishes. In the end, like the hysteric, thwarted and caught in an intrapsychic struggle, he turns away from sexuality with disgust.

In discussing Shakespeare's work, Freud reflected on possible biographical factors in its creation. He referred to Georg Brandes, the

literary critic who suggested that Shakespeare wrote *Hamlet* immediately after the death of his father. Freud then speculated that
Shakespeare's childhood oedipal feelings had been revived. Moreover, he pointed out, Shakespeare had lost a son, Hamnet, some
short time previously. In saying this, however, Freud noted that creative writing, like neurotic symptoms and dreams, has more than
one motive and thus more than one interpretation; his interpretation, he cautioned, should not be taken as a complete statement.
What he meant to account for was only "the deepest layer of impulses in the mind of the creative writer" (1900a, p. 266).

When Freud later came to believe that the man Shakespeare who
had lost his father and son was not the one who wrote the plays, he
did not delete this text from *The Interpretation of Dreams*. He simply
stated in a footnote (in 1930) that he had ceased to believe that the
author of Shakespeare's plays was the man from Stratford. Instead,
he proposed that certain personal experiences of the Earl of Oxford,
the presumptive author, had affected the poet's mind and thus the
form of *Hamlet*. To Freud, it was relevant that Edward de Vere, Earl
of Oxford, had lost a father—not immediately before writing the
play, as in the case of the man from Stratford, but while the Earl was
still a boy. Moreover, Oxford had repudiated his mother, who married again shortly after her husband's death—a biographical event
quite close to Hamlet's renunciation of Gertrude's early marriage
(see Freud, 1940a, p. 192n; Trosman, 1965).

Freud, whose own father had recently died, identified with both
Oedipus and Hamlet. As already noted, with Oedipus, Freud responded to the shared infantile complex—to the fact that "each
member of the audience was once in germ and in fantasy, just *such*
an Oedipus" (1887–1902b, p. 265). In addition, he identified with
the hero who seeks enlightenment concerning his fate and relent-
lessly purues his inquiry, even when he half-realizes the dire consequences of the truth. This is the Oedipus who is not turned from his
path by lack of moral courage. Years later, when accounting for his
discovery of the cause of dream distortions, Freud (1923) attributed
his success to just this quality of moral courage.

It is likely that Freud's identification with literary figures was a profound and perhaps even essential condition for his creativity. His interest in literature extended beyond support for his theories. Certainly he saw literary works as stimulation toward inquiry; but, more important, he used literary figures and their psychological states, expressed in the powerful language of the novelist, dramatist, or poet, as models for identification in his own work of creativity. Freud's letter of October 15, 1897 to Fliess, in which he first proposed the theory of the Oedipus complex, has been cited as a turning point in the development of psychoanalytic psychology. Yet an earlier letter, of September 21, 1897, sheds light on his movement toward this breakthrough. When he discovered the seduction theory was incorrect, he told Fliess, he was disappointed but also proud of his ability to criticize it. "Can these doubts be only an episode on the way to further knowledge?" he wondered. And here Freud referred to Hamlet's state before killing the king, when Hamlet had reason to feel equally discouraged. Freud wrote: "I vary Hamlet's words, 'To be in readiness' – to be in good spirits is all" ("Ich variiere das Hamlet'sche Wort, 'To be in readiness' – Heiter sein ist alles" (1887–1902a, p. 232).[5] Eissler (1971a) suggests that Freud's use of the quotation implies an unconscious identification with the Hamlet who was not psychologically prepared to carry out the act that had paralyzed him in the past, and yet who experienced a presentiment that he was on the threshold of a great advance (pp. 468–469).

In his letter to Fliess, Freud continued with the thought that, in giving up the belief that he had conquered the problem of hysteria, he had to renounce the grandiose fantasy of eternal fame, wealth, and independence, and come down to earth. "Rebecca," he told himself, "you can take off your wedding-gown; you're not a bride any longer" (1887–1902b, p. 218). Again, we see responsiveness to literary expressions that conveyed his own state of mind. He found satisfaction in connecting his own mood to the poet's well-wrought

---

[5]This passage has been garbled in the English translation (1887–1902b, p. 217).

phrase. The creative artist's apt expression provided, through the incentive bonus of artistic pleasure, a special opportunity to attain psychological insights lacking in the clinical context. The artist eased the route toward the expression of unconscious content against which others defended.

While still engaged in writing *The Interpretation of Dreams*, Freud ventured on another excursion into literary analysis. He wrote a short essay on *Die Richterin* ("The Woman Judge"), a novella by the Swiss writer Conrad Ferdinand Meyer, and he added a comment on another of Meyer's tales, *Die Hochzeit des Monchs* ("The Monk's Wedding") (see Freud, 1887–1902b).[6] Meyer had been recommended to Freud by Fliess, and although Freud was initially unenthusiastic, Fliess "converted" him. Indeed, Meyer soon became a favorite. Nine years later, when asked to compile a list of his ten favorite books, Freud included Meyer's *Huttens letzte Tage*. He added, however, that the story appealed to him more for its "goodness" than its "beauty," its "edification" rather than "aesthetic enjoyment" (1907a, p. 247).

As with Goethe's *Werther*, Freud viewed the plot of *Die Richterin* as not too different from the fantasy created by neurotic patients. He was again struck by the defensive function the story served for the author. Because the theme of *Die Richterin* concerns an incestuous tie between a brother and a sister, Freud assumed that Meyer was struggling with painful memories of an affair with his own sister. The story is a medieval tale of a woman judge, Stemma, who rules one of Charlemagne's alpine districts. In order to obtain the fiefdom, she poisoned her husband, Wulf. Fifteen years later, when the story begins, she is suffering pangs of guilt for her crime and demands exoneration at the hands of her son, Wulfrin. Wulfrin falls in love with Stemma's daughter, his stepsister, Palma! At the end of the story, Stemma finally confesses her guilt, even admits to adul-

---

[6]These comments unlike the remarks about *Oedipus Rex* and *Hamlet*, were not published by Freud; they came to light only through the posthumous publication of the correspondence with Fliess. Niederland (1960) sees Freud's comments on *Die Richterin* as the first application of psychoanalysis to a literary work, and he adds biographical material on Meyer to support Freud's interpretation.

tery, and denies Wulf's paternity, thus clearing Wulfrin and Palma of direct incestuous ties. When Stemma then commits suicide, the murder is revenged. A subplot weaves a parallel tale among the servants.

Freud's interest in *Die Richterin* was stirred by what he had already heard from patients, for he saw the family romance fantasy of the neurotic as closely allied to the tale told by the creative writer. (Indeed, because in German *Roman* means "novel" as well as "romance," it is implied that the neurotic who harbors a family romance fantasy has spun a story of his origins, that he is like the creative writer.) Freud moved back and forth between the structure of neurotic fantasies and the story, reflecting on the similarities. To Freud, the events of the story represented displacements of childhood fears and wishes. Stemma, the mother, is punished and condemned rather than Wulfrin, the child. When the sister, Palma, becomes anorexic, she suffers the neurotic consequence of infantile seduction. The violence of the story belongs to the violence of infantile love. An idealized father figure is suggested by the remote Charlemagne, a surrogate for the murdered Wulf. The murder of Wulf, the real father, is in the service of oedipal rivalry. Hostility toward the mother is indicated by demoting her to a stepmother position. Freud concluded, "Thus in every single feature [*Die Richterin*] is identical with the revenge and exoneration romances which my hysterics compose about their mothers if they are boys" (1887–1902b, p. 257). The parallel subplot in *Die Richterin* further suggests a neurotic fantasy striving for repeated fulfillment.

Freud believed that *Die Richterin* was closely allied to infantile fantasies because the author was writing of something close to his own conflicted experience. Even though by this time Freud had given up the seduction hypothesis, he maintained that the story related to the actuality of the author's childhood relationship with his sister. Biographical material about Meyer—about whom Freud was eager to learn more (1887–1902b, p. 270)—supports the contention of a close brother-sister tie. In fact, Meyer's only sister, Betsy, wrote that although Meyer dictated all his other stories to her, *Die Richterin* was written without her participation. Meyer's wife, whom he married late in life, found the intensity of his relationship with his sister so distressing she prohibited Betsy from visiting the house after the marriage (Frey, 1900; Meyer, 1903).

Much as Freud admired *Die Richterin*, he felt that Meyer's best novel was *The Monk's Wedding*, a work further removed from infantile events. The manifest content of the story conceals a theme of revenge and punishment. Even though infantile events are not depicted, Meyer is still concerned with brother-sister incest. At one point he says to himself, through the mouth of the monk (brother) in the story, "A brother like me should not marry, or my infantile love affair will be revenged on my wife" (quoted in Freud, 1887–1902b, pp. 258–259). According to Freud, the writer's imagination had transformed current experience into amalgams with the past "so that new figures are a continuation of the old and provide patterns for them" (p. 258). The author was concerned with his present life but recognized the hold of his past attachment and feared its consequences for the future.

Freud's interest in *Die Richterin* while composing *The Interpretation of Dreams* is further evidence of his immersion in imaginative literature during a time of great discovery. This was also the period of his self-analysis. The book on dreams, which contains so many of Freud's own dreams, is clearly an expression of Freud's journey into himself, a journey Freud could not have undertaken without relying on his literary sensibilities. I have already referred to Freud's identification with Oedipus as a relentless seeker after the truth, regardless of the cost or pain involved. One can trace his ideas on the Oedipus complex to the play as well as his stance as a psychoanalytic investigator. "In the course of the effort to explain why the play is so powerful, psychoanalysis [was] born" (Cuddihy, 1974, p. 51). Quite clearly Freud's lifelong intimacy with classical literature and the preconscious availability of its tragic themes were essential for his discoveries.

Form as a Vehicle for Hidden Content

Freud's literary and artistic enthusiasms reflected what was idealized in his society. The Greek dramatists, Shakespeare, Milton and

Goethe, Raphael and Titian—these were the members of the pantheon honored by the nineteenth-century Western intellectual. Freud's artistic tastes were deeply rooted in this tradition.

Within this tradition, a work of art was considered a repository for more than what was apparent on the surface. Although a poem might express a thought in a pleasing manner or a play might be praised for its organization or plot, these aesthetic characteristics were not considered sufficient to account for the work's impact. When Wilhelm Fliess urged Freud to learn more about the formal values in the visual arts in order to heighten his appreciation, Freud's initial efforts proved unsystematic and fitful. He did not see the formal elements as sufficiently linked with the psychically intense. The effect was understood in terms of hidden or latent qualities communicated by the author to the receptive reader.

In investigating hysterical symptoms and neurotic fantasies Freud found an opportunity to incorporate his literary interest into the scientific field. A story, in his opinion, was like a case history; the author was expressing through an elaborated fantasy a reminiscence in need of discharge. The work's universal appeal depended on the fact that mankind and the author were similarly stirred and potentially afflicted. The author could evoke the hidden fantasy in others, make it partially acceptable, and even partially gratify it. But the essential *aperçu* for Freud at this time was the link with symptom formation. It was with a sense of satisfaction that Freud declared the two phenomena similar: "The mechanism of creative writing is the same as that of hysterical fantasies. . . . The only remarkable thing is that this [the defensive mechanism in *Die Richterin*] happens exactly as it does in neurosis" (1887–1902b, p. 256).

In comparing creative writing to symptom formation, Freud brought forward the relevancy of biographical reflections concerning the author. From the clinical perspective, the connecting links between events in the patient's life and fantasy subsequently created permitted an understandable view of the symptom. With the creative work, Freud suggested, the link was established through plot elaborations, which were like associations leading to the meaning. Some creative works were "typical," that is, they had a universal appeal because their themes were part of the common experience of humankind. Indeed, Freud believed that the more "genuine" the work of art, the more likely it was that the "deepest" layer of the creative artist's mind was being revealed. His tendency was to accept the cultural achievements of the Western tradition as intimately linked with what was of greatest emotional importance to himself and his patients. The work of art was a form of "primeval dream material" and thus an alternative to neurotic symptom formation.

A full examination of the intimate connection between art and neurosis occurs in Freud's (1907b) analysis of a tale by Wilhelm Jensen, *Gradiva* (published in 1903). Carl Jung brought the story to Freud's attention. Because the story makes use of dream material, Jung proposed that Freud subject the story to analysis in order to demonstrate that the principles of dream interpretation revealed in the clinical context could be used to understand fictional dreams as well. Freud responded to the challenge.

In the story an archaeologist fantasizes about a young woman who appeared to him in a dream. Although in the dream she was buried in the eruption of Mount Vesuvius at Pompeii, upon awakening, he develops the belief that she is actually alive and wandering about in the ruins of present-day Pompeii. Freud analyzed the archaeologist's delusion as a compromise between erotic wishes and their inhibition, and he demonstrated how the author had skillfully transposed the conflict into an artistic creation. Again, Freud underlined the theme of expressing conflict through artistic fantasy, as he had with Goethe's *Werther*, *Oedipus Rex*, *Hamlet*, and *Die Richterin*. But by 1907 a new note could already be heard. Freud pointed out how Jensen used his skills as an artist to present the conflict in a way that it could be accepted by readers without arousing their defenses. Form, Freud began to recognize, was essential for expressing neurotic content in art. Thus art was superior to symptom.

5

A Claim Avowed:
Freud's Jewish Identity

In tracing the range of qualities with which Freud endowed the meaning of his Jewishness, we find a decisive link with humanism and the artisitic tradition. Freud himself referred directly to this connection on only one occassion—in an obituary notice written for the *Neue Freie Presse* in 1904, following the death of the man who had taught him the Scriptures and Hebrew, Professor S. Hammerschlag. "A spark from the same fire which animated the spirit of the great Jewish seers and prophets burned in him," Freud observed. "The passionate side of his nature was happily tempered by the ideal of humanism. . . . Religious instruction served him as a way of educating towards love of the humanities" (1903–1904, p. 225).

Although, as we have seen, Freud was reluctant to claim an identity as a literary artist, he had no reticence about asserting his identity as a Jew. He proclaimed his Jewish identity even though at times he doubted the expediency of such a claim. The fear was that his life work, psychoanalysis itself, might be viewed as parochial and dismissed as "a Jewish national affair" (Freud and Abraham, 1907–1926, p. 34). Nevertheless, he stated that it was "not only unworthy but positively senseless to deny" he was a Jew (1926a, p. 273).

It is the journeys of Sigmund Freud—and his thoughts and associations concerning journeying—that highlight his sense of Jewish identity. While traveling, he had a number of experiences that confronted him with the question of his Jewishness. Not only was he stirred by the stimulation of new surroundings, but he also became more acutely aware of aspects of his own self in response to the changing settings. The figure of the traveling Jew, the conscious and unconscious meaning of traveling and geographic locality are frequently used in his published writings, in both literary and psychoanalytic contexts. Interestingly, as Erikson (1968) has pointed out, the only time Freud used the term "identity" in anything but a casual manner, he did so to refer to his Jewish identity (see Freud, 1926a). This singular usage raises questions about both the meaning of Freud's Jewishness and the use of the identity concept in psychoanalytic writings.

The Journeys

The Freiberg Journey

The first journey to be considered is a journey Freud did not make himself, it was related to him by his father when Freud was a boy of ten or twelve (see Freud, 1900a). Jakob Freud belonged to the generation of Central European Jews who were permitted to travel for purposes of trade if proper permission were obtained from the authorities. Originally he came from Galicia, and for several years he traveled back and forth from Galicia to Freiberg in Moravia buying and selling wool. In 1844 he obtained permission to settle in Freiberg, after paying a special tax that allowed him to live somewhere other than a ghetto. He thus was identified as a "tolerated Jew," one certified as having good moral character and traveling for legitimate commercial purposes. The "toleration," however, was limited. At first he could live in Moravia only six months of the year because the Moravian authorities wished to prevent Galician Jews from settling permanently in Moravia. Jakob Freud and other "tolerated Jews"—each of whom had paid the "tolerance tax"—were forced to travel outside of town during the remaining six months or return to Galicia (Gicklhorn, 1969).[1]

In spite of increasing Jewish emancipation, the toleration granted the Central European Jew in the middle of the nineteenth century was unpredictable; his expanding movements could easily become a source of irritation to others. Jakob Freud told the young Sigmund that one day, having moved to Freiberg sometime in the decade before the birth of his son, he had donned his good clothes and a new fur hat and gone out for a stroll on the Sabbath, feeling perhaps some pride and satisfaction in having come the long distance from the ghettos of Galicia to the toleration of Moravia. Suddenly he was assaulted by a Christian, who with one blow knocked his hat off his head and ordered him into the gutter with, "Jew, get off the pavement!" (Freud, 1900a, p. 197). Jakob told the young Sigmund this story so that he would understand how insecure his father's life had once been and how fortunate his own lot was. But the young boy, Freud tells us, was eager to know how his father had acquitted himself and how one behaves under such circumstances. When Jakob stated that he calmly picked up his cap and continued on his way, the young Sigmund felt this was unheroic and disappointing. He thought of Hannibal's father, Hamilcar, who had made his young son vow vengeance against the Roman enemy—certainly a more inspiring model than Freud's own passive and humiliated father.

The incident, although certainly not neglected by psychoanalytic biographers (Jones, 1953; Erikson, 1958), has recently come under further scrutiny. It may have been true, as Erikson suggests, that the young Sigmund was confronted with the negative identity of the

---

[1]Gicklhorn informs us that the group of Jewish traders who traveled perpetually between Galicia and Freiberg were registered as Galician "wandering Jews" (*Wanderjüden*) (1969, p. 38). This was apparently a special designation for this area as well as a term commonly employed for Jewish merchants with no fixed domicile. Of interest is Freud's use of this appelation to describe himself late in his life. The term had a pejorative meaning associated with the legend of the Jew who denied Christ on the road to Calvary and was thus doomed to wander the earth until the end of the world.

Jew as anti-hero or "schlemiel," the depreciated and humiliated Jew who is not considered fit for even walking on the sidewalk, however seemly in appearance. But there is a hint of a positive quality, if not admiration, in Freud's memory of his father's story. The incident is described by the father, if not heroically, at least calmly and with composure; his rely to Freud's question, "And what did you do?," was in keeping with the belief that a Jew was expected to control his anger. His need for survival and sense of dignity demanded that he master his impulse to return the blow. This image of the Jew, provoked but not giving in to provocation, reappears in Freud's encounters many years later (M. Bergmann, in Angel, 1975).

From Freiberg to Vienna

Freud's own earliest journeys were undertaken because of Jakob Freud's business reverses. When Freud was three, his family moved from Moravia to Leipzig; when he was four, from Leipzig to Vienna. These moves have been the subject of discerning psychoanalytic examination by a number of investigators (Jones, 1953; Erikson, 1955; Lehmann, 1966; Shengold, 1966; Gedo, 1968; Lewin, 1970; Griggs, 1973; Vitz, 1983). Freud himself, in his self-analysis, related the pertinent facts. In passing through Breslau on the journey from Freiberg to Leipzig, he saw gas jets, which reminded him of souls burning in Hell—an association probably related to tales told by the Czech nanny whom he had left behind in Freiberg. During the next move, from Leipzig to Vienna, he was excited by the sight of his nude mother. The two memories became fused and served as a basis for a travel phobia later resolved through self-analysis (see Freud, 1887–1902b).

Griggs (1973) and Vitz (1983) comment on the specific Catholic notion of souls burning in Hell, for such beliefs were alien to the Judaic tradition. The young child, who was taken to the Catholic church by his nanny in Freiberg, had ample opportunity to be stirred by the liturgy, ritual, and religious sculpture and paintings. Freud's interest in Dante and his later immersion in *The Divine*

Comedy link the journey through Hell with the motto and imagery of *The Interpretation of Dreams* (Shengold, 1966).

A parapraxis Freud (1901) described later is relevant. In a conversation with a stranger on a trip, Freud had difficulty in recalling the name of Signorelli, the painter of the frescoes in the cathedral at Orvieto. The frescoes contain graphic scenes of the punishments of Hell. The parapraxis occurred on a journey while Freud was restraining himself from relating a sexual anecdote to his traveling companion, a stranger.

Freud was to visit Freiberg again at sixteen. He described the return train journey to Vienna, this time with unmistakable reference to his fellow Jews. Dissatisfied with his first traveling companion, a young girl whose face was disfigured by boils, he changed compartments. "This being my lucky day," he wrote:

> I ended up in the company of a most venerable old Jew and his correspondingly old wife with their languorous darling daughter and cheeky young 'hopeful' son. Their company was even more unpalatable. . . . Now, this Jew talked in the same way as I had heard thousands of others talk before, even in Freiberg. His very face seemed familiar — he was typical. So was the boy, with whom he discussed religion. He was cut from the cloth from which fate makes swindlers when the time is ripe: cunning, mendacious, kept by his adoring relatives in the belief that his is a great talent, but unprincipled and without character. . . . I have enough of this lot. In the course of the conversation I learned that Madame Jewess and family hailed from Meseritsch [a town in Moravia between Freiberg and Vienna]: the proper compost heap for this sort of weed [1969, p. 420].

This contemptuous opinion of the Jewish family is not dissimilar from the anti-Semitic writings of the period. The blanket repudiation, the attitude of intolerance, especially toward the young boy who had been raised in the belief that he had a "great talent" (similar to a belief impressed upon the young Freud), suggest a feared identification and a need to distance himself from what he saw as odiously and repugnantly Jewish.

A few months later Freud was to write in a totally different tone of a household celebration on the occasion of Purim, the Jewish holiday celebrating the success of the Jews and the defeat of the tyrant Haman described in the Book of Esther. He also established a link between the Jewish and classical Roman traditions. He described "a little theatre performance [we had] at our house on the occasion of *Purim* (which, moreover, fell on the 13 of March so sacred to us all; the day, too, when Caesar was murdered)" (1969, p. 423). The connection in his thoughts between Jewish victory and Roman assassination results in advancing the aggression by a couple of days. The same letter expresses his intent to prepare himself for his graduating examination from the Gymnasium by reading Sophocles' *Oedipus Rex*. It is likely that, at a time when intellectual content for his Jewish identity appears to have been meager, he substitued a familiarity with Greek and Roman history and literature.[2]

"I Was Quite Prepared to Kill Him"

Eleven years later, at the age of twenty seven, again on a train journey, Freud was confronted with another variant of what it was to be Jewish (Freud, 1873-1939a, pp. 77-80). In December 1883, he was on his way to Leipzig to meet with his half-brother Emmanuel, who was visiting from England. As the train passed between Dresden and Riesa, Freud, finding the confined coach oppressive, opened a window to get a breath of fresh air. Immediately, other passengers in the compartment demanded that he close it. Freud agreed, provided another window were opened. In the ensuing discussion, which soon added to the heat, someone shouted, "He's a dirty Jew" (p. 78).[3] The matter then took a different turn.

One man declared, "We Christians consider other people; you'd better think less of your precious self!" Another, the one who had shouted "dirty Jew," vowed to climb over the seats and show Freud a

---

[2]Note Freud's attribution of Semitic identity to Hannibal (1900a, p. 196).

[3]"Das is ein elender Jude!" (1873-1939b, p. 84). "Miserable" rather than "dirty" — but the drift is unmistakable.

thing or two. Freud, however, was not intimidated by the mob; he told the man who recommended altruism to keep his words to himself, and he invited the man who had threatened him to step up and take what was coming to him. "I was quite prepared to kill him," stated Freud. The man did not accept Freud's challenge. Finally, a conductor decided that in winter all windows were to be closed. When the crowd hooted at Freud's defeat, he again invited the ringleader to come over and make his acquaintance. In spite of the unpleasantness, Freud was pleased with himself. He felt that he had handled himself well in his "battle with the infidels" (p. 79). He had not been frightened; indeed, he had behaved courageously and not lowered himself to their level. That Freud saw his militant reaction as consistent with his Jewish identity is revealed by a remark made to Martha about two years later: "I have often felt as though I had inherited all the defiance and all the passion with which our ancestors defended their Temple and could gladly sacrifice my life for one great moment in history" (p. 94).

A quite similar episode, several years later, is reported by Freud's son Martin. While on a summer vacation in the Austrian Alps, the family was subjected to anti-Semitic slurs. One day, after docking their boat, their way was barred. Freud charged into the anti-Semitic mob blocking his path. "The crowd gave way before him and promptly dispersed, allowing him a free passage" (M. Freud, 1957, p. 71). What Martin recalled most vividly was the enraged and threatening visage of his father as he charged the crowd.

Freud's battle for fresh air on his train journeys also appears in the associations to the "Hollthurn" dream reported in *The Interpretation of Dreams* (1900a). On the night of July 18, 1898, he was traveling from Vienna to Marburg in Styria, first class, on a crowded train. He had to share a compartment with an elderly lady and gentleman of aristocratic mien but lacking in civility. They were clearly annoyed by Freud's intrusion when he entered the compartment. Doubtless sensing a fresh-air enthusiast, the woman quickly placed her umbrella on the seat next to the window, and both made pointed remarks on the undesirability of opening windows. The distinguished couple, it soon developed, were traveling on a free ticket;

thus they had some official connection and were not Jewish. The atmosphere in the closed compartment became stifling, but this time Freud stuck it out, held his tongue, and fell asleep. He took his revenge by including in the content of his dream a wealth of insults and humiliations for the disagreeable pair.

The sense of estrangement, the discomfort in being confined, the mobilization of aggressive impulses—expressed directly in the first incident; indirectly, through the dream, in the second—contrast with an anecdote of a Jewish encounter on journey described in *Jokes and Their Relation to the Unconscious:*

> A Galician Jew was traveling in a train. He had made himself really comfortable, had unbuttoned his coat, and put his feet up on the seat. Just then a gentleman in modern dress entered the compartment. The Jew promptly pulled himself together and took up a proper pose. The stranger fingered through the pages of a notebook, made some calculations, reflected for a moment, and then suddenly asked the Jew, 'Excuse me, when is Yom Kippur (the Day of Atonement)?' 'Oho,' said the Jew, and put his feet up on the seat again before answering [Freud, 1905b, pp. 80–81].

One may see in all these incidents a reflection of the lot of the recently emancipated Jew, for whom geographic mobility and unhindered travel were an expression of freedom from the confines of the nineteenth-century ghetto. Several authors have recently pointed out Freud's concern with his own marginal status as a Jew and how it affected both his choice of a career and his political and psychoanalytic thinking (McGrath, 1974; Schorske, 1975). Indeed, these authors consider psychoanalysis in terms of its political implications as an attempt to subvert the existing social order and to legitimate the claims of the marginal Jew for equality (Rothman and Isenberg, 1974a, 1974b). It is also suggested that the task of the emancipated Jew was to adapt to bourgeois civility, and one form of this adaptation was to highlight the uncivilized unconscious impulses which Jew and Gentile had in common (Cuddihy, 1974).

These wider political and social issues are not to be disregarded. Nevertheless, these studies tend to explain shifts in identity in terms of external factors or "common sense," without accounting for intrapsychic factors. Witness Schorske's (1975) position that Freud's immersion in science was a response to waning opportunity for politically ambitious Jews. Also consider McGrath's (1974) remark that Freud was hostile toward his father because "he was not even able to provide for his family" (p. 55). Even worse is the descent into the fatuous. Cuddihy (1974) offers the aperçu that Freud conceived the "id" along the lines of the uncivilized "Yid," whom he was attempting to socialize—an insight that disregards the fact that the German word for the id is *das Es*. Certain problems in the use of the psychoanalytic concept of identity emerge in these writings. Undue emphasis is placed on social content of self at the expense of dynamic factors that affect the individual in a genetic context or a developmental sequence.

From Delphi to Daulia

Shengold (1966) and Mahony (1982) have perspicaciously noted that the metaphor of a journey runs through *The Interpretation of Dreams* as a unifying figure of speech. In August 1899, Freud wrote Fliess that the book was to be "planned on the model of an imaginary walk. First comes the dark wood of the authorities (who cannot see the trees), where there is no clear view and it is very easy to go astray. Then there is the cavernous defile through which I lead my readers—my specimen with its peculiarities, its details, its indiscretions, and its bad jokes—and then, all at once, the high ground and the prospect, and the question: 'Which way do you want to go?' " (1887–1902b, p. 290).

After describing the dream of "Irma's injection" and its wealth of associations, Freud commented, "When, after passing through a narrow defile, we suddenly emerge upon a piece of high ground, where the path divides and the finest prospects open up on every side, we may pause for a moment and consider in which direction we shall first turn our steps" (1900a, p. 122). Then, after proposing the wish-fulfilling function of dreams and before examining the material and sources of dreams, he suggested, "Having followed one path to its end, we may now retrace our steps and choose another starting-point for our rambles through the problems of dream-life" (p. 163). To introduce the theoretical portion of the book, Freud wrote:

> Before starting off along this new path, it will be well to pause and look around, to see whether in the course of our journey up to this point we have overlooked anything of importance. For it must be clearly understood that the easy and agreeable portion of our journey lies behind us. Hitherto, unless I am greatly mistaken, all the paths along which we have traveled have led up towards the light — towards elucidation and fuller understanding. But as soon as we endeavor to penetrate more deeply into the mental process involved in dreaming, every path will end in darkness [p. 511].

The oft-quoted epigram that the dream is the royal road to the unconscious perpetuates the metaphor.

Shengold (1966) correctly points out that the symbolic image of the journey can be understood in several ways. A journey may represent death, sexual intercourse, or oedipal victory. Traveling can stand for the dissolution of the symbiotic tie with the mother and the forming of individual identity. More specifically, a journey may represent a voyage into the interior of one's mind, a self-exploration. For Freud, the attraction toward Rome and the neurotic reluctance about visiting the city was related to the longing for the Catholic nanny of his childhood and the sexual interest in his mother (Gedo, 1968; Griggs, 1973; Vitz, 1983).

Of climactic importance in *The Interpretation of Dreams* is Freud's elucidation of Sophocles' drama *Oedipus Rex* as a clue to the meaning of the typical dream of the death of a loved person. Oedipus was warned by the Delphic oracle that he was to avoid his home because he would murder his father and marry his mother. After leaving the oracle, Oedipus resolved to avoid Corinth, the home of his presumptive father. On the road between Delphi and Daulia he met his true father, King Laius, and killed him in a sudden quarrel. The text of the play informs us that as Oedipus is coming down a steep narrow road he meets a herald walking in front of a carriage and is ordered out of the way. When he is pushed aside by the herald, Oedipus strikes back. The old man in the carriage, Laius, sees the fight, and as the carriage passes, he strikes Oedipus on the head with his weapon. Oedipus returns the blow, and thus slays his father.

The parallel between the encounter between Oedipus and Laius and the episode described to Freud by his father, when he was ordered off the pavement by an anti-Semite in Freiberg, is striking (Cuddihy, 1974). In *Oedipus Rex*, Freud seemed to find a heroic prototype for the response he wished his father had made when provoked. Oedipus became a substitute for his submissive father. The fantasy father returned the blow, and thus defied the insulting Christian. From this perspective, we can see why the incident described by Jakob Freud made such an impression on the young Freud of ten or twelve. It is likely that he recognized something of himself in the Christian who struck his father on the head and knocked off his new fur cap. The remobilization of hostile feelings toward his father reactivated by the oedipal stirrings of adolescence was expressed in the form of hostile Jew-Gentile relations. Wishes to surpass his father, whom Freud saw as an obstacle to his success, took the form of a repudiation of the Jewish traits he identified with the old Jewish man on his journey from Freiberg at sixteen. The underlying erotic nature of the encounter is further supported by Freud's statement that "getting in someone's way can serve as a form of pursuing sexual aims" (1901, p. 176).

The link between the encounter in the narrow defile between Delphi and Daulia and the incident on the street in Freiberg also sheds light on Freud's fascination with Sophocles' *Oedipus Rex*. Long before he became a psychoanalyst, Freud referred to the play and recommended it. When the time came to give a name to the particular emotional and ideational complex so crucial to early development, he was stirred by the image of an encounter on a narrow road in the midst of a journey. Years later, when Abraham (1922) pointed out that the place of meeting between Oedipus and Laius is a representation for the female genitalia, Freud commented that he had been troubled by the passage relating the murder in *Oedipus Rex*. Does the Greek text refer to the place as a "hollow way" or a "cross-roads," where giving way is not difficult? In other words, must one return the blow or can one step aside? (Freud and Abraham, 1907–1926, p. 326).

Moses in Rome

After Freud freed himself from his inhibition about visiting Rome in 1901, he became a constant visitor. In 1897 he had written, "My longing for Rome is deeply neurotic" (1887–1902b, p. 236). He studied the topography of Rome – "my longing for which becomes more and more acute" (p. 269). Frequently he compared himself to the poor Jew who had stowed away without a ticket on the express train to the health spa, Karlsbad. He was continually caught, thrown off at each stop, only to climb back on, each time being treated more harshly. "At one of the stations on his *via dolorosa* he met an acquaintance, who asked him where he was traveling to. 'To Karlsbad,' was his reply, 'if my constitution can stand it' " (Freud, 1900a, p. 195). Rome and Karlsbad became synonomous. In 1900 Freud closed a letter to Fliess with "Next Easter in Rome," an allusion to the prayer at the Passover service, "Next year in Jerusalem" (1887–1902b, p. 317). Rome was "the promised land seen from afar" (1900a, p. 194).

Between 1901 and 1923 Freud visited Rome eight times. He preferred ancient Rome to Christian Rome, but an abiding source of interest became Michelangelo's statue of Moses in the Church of San Pietro in Vincoli. Although he was enamored of the sculpture as early as his first visit, as time went by his interest increased. "No piece of statuary has ever made a stronger impression on me than this," he affirmed (1914c, p. 213). Often he climbed to the deserted church and found himself having "to support the angry scorn of the hero's glance." After much study, he offered an interpretation somewhat at variance with other versions as well as with the biblical account of the events the Moses statue is presumed to depict.

Freud believed that the sculpture catches the moment when Moses, on his descent from Mt. Sinai with the Ten Commandments, first sees the Jews worshipping the Golden Calf. His immediate impulse is to rise in fury, and he is about to do so when, with his sudden movement, the Tables almost slip from his grasp. To save the Tables, he controls his passion, restraining the violence of his rage. Freud's interpretation proposes a developmental change in the personality of Moses. He points out that, when Moses was a younger man, in "a transport of divine wrath" he slew an Egyptian who was maltreating an Israelite (1914c, p. 233). Freud sees Michelangelo as "correcting" the biblical version that Moses fell into an uncontrollable rage and broke the Tables. "The giant frame with its tremendous physical power," he alleges, "becomes only a concrete expression of the highest mental achievement that is possible in a man, that of struggling successfully against an inward passion for the sake of a cause to which he has devoted himself" (p. 233).

Freud's art-critical essay has become so fully accepted by psychoanalysts as a response to the dissensions of Adler and Jung that the point is even cited editorially as a footnote in the *Standard Edition* (1914c, p. 230n). There is no reason to reject such a biographical allusion. Indeed, Freud himself was conscious of the connection, for he wrote to Ferenczi at the time of the split from Stekel, "At the moment the situation in Vienna makes me feel more like the historical Moses than the Michelangelo one" (Jones, 1955, p. 367). Yet, again, the conception of a Moses who struggles to control his wrath may have reactivated for Freud the memory of his father in Freiberg. Jakob Freud did not do battle with the infidel when his Sabbath cap was knocked from his head; he controlled his wrath instead. In this period of his life, through the identification with the passionate but controlled Moses, Freud could find a renewed regard for the father whom, as an adolescent, he had seen as unheroic.[4]

Rest for the Wandering Jew

After 1923 Freud's physical difficulties severely limited his travels, although his longing for travel continued unabated. In 1928 he

---

[4]I am indebted to Martin Bergmann, who has established the link between Freud's paper on Moses and the incident described to him by his father (Angel, 1975).

wrote, "If I were . . . healthy and strong . . . I would after hard work strive for the strenuous pleasures of a long journey to places which I don't yet know" (in Deri and Brunswick, 1964, pp. 104–105). In 1933 he complained, "One of the consequences of my failing health difficult to bear is that I can no longer come to Rome" (1873–1939a, p. 416). A few years later, in 1936, he discussed the emotional pressures behind a longing for travel, comparing them with forces that drive adolescents to run away from home. "A great part of the pleasure of travel lies in the fulfillment of these early wishes," he reflected. "It is rooted in dissatisfaction with home and family. When first one catches sight of the sea, crosses the ocean and experiences as realities cities and lands which for so long had been distant, unattainable things of desire—one feels oneself like a hero who has performed deeds of improbable greatness" (1936, p. 247). He then related his difficulty in enjoying to the full the experience of being on the Acropolis in Athens to a form of filial piety, a sense of guilt in having "gone such a long way" from the life and values of his father, who would not have appreciated the significance of the journey.

This growing sense of reverence for his father also appears in Freud's later concerns with Jewish identity. In his address to the Society of B'nai B'rith, he stated that he was bound to Jewry neither by religion nor nationalism but by "obscure emotional forces, which were the more powerful the less they could be expressed in words" (1926a, p. 274). For him, the attraction of Jewry was a "clear consciousness of inner identity, the safe privacy of a common mental construction" (p. 274).[5]

Later, in response to the growth of anti-Semitism in the 1930s, Freud (1938) wrote in defense of Jews—as if through the eye of an outsider—that Jews were no worse than other people. In some ways they were better: they drank less; crimes of brutality, murder, robbery, and sexual violence were rare among them; they had close familial ties; they took care of the poor; and they had made important

---

[5]The translator here appears to have thrown up his hands in the face of "die Heimlichkeit der gleichen seelischen Konstruktion" (1926b, p. 52). "The secret familiarity of the same mental structure" may do more justice to Freud's sense. See Erikson (1968, pp. 20–21) for the problems involved in the translation.

cultural contributions. Here his emphasis was less on his own subjective and inner sense of identity and more on observable traits.

Finally, in preparation for his last journey, the trip from Vienna
to London following the Nazi occupation of Austria, Freud commented that he felt like Rabbi Jochanan ben Zakkai, who after the
destruction of the Temple in Jerusalem by Titus in 70 A.D., asked
permission to open a school for the Torah at Jabneh. He was condi-
tioned to respond to persecution by moving on in order to continue
the psychoanalytic school (Jones, 1957, p. 221). He felt like Jacob,
who as an old man was taken by his children to Egypt. He also compared himself to Ahasuerus, the wandering Jew of medieval legend,
who is said to have denied Christ on his way to Calvary and was
thus doomed to wander the earth for eternity. "It is high time,"
Freud wrote, "that Ahasuerus came to rest somewhere" (1873–
1939a, pp. 442–443).[6]

The Concept of Identity

In looking at the nature of Freud's Jewish identity, I have so far
considered identity issues from a subjective point of view. Freud was
deeply affected by his father's account of the anti-Semitic provocation in Freiberg, both because of his disillusionment in an idealized
father and because of his identification with the anti-Semitic at-
tacker. During early adolescence he passed through a period of critical repudiation of Jews, whom he regarded as unheroic and inferior.
Yet this view vied with another—that of the Jew as a militant aven-
ger, courageously facing a hostile mob and overpowering it through
fearlessness. The Jew of untamed passion then gave way to the image of a mature Moses, for whom the content of heroism had
shifted. Freud could now identify positively with his father's control
of rage and need to maintain his dignity and survival rather than
succumb to his impulses. Finally, with his last journey, Freud voiced
the need, as a Jew, to preserve intellectual continuity, perpetuating
learning and scholarship.

---

[6]For a full treatment of the legend of the wandering Jew, see Anderson (1965).

In reflecting on the complexities of Freud's Jewish identity, it may be helpful to consider the meaning of "identity" in psychoanalytic writings.[7] Although the concept of identity defies consensus and precise definition in psychoanalysis, it continues to reappear in the literature. Erikson (1956, 1968), who has probably done more than others during the last two decades to grapple with the notion, has used the term in a number of different ways, covering both clinical and theoretical grounds. Under the rubric of identity, he has included the sense of uniqueness or individuality, the sense of "I-ness," as consciously experienced. Erikson has also used the term to cover the experience of continuity over time, the sameness of personality or self in a developmental context. He sees this sense of continuity as being consolidated during the phase of postadolescence. On a different level, he gives identity a psychosocial meaning by noting the link an individual frequently establishes with a reference group; thus identity also implies a sense of solidarity with a set of commonly shared and accepted values. From this viewpoint, the journey, a temporary break in familiarity over time and space, leads to a heightened awareness of aspects of the self. In the absence of customary relations between self and object, attributes of the "I" experience become hypercathected.

In a panel discussion on "Problems of Identity," Erikson's work served as a stimulus for a number of other investigators (see Rubinfine, 1958). K. R. Eissler proposed that in addition to the three structures of the personality (the id, ego, and superego) another differentiation of the ego — the self — is added at puberty. He suggested that the "I am I" experience be considered as "self-cognizance," describing the consolidation of the ego's relation to itself. Although this proposal has not been widely accepted — indeed, adherents of self psychology have pursued paths independent of the tripartite model — it offers a perspective on certain disturbances in identity. For example, the "Capgras psychosis," in which one is unable to recognize

---

[7]My account of Freud's Jewish identity is by no means exhaustive. For a further consideration of this heritage, including its effects on the nature of psychoanalysis, see Simon (1957), Bakan (1965), Grollman (1965), Berkower (1969), Robert (1976), and D. B. Klein (1981).

the separate identity of another person and believes the other to be a double for oneself, implies an extension of the sense of self-cognizance beyond the bounds of the ego to include the object world. In current parlance, we may refer to such a state as a regression to archaic states of self and self-object dedifferentiation, or merging.

In the same discussion, Paul Kramer emphasized the quality of separateness and distinction as central to the sense of identity. He called attention to the experience of identity when one is separated from one's accustomed environment and forced to rely on one's own resources. For Kramer, the experience of separation from the first object – the mother – and the consequent sensation of aloneness are among the generative factors in the creation of a sense of identity (Rubinfine 1958, p. 133). Margaret Mahler also pointed to the separation-individuation phase as crucial in the development of a sense of identity, whereas Phyllis Greenacre and R. C. Bak underlined the phallic-oedipal phase as instrumental, particularly with regard to sexual identity. Another note was struck by Edith Jacobson, who viewed identity as a resolution of opposites: "I am different" and "I am similar" are both necessary components. She proposed a differentiation between a sense of identity and self-representation. For her, the sense of identity consists of the inner experience of individual wholeness and separateness, and this uniqueness is contrasted with the varying self-images.

There are others, however, who have questioned the usefulness of the notion of identity. Kohut (1971) suggests that the concept may be more suitably considered within a framework of social psychology and conscious or preconscious interactions with others than in an intrapsychic context. From a different viewpoint, Schafer (1973) has also addressed the problems regarding the use of "self" and "identity" in psychoanalytic formulations. He is particularly opposed to the tendency toward reification and personification in analytic theorizing. Nevertheless, he considers that the emphasis on identity may be a logical development within modern ego psychology in that it gives concerns about representation an experiential significance. There is a heightened readiness, he believes, "to accept and use theoretical concepts that seem to be closer to subjective experience and actual clinical work. Self and identity appear to be such concepts" (p. 55).

The varying distinctions of "identity" and "self" are examined by Abend (1974) in a comprehensive review of the relevant literature. He suggests that identity be considered as a "loosely organized set of conscious and preconscious self-representations that serve to define the individual in a variety of social contexts" and that "by definition we include only features available to consciousness" (p. 620). He differentiates this conception of "identity" from a "sense of identity," which refers to the "feelings and thoughts" people report about their "identities." For Abend, "self" is a conceptual term, "a theoretical abstraction" that has no "actual psychic existence" (p. 618), and should be differentiated from self-feelings.[8] Thus, identity refers to a specific part of the self; it is a subgroup of a larger entity defined in terms of structural theory.

What can we distill from all these varying perspectives? In my opinion, although there is no difficulty in conceiving of identity as a part of the self, the attempt to separate "the self" from experience and to introduce "a sense of self" or "a sense of identity" as the experiential referent does a disservice to the empirical basis of the psychological state we are considering. Both self and identity should be understood in terms of their representations, whether these are conscious, preconscious, withdrawn behind the repression barrier, or split. "Sense of" can then refer to topographical awareness—how close the experience is to consciousness.

Identity thus implies an experience, the essence of which cannot be known; only manifestations and attributes are discernible. The essential core relates to archaic states of self which are reactivated by later, unfamiliar psychosocial contexts. We can see the experience of identity as an expression for cohesion of the self at progressive stages of its development.

---

[8]"It is altogether misleading and incorrect," writes Abend, "to treat it [the self] as if it had an actual psychic existence and to speak as though people can be in touch with or directly aware of any such entity within *themselves*" (p. 618; my italics). But is not the final "themselves" treated as having "actual psychic existence"?

But is this viewpoint helpful in understanding the issues raised by Freud's Jewish identity? In writing of his "clear consciousness of inner identity," Freud was describing a sense of solidarity with a social group; yet he was simultaneously describing an intrapsychic state. Although the "essence" of this state was unknown, its consciousness was "clear." In other words, this "inner identity" might well require a fresh and unfamiliar social context to reach consciousness, such as journeying. Its roots, however, extended into the depths of the personality.

With regard to a particular form of identity, such as that designated "Jewish," one might say that it is the specifically unknown and preverbal nature of the essence that contributes to its permanence and definiteness over time. This essence probably derives from periods in development before clear differentiation between self and object. Developmental transformations of these early experiences become known in terms of attributes or, in subjective psychological terms, as experiences of "secret familiarity" (*Heimlichkeit*), and these make up the core experience of identity. Particular psychosocial contexts may repeat early self and self-object amalgams, thus reinforcing their "essential" nature. In this light, the shifting expression of Freud's Jewish identity can be seen as a longitudinal extension of archaic, unconscious self-experience. The sense of identity remains constant although the content of identity is variable.

By way of conclusion, one should note the link between Freud's Jewish identity and his immersion in the humanist tradition, for Freud's shifting sense of identity owed much to influences he absorbed from scholarship and the arts. He combined what he experienced as part of his essential nature with attributes belonging to the artistic tradition.

PART II

Psychoanalysis and the Arts

6

Freud's Style and the Matter of Style

Thus far we have focused on the impact of the arts and the humanist disciplines on Freud and his intellectual development. In turning to psychoanalytic contributions to the arts, it seems fitting to begin with a discussion of Freud's style.

An examination of Freud's own comments on style reveals his appreciation for literary devices that would heighten the effectiveness of his exposition. He saw metaphorical figures of speech as facilitating creativity and as a means to explore connections between seemingly disparate and unrelated psychological states. Style, like character, is conceptualized as a production of the synthetic ego function. It is a configuration formed from experience and addressed to an expressive, communicative task.

Freud, at seventeen, informed his boyhood friend Emil Fluss that he had received the grade *Excellent* for his composition "Considerations Involved in the Choice of a Profession on the *Matura*," his final examination on leaving the Gymnasium. He added, with evident delight and youthful humor, that in praising his paper, his professor had pointed out that the young Freud possessed "what Herder so nicely calls an *idiotic* style[1] — i.e., a style at once correct and charac-

---

[1]By "idiotic" (*idiotitsch* from *Idiotismen*), Johann Gottfried von Herder, the eighteenth-century German poet and philosopher, meant the grammatical and stylistic features peculiar to a language, those which are essentially untranslatable and inseparable from the historical context. He indeed used the term to denote a prized ability, although he emphasized what is "characteristic" over what is "correct" in a

teristic." "I was suitably impressed by this amazing fact," wrote Freud, "and do not hesitate to disseminate the happy event, the first of its kind, as widely as possible—to you, for instance, who until now have probably remained unaware that you have been exchanging letters with a German stylist. And now I advise you as a friend, not as an interested party, to preserve them—have them bound—take good care of them—one never knows" (Letter of June 16, 1873, in 1873–1939a, p. 4).

The manner in which ideas are expressed and the suitability of the expression to the content continued to be of abiding interest to Freud. Occasionally he wrote critically of his own style. He recommended a variety of approaches for scientific writing and proposed stylistic criteria for discerning mastery of a body of thought. His own style, although highly distinctive, shifted with context and purpose, and continued to be admired for its literary merit throughout his life.[2]

Freud's Comments on Style

Although at seventeen Freud wrote with evident pleasure about the recognition his essay had received and even considered that his style might contribute to his immortality, the tone of his remark is ironic and self-mocking. Clearly he did not put style above content, nor make stylistic skill an end in itself. Indeed, when he came to colloborate with Breuer on *Studies on Hysteria*, he seriously questioned the effect his style would have on the scientific community. I have already noted his remark: it "strikes me myself as strange that the case histories I write should read like short stories," and not like scientific accounts (Breuer and Freud, 1893–1895b, p. 160). He in-

---

grammatical sense. In English, "idiomatic" carries a similar sense, and is similarly derived. I am grateful to Professor Samuel Jaffe of the Department of German Languages and Literature, at the University of Chicago, who found the appropriate passages in Herder's *Fragmente über die neuere Deutsche Literatur* (1768).

   [2]It is pertinent that one of the few public honors Freud received, the Goethe Prize of 1930, was awarded for his literary skill (Freud, 1930b).

sisted that in choosing this mode of presentation, which resembled that of imaginative writers who describe the details of a character's thoughts and feelings, he was responding to the thrust of his *clinical* findings. To write in the contemporary fashion of the usual psychiatric case history would be a disservice to the discovery of the "intimate connection between the story of the patient's sufferings and the symptoms of his illness" (p. 161).

Freud uses the short story as a model for the case history of a serving girl, Katharina, who presented herself to him as a patient while he was on a summer vacation, after he had climbed a mountain to escape medicine and the neuroses. The report is given in dialogue form, and he even attempts to set down Katharina's speech in the dialect of the region. As Freud tells it:

> In the summer vacation of the year 189–I made an excursion into the Hohe Tauern so that for a while I might forget medicine and more particularly the neuroses. I had almost succeeded in this when one day I turned aside from the main road to climb a mountain which lay somewhat apart and which was renowned for its views and for its well-run refuge hut. I reached the top after a strenuous climb and, feeling refreshed and rested, was sitting deep in contemplation of the charm of the distant prospect. I was so lost in thought that at first I did not connect it with myself when these words reached my ears: 'Are you a doctor, sir?' But the question was addressed to me, and by the rather sulky-looking girl of perhaps eighteen who had served my meal and had been spoken to by the landlady as 'Katharina.' To judge by her dress and bearing, she could not be a servant, but must no doubt be a daughter or relative of the landlady's.
>
> Coming to myself I replied: 'Yes, I'm a doctor: but how did you know that?'
>
> 'You wrote your name in the Visitors' Book, sir. And I thought if you had a few moments to spare. . . . The truth is, sir, my nerves are bad. I went to see a doctor in L____ about them and he gave me something for them; but I'm not well yet.'
>
> So there I was with the neuroses once again [Breuer and Freud, 1893–1895b, p. 125].

Did ever a case report begin thus? The very setting of the stage, on the remote mountain top, evokes for us the insistence with which the story of the hysterical girl must be told. We, too, become reluctant listeners whose resistance is gradually overcome by the strangeness of the tale and the need to find a solution. Along with Freud, we realize that the neuroses are not confined to middle-class, cosmopolitan Vienna. They are everywhere.

In the same volume, Freud describes the thoughts of the distraught Fräulein Elisabeth von R.:

> She had thought herself strong enough to be able to do without the help of a man; but she was now overcome by a sense of her weakness as a woman and by a longing for love in which, to quote her own words, her frozen nature began to melt. In this mood she was deeply affected by her second sister's happy marriage—by seeing with what touching care he [her brother-in-law] looked after her, how they understood each other at a single glance and how sure they seemed to be of each other [p. 155].

Lest the reader wonder if Elisabeth spoke in purple prose, really saying "my frozen nature began to melt," I should note that Freud actually wrote "ihr starres [obstinate or unbending] Wesen zu schmelzen begann" (Breuer and Freud, 1893–1895a, p. 220). Strachey could not resist extending the metaphor from "melting" to "frozen." Indeed, in considering the translation of the *Standard Edition*, one must recall Strachey's disclaimers. Although fully aware of Freud's literary ability, he generally opted for accuracy over artistic elegance. When he thought of an imaginary model for Freud as a stylist, he always kept before him "the writings of some English man of science of wide education born in the middle of the nineteenth century." "And I should like," he added, "in an explanatory and no patriotic spirit, to emphasize the word 'English'" (Strachey, 1966, p. xix).

The question has arisen: To what extent have the English translations of Freud—particularly the one under the editorship of James Strachey—done a disservice to Freud's style by underplaying the humanist tradition? Critiques by Ornston (1982) and Bettelheim

(1983) reveal that Freud avoided the impersonal, mechanistic, and neologistic forms of expression found in Strachey's translation. *Fehlleistungen* became "parapraxes," instead of "faulty achievements"; *Besetzung* became "cathexis," rather than "occupation" or "investment"; *das Es* became "the id," not "the it"; and *Trieb* became "instinct," instead of "drive" or "impulse." A style originally crisper, more vibrant and more human, became technical, stiff, even turgid.

But let us return to Freud's introduction of a new style of case reporting, one strange to psychiatric literature, whose antecedents lay more in the nineteenth-century novel. We learn about Elisabeth through a series of events glimpsed through her mind's eye, as she changes internally. Subtly Freud reveals her longing and hints at her envy; the reader by identification experiences emotions similar to her own. And Freud prepares us for the guilt and shame she later experienced when her sister died, as we follow the unconscious feelings revealed by the treatment. We feel the impact of her irresistible thought at her sister's deathbed, "like a flash of lightening in the dark: Now he is free again and I can be his wife" (1893–1895b, p. 156).

Freud's concern with presentation emerges, in a different way, in his criticisms about the writing of *The Interpretation of Dreams*. He complained to Fliess, "What I dislike about it [*The Interpretation of Dreams*] is the style. I was quite unable to express myself with noble simplicity, but lapsed into a facetious, circumlocutory straining after the picturesque" (1887–1902b, p. 297).[3] Ten days later he wrote that because of his appreciation for form and beauty he was particularly upset that 'the toturous sentences of the dream-book, with its high-flown, indirect phraseology, its squinting at the point, have

---

[3] "Noble simplicity" calls to mind the "calm grandeur and noble simplicity" that J. J. Winckelmann saw as the hallmark of classical Greek style. Two years later, complimenting Fliess on his latest work, Freud wrote, "you are able to put your riches aside and confine yourself within the limits laid down. I think that is the hallmark of the classic style" (1887–1902b, p. 338). Freud himself refers to Winckelmann in *The Interpretation of Dreams* as one who shared his passion for Rome and antiquity. And as we saw in Chapter 1, the neoclassical movement, which Winckelmann enthusiastically supported, dominated Freud's Gymnasium education and served as a model for restraint and clarity.

sorely offended one of my ideals" (p. 298). For him, these deficiences
indicated poor mastery of the material.

What passages did Freud have in mind? Certainly not the review
of the dream literature, which is a model for how any literature review should be done. Nor in all likelihood was he referring to the
presentation and analyses of the dreams; the reader does not even
stumble over the clinical dream theory. Most probably Freud was
thinking of Chapter VII and the difficulties he encountered in
describing the topographic model and attempting to reconcile the
new findings of dream psychology with the antiquated model from
his physicalistic neurological background. Perhaps he had in mind
such vague disclaimers as:

> Ideas, thoughts and psychical structures in general must never be re-
> garded as localized in organic elements of the nervous system but
> rather, as one might say, *between* them, where resistances and facili-
> tations provide the corresponding correlates. Everything that can be
> an object of our internal perception is *virtual*, like the image pro-
> duced in a telescope by the passage of light rays. But we are justified
> in assuming the existence of the systems (which are not in any way
> psychical entities themselves and can never be accessible to our psy-
> chical perception) like the lenses of the telescope, which cast the im-
> age [1900a, p. 611].

Here literary exuberance became a substitute for scientific precision. Freud fell into error when he adhered too strictly to his metaphor in assigning the properties of lenses to the psychic apparatus
(Eissler, 1969). The metaphor took on a factual reality. Contrary to
Freud's assertion, the image is not produced in the telescope; it is
not substantive and cannot be conceived as occurring "between"
the lenses any more than thought occurs in the synapses between
neurons (Basch, 1976). The problematic nature of the metaphor
contributes to the hesitancy of expression and the vagueness of
meaning. Indeed, the translator's difficulties are evident in the
added parentheses to compensate for the convoluted sentence.

A year after his self-critical remarks about *The Interpretation of
Dreams*, Freud offered an interesting psychological observation

about style: "A clear and unambiguous manner of writing shows us that . . . the author is at one with himself; where we find a forced and involved expression which (to use an apt phrase) is aimed at more than one target, we may recognize the intervention of an insufficiently worked out, complicating thought, or we may hear the stifled voice of the author's self-criticism" (1901, p. 101). The suggestion that lack of clarity in expression may be the result of failure of integration between conflicting aims could be applied to Freud's own difficulties with *The Interpretation of Dreams*. In spite of his wish to free himself from a neurological model and establish a psychological system, the pull of the past was still forceful.

Freud continued to comment, throughout his work, on his manner of expressing scientific ideas, and he often compared and contrasted these means with the style of imaginative writers. After revealing Dora's ambivalent love for Herr K., for instance, he introduced his exploration of Dora's homosexual attachment to Frau K. in the following manner:

> I must now turn to consider a further complication to which I should certainly give no space if I were a man of letters engaged upon the creation of a mental state like this for a short story, instead of being a medical man engaged upon its dissection. The element to which I must now allude can only serve to obscure and efface the outlines of the *fine poetic conflict* which we have been able to ascribe to Dora. This element would rightly fall a sacrifice to the censorship of a writer, for he, after all, simplifies and abstracts when he appears in the character of a psychologist. But in the world of reality, which I am trying to depict here, a complication of motives, an accumulation and conjunction of mental activities – in a word – overdetermination is the rule [1905a, pp. 59–60; my italics].

Freud's seemingly distances himself from the romantic writer here; his account must adhere to all the "facts." The reader is not to be compelled by a singular drama. Rather, he wishes to engage the reader in objectively examining the total complex of the patient's state as a scientist should. But, contrary to his disclaimer, there is no falling off in his expository style as he presents the homosexual theme. For although it adds a complication, its import is quite clear.[4]

At another point Freud stated that he had no skill in writing polemics to defend psychoanalysis when it was under attack. He denied that his failure was due to his good nature or to his being easily intimidated. In fact he asserted, "I can be as abusive and enraged as anyone; but I have not the art of expressing the underlying emotions in a form suitable for publication and therefore prefer to abstain completely" (1914b, p. 39). One does sense a bitter enmity in Freud's comments at the time of Adler's death. "I don't understand your sympathy for Adler," he wrote Arnold Zweig. "For a Jew boy out of a Viennese suburb a death in Aberdeen is an unheard-of career in itself and a proof of how far he had got on. The world rewarded him richly for his services in having contradicted psychoanalysis" (Jones, 1957, p.208).[5] Yet such animosity was confined to a personal letter; Freud could not turn it into a form suitable for scientific argument.

A further comment on expository style appears in the introduction to an unfinished paper, "Some Elementary Lessons in Psychoanalysis" (1940b). Freud explained that there are two main styles a writer can use to present knowledge to an uninformed public: "the genetic approach" and "the dogmatic approach." Using the genetic approach, the author starts with what all readers think they know, and gradually makes them aware of what they have neglected or disregarded. Then the writer slowly exposes the readers to new knowl-

---

[4]One might well question Freud's linking good literary style to avoiding complications in plot construction. He makes a similar comment about Meyer inappropriately complicating the plot of *Die Richterin* by introducing a subplot which, he fears, detracts from the action of the main characters (1887–1902b; see also Chapter 4). Surely subplots and complexity as literary devices, if used judiciously, enhance the aesthetic effect rather than dispel it.

[5]Eissler (1971b) points out that Freud used the word *Judenbube*, which could be translated as the milder "Jewish boy," thus reducing the contempt somewhat. However, even with the emendation, the comment is chilling and indicative of Freud's difficulty in publishing a scientific disagreement with Adler. Incidentally, the book referred to in this footnote offers an excellent example of the style of writing Freud found so alien.

edge, and so allows them to expand on their earlier judgments. In this way the readers take part in building up the new subject, and their objections are met at each step. Here the writer follows the same path he has traveled as a discoverer. The defect of the method—which Freud nevertheless saw as having many advantages —rests in the possibility that readers will be unimpressed by the integrated, well-organized body of new information. They may think instead, "I've known that all along."

The other approach, the dogmatic method, emphasizes the organization. Conclusions are stated boldly, without permitting readers to follow the steps by which the conclusions are reached. The difficulty here is that readers may think, "All this sounds most peculiar: where does the fellow get it from?" (1940b, p. 281).

In his writings Freud made use of both methods. *The Interpretation of Dreams*, or at least its first six chapters, is an example of the genetic method. The late *Outline of Psycho-Analysis* takes the dogmatic approach. Freud was conscious of the reader's response to changes in his style, and he often varied his style in line with the purpose he had in mind. He also recognized style as a representation of the content. For instance, the form he chooses for the reporting of a dream is often an indicator of the latent dream thoughts (see Freud, 1900a, pp. 310–338).

Freud's Prose

Although it is generally agreed that Freud's prose was appropriate to scientific discourse, his style was distinct from that of other scientists. To tie his clinical work to his theoretical elaboration, he needed to develop a style permitting subjective states to be viewed as objective data. In addition, Freud wrote a number of works that fit only loosely within a scientific framework—leading to further variations in his style.

Overall Freud aimed at clarity and simplicity; there is little that is ornamental or elegant for its own sake. Nor was Freud a "prose polisher"; although he experienced difficulties with *The Interpretation of*

Dreams, in general he wrote easily, without any need to correct or revise (A. Freud, personal communication). Insofar as he attempted a conscious mastery of style, he followed the lead of Gotthold Ephraim Lessing, avoiding awkward Germanic involutions (Wittels, 1931; Wortis, 1954). In this sense, although Freud's aims and content were scientific, his style developed from literary models (Wolf, 1971).

The importance of Freud's way of presenting his scientific findings emerges clearly in a comparison with the prose of his collaborator, Josef Breuer, in *Studies on Hysteria*. Breuer was a careful scientist, but when he wrote the theoretical section of the *Studies on Hysteria*, he made many more unsubstantiated assertions than did Freud. Freud confined himself to low-level speculations and usually cited the data upon which his assertions were based (Schlessinger et al., 1967). A difference can also be seen in comparing Breuer's report of Anna O. and Freud's cases in the clinical section of the book. Breuer fails to organize the wealth of psychological material in a meaningful sequence; he appears overwhelmed by the isolated results of the cathartic method. Freud, on the other hand, links the emotional life of his patients with the method of treatment. In the absence of a theory not yet adequate to the findings, it is essentially Freud's use of a coherent narrative style that unifies the material.

Freud's choice of literary devices and narrative style has already been examined closely in his Dora case (1905a), which is similar in style to the imaginative literature of the time (Ellenberger, 1970a). Marcus (1974), as already noted, concludes that this case history is a great work of literature (p. 12). Both Ellenberger and Marcus are struck by the similarity to Ibsen's plays. An apparently benign situation is revealed as harboring a wealth of unpleasant and distasteful secrets. The scene is set in a "remote provincial town" (1905a, p. 8). Freud even goes so far as to disavow anything remarkable: "No doubt this case history, as I have so far outlined, does not upon the whole seem worth recording" (p. 23).

What differentiates Freud from Ibsen and fiction writers is that he, the author, is also a participant in the drama. As we have seen, he characteristically disavows all literary pretensions. His is a scientific account. Yet Freud underlines the dubious and uncertain nature of his undertaking with his very title, reminding us that it is but a "Fragment of an Analysis of a Case of Hysteria." He begins the analysis "by asking the patient to give the whole story of [her] life" (p. 16), although he realizes that a coherent story is beyond the patient's ability. Indeed he states that the impairment in the patient's narrative ability is connected with the nature of the illness. The symptoms are a sign of a deficient narrative flow, and the purpose of treatment is related to making the story unfold in a more coherent manner. Transferences are described as "new editions or facsimiles" (p. 116). When, as part of her transference revenge, Dora breaks off the treatment, a Faustian Freud writes, "no one who, like me, conjures up the most evil of those half-tamed demons that inhabit the human breast, and seeks to wrestle with them, can expect to come through the struggle unscathed" (p. 109). Insofar as the Dora case, like Freud's other case histories, is a source of continuous reinterpretation, Marcus (1974) concludes that "Freud's case histories are a new form of literature. . . . They can be read and reread. The material they contain is always richer than the original analysis and interpretation that accompany it" (p. 108).

Freud's mastery of narrative style is again revealed in a short vignette he used to illustrate the paradox of people who are wrecked by success:

> I had an opportunity of obtaining an insight into a woman's history, which I propose to describe as typical of these tragic occurrences. She was of good birth and well brought up, but as quite a young girl she could not restrain her zest for life; she ran away from home and roved about the world in search of adventures, till she made the acquaintance of an artist who could appreciate her feminine charms but could also divine, in spite of what she has fallen to, the finer qualities she possessed. He took her to live with him, and she proved a faithful companion to him, and seemed only to need social rehabilitation to achieve complete happiness. After many years of life together he succeeded in getting his family reconciled to her, and was then prepared to make her his legal wife. At that moment she began to go to pieces. She neglected the house of which she was now about

to become the rightful mistress, imagined herself persecuted by his relatives, who wanted to take her into the family, debarred her lover, through her senseless jealousy, from all social intercourse, hindered him in his artistic work and soon succumbed to an incurable mental illness [1916a, pp. 316–317].

How direct and unimpeded the flow of the narrative and how much of the woman's story Freud manages to include in one paragraph! In the beginning, the responsive reader is likely to be moved by the suggestion of potential fulfillment in the woman's life. The climax of the tale comes in the brief sentence: "At that moment she began to go to pieces." The long last sentence is perfectly constructed to evoke the unhappy decline of the woman. The language is clear, unadorned by unnecessary adjectives or other qualifiers which might detract from the directness of the presentation. At the end one is left with a sense of sadness and regret, and this dissatisfaction serves as an excellent preparation for the eagerly awaited explanatory section that follows.

In addition to the unadorned narrative, Freud used a number of other stylistic devices to heighten the effectiveness of his prose. To confront objections to a train of thought he was developing, he frequently resorted to direct or indirect dialogue. His imagined antagonists take on lives of their own; they are portrayed in various states of defiance or acquiescence, benign skepticism or unruly disbelief, depending on the "outrageousness" of Freud's argument. In the *Introductory Lectures on Psycho-Analysis* (1916–1917), for example, Freud many times addresses the skeptical reader or listener directly: "I know you will say that these ideas are both crude and fantastic" (p. 296). In *The Question of Lay Analysis* (1926d), the interlocutor whom he is addressing has a definite voice and a personality. This fictional antagonist, ironically referred to as an Impartial Person, is often filled with disdain and contempt. When Freud tells him that in psychoanalytic treatment the analyst cannot count on the patient's collaboration because the patient has no wish to be cured, the Impartial Person is beside himself. "That is the craziest thing you have told me yet," the listener cries out, losing his impartiality. "Calm yourself," replies Freud, "the patient wants to be cured—but he also wants not to be" (p. 221). In despair at the buffeting about, Freud's antagonist finds himself quoting disconnected pieces of dramatic poetry. Freud then points out that the neurotic patient has lost his sense of unity—"if that were not so he would be no neurotic." The Impartial Person, by this time far gone, can only acquiesce, "Were I sagacious, I should not be Tell!," identifying with Wilhelm Tell, or, more likely, his apple-headed son (p. 221). Like a patient in analysis, the antagonistic reader is pictured working through resistances toward discovery.

Freud's frequent use of analogies suggests that they are more than mere literary devices or instruments of exposition employed for purposes of clarity (Wolf, 1971). "In psychology," he explained, "we can only describe things by the help of analogies" (1926d, p. 195). As already noted, occasionally Freud leaned toward excessive attachment to a metaphor, thereby confounding his theoretical clarity. Indeed, it may have been a peculiarity of his creativity to follow an analogy beyond its usual limit in order to obtain additional insights. With the analogy between the psychic apparatus and a telescope in *The Interpretation of Dreams*, we saw that Freud fell into the error of locating the virtual image between the lenses inside the telescope. Clearly the image exists only as projection in the field of the viewer. Other analogies in the dream book, however, are more successful. Through the image of a picket fence, for instance, Freud differentiates memory traces from perceptions; he explains how memory traces, whose excitation moves "backward"—as along a fence—can obtain perceptual quality and hallucinatory vividness. Thus the unique relation between memory trace and perceptual quality in the dream is given a spatial form. Throughout *The Interpretation of Dreams* Freud offers the metaphors of disentangling a woven fabric, explicating a written text, and following an obscure path as unifying images to describe both the progress of his thoughts and the activity of dream interpretation (Edelson, 1983).

Freud's use of metaphor is so extensive and so unusual in scientific writing that it must be accounted for as an idiosyncratic, specific ability to relate psychological reality to concrete image by grasping links between seemingly disparate phenomena. As an example, one may take Freud's comparison between the mechanism of repression, as it relates to resistance, and the ejection of an ill-mannered intruder. While addressing the audience of Clark University in 1909, he imagined:

> . . . in this lecture room and among this audience . . . there is . . . somene who is causing a disturbance and whose ill-mannered laughter, chattering and shuffling with his feet are distracting my attention from my task. I have to announce that I cannot proceed with my lecture; and thereupon three or four of you who are strong men stand up and, after a short struggle, put the interrupter outside the door. So now he is 'repressed,' and I can continue my lecture [1910a, p. 25].

Should the man who was expelled attempt to reenter, chairs would have to be put against the door to keep him out. In a similar way, the forces of repression have to be alerted and mobilized to deny entry to unacceptable intruding thoughts.

Here abstract content is given an immediate concrete form vividly related to the situation in which Freud found himself. From his previous experience of addressing unsympathetic audiences, Freud was sensitive to the latent objections of his listeners and their silent repudiation. Simultaneously he identified with the noisy intruder; in fact, he spoke of himself as one who "disturbed the sleep of the world" (1914b, p. 21). Freud used a quotation from Virgil's *Aeneid* about intrusion as a motto for *The Interpretation of Dreams*: "Flectere si nequeo superos, Acheronta movebo" (If I cannot influence the celestial gods, I will set in motion the infernal regions). He also depicted himself as a childhood intruder into the parental bedroom (1900a, p. 216). The figure of speech thus becomes the vehicle connecting the thought to its origin in his own experiences.

Among his many literary skills, Freud was a master in the use of apt expression, aphorism, and epigram. Although non-German readers may be hindered by the interposition of a translation, they can still appreciate the special qualities of rhythm and balance, irony and bite. In describing the thought content of the depressed patient, for instance, Freud writes, "When he describes himself as petty, egoistic, dishonest, lacking in independence, one whose sole aim has been to hide the weaknesses of his own nature, it may be, so far as we know, that he has come pretty near to understanding himself; we only wonder why a man has to be ill before he can be accessible to a truth of this kind" (1917b, p. 246). Here Freud deliberately surprises and shocks the reader by not contradicting his prototypical depressive. In effect, the wry comment, suggesting that Freud accepts the patient's self-evaluation, establishes the importance of the patient's psychic reality, it invites the reader to puzzle about the illness rather than to dismiss or minimize the psychic content. We experience an expansion of outlook; we grasp that a truth lies dormant in psychopathology.

A seemingly ideal balance between the abstract and concrete is struck in a section in which Freud describes the failure of resistance: "He that has eyes to see and ears to hear may convince himself that no mortal can keep a secret. If his lips are silent, he chatters with his fingertips; betrayal oozes out of him at every pore" (1905a, pp. 77–78). The mental and the physical assume equal weight, and the experience of listening to a patient takes on an immediacy in the direct, physical observation of the other person.

Freud's literary style was usually subordinated to his scientific intentions, but he did write a number of philosophical essays and literary pieces. In considering the short essay "On Transience" (Freud, 1916b), Schönau (1968) is so impressed with its poetic mood that he casts doubt on whether the conversation Freud reports with the taciturn friend and the young poet ever took place.[6] The essay reflects a personal reaction to the experience of loss, underlining the need to accept the inevitable pain of mourning rather than denigrate the loss by denying the value of the lost object. The style is elegiac, nostalgic, and restrained. The conversation is said to have taken place "in the summer before the war"; it is a reflection on loss from a time that is itself lost. "The war broke out and robbed the world of its beauties. . . . It revealed our instincts in all their naked-

---

[6]Roazen (1969, p. 33) states that the other participants in the conversation were Lou Andreas-Salomé and Rainer Maria Rilke.

ness and let loose the evil spirits within us which we thought had been tamed forever by centuries of continuous education by the noblest minds" (1916b, p. 307). In this essay, written for a commemorative volume issued by the Berlin Goethe Society in 1916, Freud offers a metaphoric condolence note to Western civilization, in response to his own deep disappointment at the outbreak of the First World War.

In light of the richness of Freud's style, critics and literary figures such as Thomas Mann and Walter Muschg have questioned whether Freud in actuality subordinated style to scientific considerations. Indeed, they have been inclined to consider Freud primarily as a writer. Muschg (1930) claims that the writer cannot be separated from the psychologist; he attributes the power of conviction that seized him when he read Freud as a response to the literary form of the work. Here Muschg points out that as Freud felt more secure about his scientific contribution, disclaimers about the literary quality of his work decreased.

Freud varied his style with the nature of the work, moving from the cold, objective, relentless style of *Three Essays on the Theory of Sexuality* (1905c) to the confiding, personal style of his *Introductory Lectures* (1916–1917) and *The Question of Lay Analysis* (1926d). Some, such as Holt (1965), have described Freud's style in terms of rhetorical devices meant to persuade the reader rather than to prove a proposition. Holt believes that when, as a student, Freud was exposed to Aristotle in Brentano's philosophy courses, he mastered the devices of rhetoric, which then became second nature to him. Ricouer (1976) also remarks on the rhetorical means at Freud's disposal.

Mahony (1982), in the first full-length study in English devoted to Freud's style, argues that attempts to describe Freud's style as merely secondary to scientific aims do an injustice to the artistic richness of his writing. "Freud's writing *produces* knowledge rather than merely describing it," he asserts (p. 14). In the sense that literary language characterizes and communicates with the unconscious ego, Freud's style is more than an appeal to secondary-process, rational thinking. The style affects the reader, rhetorically, below consciousness. In agreement with Derrida (1978), Mahony demonstrates that Freud's style at times mimics what he writes about. As an example, he points to how, in *Beyond the Pleasure Principle* (1920a), the tendency to move back and forth in the argument, to turn the text on itself, repeats the game Freud observed his one-and-a-half-year-old grandson playing. When the child's mother left him, he threw a wooden reel on a string outside his crib and then with great satisfaction retrieved it. This, Freud noted, was an attempt to overcome the trauma of temporary separation by the mastery of play. In presenting the argument for the repetition compulsion and the death instinct, Freud repeats the *fort/da* game of his grandson; he displays a *fort/da* style in his exposition.

Mahony also points out that Freud's form of composition is processive—he portrays his own mind in the process of thinking. As we read him, we are caught up in a movement that is ongoing, always evolving and unfolding. We reread Freud "because our act of reading constantly affords us the pleasure of the psychoanalytic experience" (1982, p. 173). We share the experience of having our understanding enlarged.

The Psychoanalysis of Style

The comment made in 1753 by the French naturalist Buffon—"Le style est l'homme même"—appears to state the case, quite succinctly, for those who believe that style reflects personality. Actually, Buffon did not pursue this very far. He was interested in why writers are remembered by posterity; his point was that literary fame does not depend on content of knowledge, which is common property, but on the quality of style, which is the contribution of an individual author (Abrams, 1953). Nevertheless, the maxim is too pithy to ignore; it can serve as an epigram for an investigation into the link between style and personality attributes.

The term "style" has a wide range of meanings, but let us look first at the literary meaning of style. Here style refers to the manner of linguistic expression (Abrams, 1971). It includes diction or the choice of words, sentence structure and syntax, figures of speech, rhythms and sound, rhetorical aims and devices. Through these means language can be manipulated for expressive effect, as well as to communicate an idea. Each expressive communication is readily found in Freud's use of sentence structure. For instance, to demonstrate his impatience with the recalcitrance of Fräulein Elisabeth von R. when she would not reveal her thoughts, he sums up his state in a short phrase: "It was an unfavorable day; we would try another time" (Breuer and Freud, 1893–1895b, p. 153).[7]

Scientific thought may lend itself to the use of parallelisms in sentence structure, particularly where relations and comparisons are called for. Freud was skillful at such stylistic construction, emphasizing his point through poetic rhythm. "Pain is the actual reaction to loss of object," he proposed, "while anxiety is the reaction to the danger which that loss entails" (1926c, p. 170). Or similarly: "A denial is not a refutation, an innovation is not necessarily an advance" (1939b, p. 131).[8]

Within the sentence structure, word order can mirror the psychological process in the author. Emphasis and suspense may be added when an important idea is left to the end. By choosing new word forms or appropriating old words for new ideas, a writer can heighten the evocative effect (consider Freud's use of *Ich*, superior to the less subjectively apt translation "ego," or his *Übertragung* for the idea of carrying-over as in transference). Of course, too obvious a poetic effect detracts from the effectiveness of good scientific prose; thus Freud's use of alliteration, quotations, or imagery is not excessive.

I have already pointed out that Freud relied on figures of speech not only as stylistic devices but also as a means of developing his thinking. Among such stylistic devices, he favored the simile, metaphor, and comparison. Rhetorically, these stylistic devices are useful in enlarging the sphere of the reader's awareness and bringing into association the reader's available preconscious experiences. But

---

[7]This is even more effective in the original: "Der Tag sei nicht gunstig: ein andermal" (Breuer and Freud, 1893–1895a, p. 218).

[8]Note the assonance and alliteration in the original: "Ein Widerspruch is noch keine Widerlegung, eine Neuerung nicht notwending ein Fortschritt" (1939a, p.t/240).

Freud's figures of speech are more than rhetorical; they reveal important psychological connections. When Freud comments, "Writing is . . . the voice of an absent person" ("die Schrift is . . . die Sprache des Abwesenden" [1930d, p. 450]), he is clearly employing a metaphor. By adding *ursprunglich* ("primitively" or "originally") to the sentence, he converts the figure of speech into a genetic explanation. Again, there is a caution: A metaphor overused becomes a cliché, and the repetition stultifies the associational pathways. With time it has become hard to hear what it means that dreams are "the royal road to the unconscious." The stylist must be parsimonious in the use of figurative language, maintaining a balance with direct exposition.

From a broad view, however, style need not be confined to literary style, or to the work of an individual. One may speak of style as the constant forms of expression of a group or culture. In the arts, the description of a style refers to characteristic motifs. Investigators of style search for an organizing principle that determines the nature of the elements and their patterning into a whole (Schapiro, 1953). In the visual arts, style may be described in terms of cycles, such as archaic, classical, baroque, or archaistic; or it may be considered evolutionary, progressing from geometrical to naturalistic forms. Any number of organizing principles might be cited, such as increasing attention to the position of the observer or the viewer's responses. Style may also be regarded as embracing content in the sense that it serves as an objective vehicle for subject matter or embodies characteristic modes of thoughts or belief systems that underlie content. From this perspective, one may say that a characteristic of Freud's cognitive style was to conceptualize in terms of dualities, such as unconscious and conscious, sex and aggression, latent and manifest, drive and defense, self and object, ego and id. As he himself stated, "Our views have from the very first been dualistic and today they are even more definitely dualistic than before" (1920a, p. 53).

Within the context of ego psychology, style can be defined as a progressive synthesis of form and content in an individually typical manner, an expression of the organizing, synthetic and differentiating function of the ego (Rosen, 1961). An individual style results from idiosyncratic experiences. Kris (1952), for instance, suggests that Leonardo da Vinci's relatively innovative use of the pyramidal configuration in Renaissance painting can be understood as a response to his childhood situation. As an infant, he had been raised by two mothers; this emotionally crucial experience became a factor in spatial design of his work.[9] According to Rosen (1961), an "incentive from the life history is fused with the stringencies of the artistic problem" through the synthetic ego function, resulting in an individualized style (p. 448).

The study of style offers a deepening of psychological understanding because of the constancy associated with style. The habitual aspects of style may have been initially responsive to fundamental psychological needs; attempts at finding appropriate techniques for need satisfaction account for characteristic modes and styles of expression. As development progresses and ego functions attain autonomy, a discontinuity between fundamental needs and stylistic form may occur. Subsequently, however, under traumatic pressure and stress these forms may lose their autonomy, once more become drive-connected, and be influenced by conflict or illness. Kris and Pappenheim offer an example of a schizophrenic artist who, in his regressive withdrawal, continued the same subject matter in his drawings as in his normal state; however, the formal features of his style shifted back to more primitive modes of expression (Kris, 1952).

A number of stylistic phenomena appear in the psychoanalytic situation, and they may be looked at in terms analogous to the analysis of literary or artistic style. Characteristic forms of speech, mannerisms, and modes of dress bear the marks of symptomatic actions, carrying a content meaning. Yet a caution must be added, for there is a difference between individual character structure and style as used in the creative arts. The latter is influenced by artistic tradition as well as the exigencies requiring solution in the artistic task. Although the creative artist's style may have its origins in the matrix of his or her own experience, it is also appropriate to the task. An excessive concern, fending off anxiety or protecting against trauma or

---

[9]See Chapter 8 for a futher development and critique of this position.

danger, may in fact limit the artist's formal resources, so that the work comes to reflect only the idiosyncratic and not a larger purview. In this sense, Buffon's aphorism is a statement about the limitations of style.

Neverthelesss, if style is both the product of the personality and the appropriate vehicle for expressing the ego's activity in executing a task, then one may appropriate Buffon's maxim in a larger sense. Freud himself saw stylistic considerations as wedded to the "nature of the subject" as well as reflecting a preference of his own (Breuer and Freud, 1893–1895b, p. 160). If his case histories read like short stories, it is because his emergence as an analyst was coterminous with the development of his mature literary style (Schwaber, 1976). His emerging psychoanalytic view required a prose considered appropriate to the literary tradition, a tradition more concerned with the understanding of human experience than the science of the day.

7

The Psychoanalysis of
Aesthetic Response

How may the psychoanalytic view be used to deepen our understanding of art? Some analysts have interested themselves in creativity itself and the process whereby contents of the artist's mind transformed into a work of art. Here the psychoanalyst may profit from
the comparison between fantasy expressed as symptom and fantasy
expressed as art. Of course, despite its resemblances to a neurotic
symptom or a dream, the work of art is different: it is a formed
communication, addressed to an audience who responds aesthet-
ically.

From a similar vantage point, given that the work of art shares at
least some common features with symptomatic activity, the psychoanalyst may discern aspects of the biography of the creator. The art
work may reveal characteristics of style, values, or artistic personality, as well as deeper preoccupations, unconscious conflict, developmental deficiencies, attempts at conflict resolution, and patterns of
mastery.

Psychoanalysis may also be of use in accounting for the artistic
power of the work itself. Members of an audience may respond to a
work because it expresses imaginatively a universal fantasy or
shared preoccupation. Recall Freud's words about our response to
Oedipus in Sophocles' play: "His destiny moves us only because it
might have been ours—because the oracle laid the same curse upon

us before our birth as upon him" (1900a, p. 262). The reader, the hero, and the creator are linked by their common destiny, by the unsatisfied and repudiated infantile fantasies that activated (and activate) the work of art.

But the audience's response to the drama does not depend "only" on the similarity of content. The artist's gift lies in the capacity to present the shared fantasy in such a manner as to overcome the tendency toward repudiation. Although the wish itself is not gratified directly, there is another satisfaction, which depends on the repertoire of formal means at the artist's disposal. The artist's skill in finding an apt rhyme or enriching metaphor, in organizing the color harmony or controlling the expression of line, combines with the evocative content to yield an integrated aesthetic response.

Although early attempts at a psychoanalytic investigation of aesthetic response—as in Freud's book on jokes (1905b)—laid the groundwork for an understanding of the effect of the formal devices in a work of art, this approach has largely been neglected. Most psychoanalytic criticism has focused on the analysis of unconscious content rather than the means by which such content is expressed. Frequently the work of art has been treated as if its most pertinent reference point were the dream or the neurotic symptom. That the psychoanalytic theory of aesthetics has its base in the analysis of jokes is in part responsible for this one-sided emphasis. Moreover, too often the work of art has been approached for evidence of a specific emotional constellation. Freud, in finding the Oedipus complex in *Oedipus Rex*, *Hamlet*, and *The Brothers Karamazov*, believed that he had discovered the "deepest" meaning of these works; he was thus less interested in the uniqueness of each work and the differences among them (aside from the clarity or obscurity with which the complex was presented).

Yet clearly an aesthetic response cannot occur without the deployment of complex formal devices that communicate and express, conceal and reveal, the deepest layers Freud referred to. The analyst's recognition that the work expresses the solution of an artistic problem adds a further dimension to the psychoanalytic understanding of art. The aesthetic response to the form of a work is contingent on the perception of a constructed unity, which resonates with the coherence and form given to the self.

The Economics of the Aesthetic Response

Freud wrote, "The first example an application of the analytic mode of thought to the problems of aesthetics was contained in my book on jokes," and he promised workers who devoted themselves to this field "a particularly rich harvest" (1914b, p. 37). At first blush, it may seem strange that Freud entered the field of aesthetics through the pathway of jokes and humor. Yet once he had established a common link between the neurotic symptom and a work of artistic creation, it was but a short step to find that dreams shared features common to both. He then wrote, "all dreamers are insufferably witty and they have to be, because they are under pressure, and the direct way is barred to them" (Letter of September 11, 1899, in 1887–1902b, p. 297). The dream resembles a bad joke whose point has been lost because the dreamer did not take sufficient care with the communicative effect. Nevertheless, the mechanisms of the dream work are similar to those of the joke; latent meaning is present in each.

Among the shared mechanisms, Freud singled out condensation. A poor lottery agent, for instance, is asked how he was treated on his visit to the great Baron Rothschild. "Quite famillionairely," he replies. Ostensibly he is stating that the Baron treated him as an equal; on a deeper level, he implies he was treated as a poor relation. In addition to condensation, Freud pointed to displacement, indirect representation, symbolism, and representation by the opposite as shared mechanisms in the dream and the joke (1905b, pp. 12–13).

Although the mechanisms are shared, clearly the purposes differ. A dream fulfills an expressive function, with communication secondary. A joke, on the other hand, must take into account the response of an audience. It is the pleasurable quality of the response that provides the link between the joke and the work of art. The joke evokes this directly, in laughter; the work of art, by a more complicated route. Both, however, aim at pleasure not through satisfaction of a vital need but through the economic use of mental processes themselves. One gains a maximum of satisfaction through a minimum of means.

Not only is the joke enjoyable for its own sake, but it also provides satisfaction to hidden aims of the personality. Hostile and sexual wishes that have been partially renounced retrieve an opportunity for expression. The form of the joke and the opportunity to share it in collusion with a sympathetic listener permit the surmounting of inhibitions against such wishes.

There are, then, two different types of pleasure in jokes. With tendentious jokes, jokes with the purpose of satisfying repudiated wishes, the pleasure comes from the lifting of an internal inhibition. Energy previously used to maintain a repressive defense is suddenly freed—discharged as laughter. With innocent jokes, jokes with no hidden aim in view—and Freud questioned whether in fact such jokes exist—the pleasure is akin to that experienced by the child in playing with sounds of words rather than meanings. The adult finds satisfaction in returning to the realm of the imagination and giving up the demand for logic and reality characteristic of adult life. Nonsense can once more be enjoyed for its own sake. Rhymes, alliterations, and refrains permit one to recapture the childhood pleasure in repetition of the familiar and rediscoverable. The superficial meaning of a joke, its conscious sense, serves as a protection against the criticizing agency that denigrates such childhood wishes.

In sum, with jokes, one finds a pleasure in playing with words and resorting to primitive forms of mentation; this delight serves as a forepleasure, facilitating further pleasure by lifting repression. The pleasure in the form of the joke, the manner in which it is told, thus serves as an incentive bonus, assisting in the freeing of the repressed. The hearer then "laughs with the quota of psychical energy which has become free through the lifting of the inhibitory cathexis" (Freud, 1905b, p. 149). Indeed often, in listening to a joke, one mobilizes one's defenses to resist the joke's effect, but—if the joke is well constructed—this attempt at inhibition proves futile. The power of the joke overwhelms the defenses, and one laughs in relief. One might compare the teller of a joke to a religious evangelist who, through his oratorical skill, arouses the demonic appetites of his audience, frightens it with a tally of punishments and threats of damnation, and then offers it release through the promise of salvation. After all, it is only a joke.

Freud applied his theory of an incentive bonus and forepleasure to an understanding of the response to artistic creation. Through the use of *ars poetica*, Freud explained, the creative writer alters and disguises his daydreams; "he bribes us by the purely formal—that is, aesthetic yield of pleasure which he offers us in the presentation of his fantasies." This inducement makes possible still deeper pleasure. "All the aesthetic pleasure which a creative writer offers us has the character of a fore-pleasure . . ." (1908, p. 153). We can then enjoy our own daydreams more freely; our conflicts over our hidden wishes are overcome by the formal devices.

Again, Freud distinguishes between two types of pleasure. Aesthetic pleasure—the pleasure of a person in experiencing a subtle rhyme, an apt color modulation, or a well-planned compostiton—is to be differentiated from another pleasure, associated with the satisfaction experienced by a deeper stratum of the personality. This conception of levels of pleasurable experience was compatible with the topographic model of the mind with which Freud dealt in the early years of psychoanalytic work. It emerges in Freud's comment on his oedipal interpretation of *Hamlet* quoted earlier: "All genuine creative writings are the product of more than a single motive and more than a single impulse in the poet's mind, and are open to more than a single interpretation. . . . I have only attempted [in revealing the oedipal theme] to interpret the deepest layer of impulses in the mind of a creative writer" (1900a, p. 266).

Psychological Structure and Aesthetic Response

In spite of Freud's care to describe the aesthetic response as an integration of the formal and content elements, many critics responded to the psychoanalytic contribution as if it proposed a view of art that encompassed only the "deepest layer," the repudiated drive content. Admittedly, much psychoanalytic writing on art did concentrate exclusively on an analysis of "the deepest layer." For the aestheticians, this position overlooked what was fundamental in art.

The shortcomings of a conflict model applied to aesthetics soon became apparent. According to Roger Fry (1924), Freud, in his concern with the deepest layer of mental impulses, short-changed the pleasure derived from the formal relations of a work. In Fry's opinion, the aesthetic emotion is to a large extent detached from primal origins in instinctual life; it is an emotion about form itself. Even though these formal relations may have associational links with drive-related strata of the personality, Fry pleaded that "the accumulated and inherited artistic treasures of mankind are made up almost entirely of those works in which formal design is the predominant consideration" (1924, p. 9). Pleasure in form, he contended, is less likely to be successfully traced back to libido than to the necessity in recognizing order and harmony, the inevitability of formal sequences.

No attempt was made to defend the economic and topographic view against this criticism, but the development of a structural point of view did add a new dimension to psychoanalytic understanding of the artistic response. With the assignment of mental functions to the agencies of id, ego, and superego, the psychoanalyst could reassess art in terms of the contribution of each agency. Even before the development of the structural point of view, Freud had evaluated the social value of the artist. Not only was the artist the keeper of a wildlife preserve, "who allows his erotic and ambitious wishes full play," he also "finds the way back to reality," and he moulds "his phantasies into truths of a new kind, which are valued by men as precious" (1911, p. 224). In discovering the way back to reality the artist accepts renunciation as necessary, and the ensuing dissatisfaction is an integral part of the reality the artist reflects. From the structural perspective, although the id's contribution to aesthetic response was still seen as substantial, the vicissitudes and deflection to which the repressed or condemned wishes were exposed also had to be considered. Not only external reality, which interferes with satisfaction, but the ego, which repudiates or attenuates the repressed wishes, also makes a contribution to aesthetic response.

The task of the ego is not only to repress unconscious and unacceptable wishes, but also to serve as a mediator between impulse and reality. The ego's success in resolving this psychological dilemma can have an aesthetic dimension. Because the ego is a problem-solving agent, argued Waelder, "quality of performance lies, first, in the fact that a solution has been found when the task had seemed insolvable or would have been unsolvable by ordinary human effort; second, in the perfection of a solution; and finally, in its elegance, the economy of means. These are the characteristics that make the beauty of a solution and . . . they constitute the ego aspect of beauty" (1965, p. 44).

Economic factors thus are relevant in considering the ego's regulatory functions as well as its defensive functions. In addition to the release from inhibition, there is satisfaction in the parsimony of an artistic solution. The ego's ability to express latent content, to order and reconcile opposing trends, becomes an important source of aesthetic pleasure (Weiss, 1947; Noy, 1979).

The psychoanalyst who is inclined to consider experiences of pleasure as the fulfillment of an instinctive drive may have some difficulty in conceiving of *aesthetic* pleasure, the locus of which is the ego. Such pleasure has at times been considered the result of sublimation: the aim of a drive is displaced onto a nonsexual object that is socially acceptable. In this view the pleasure is seen as a satisfaction of a drive derivative. Waelder (1965), however proposes an alternative conception. He suggests that certain ego activities— those, say, involved in responding to art—are stimulated by instinctual drives but then lose the drive connection. Thus the satisfaction of the aesthetic response has both drive and ego components.

An additional satisfaction in art comes from the contribution of the superego, the value maintaining agency of the personality. Aesthetic appreciation is essentially a normative activity. Standards of beauty incorporated by the connoisseur or even by one unsophisticated in an artistic tradition provide an ideal against which the worth of a work can be measured. Moreover, there is a tendency to attribute a transcendent meaning to a work of art. Freud believed that the artist was capable of insights that science could arrrive at only through lengthy and laborious means. We speak of art as illuminating reality, and we treasure the aesthetic response as a sign of man's higher nature. The artist who stives for perfection of form is preserving some aspect of infantile narcissism in the work, which is an ideal extension of his or her self.

The structural point of view highlights the contribution of both content and form to aesthetic appreciation. Freud's initial interest in the gratification of unconscious drives emphasizes the pleasure in the content, the fulfillment of the ideational component of a latent wish based on an infantile prototype. The question arises: How much of the pleasure in art is specifically associated with the formal means employed by the artist? A first step in approaching this problem is an attempt at a more precise definition of form. In discussions of aesthetics, the term "form" is used in at least three different ways (Bush, 1967). Form refers to a particular structural element in an artistic work, such as a metaphor in poetry or a shape in painting. In addition, form may refer to a mode of presentation, such as ambiguity or clarity, or it may refer to the overall organization, the organic unity. When we consider the aesthetic effect of an art work, each of these definitions must be taken into account.

If, then, we take form as the means of expression of content, then, from a structural viewpoint, we can see the formal component of aesthetic pleasure as derived from the exercise and mastery of ego functions. These ego functions—perception, cognition, execution, synthesis, and integration—provide a source of gratification in their own right. The more successfully each function is exercised, the greater the pleasure experienced. Although initially the ego functions may be in the service of drive gratification, with experience and personality development, the drive component accounts for only a limited portion of the total pleasure. The work of art, insofar as it is successful, mirrors the ego, which strives for a successful mediation of tendencies within the personality (Rose, 1980). In other words, the formal pleasure in the work of art is an expression of ego functioning in an ideal state.

From the structural point of view, we also gain insight into the manner in which a work is perceived. Ehrenzweig (1965, 1967), drawing partially on Gestalt psychology, suggests that there may be two dominant modes of perceiving artistic forms: a tendency to react in terms of organized, secondary-process configurations and a tendency to react at unconscious levels to stimuli that evoke primary-process mechanisms. When we look at the late work of Cézanne, for example, although the manifest distortions in space and shape may be jarring, the final aesthetic response stems from the integration of fresh, undifferentiated infantile sensations, much as reality is probably comprehended in early life. Cézanne, in fact, maintained that he was interested in including in his art "the confused sensations with which we are born" (Kanzer, 1957, p. 518).

With the shift in psychoanalytic thought toward a conception of the ego as a synthesizing and integrating agency, the mode with which drive satisfaction occurred attained new importance. This is seen most readily where much of the aesthetic impact depends on the revelation or development of character. Here the aesthetic effect is often brought about by an element of constraint, with concealment and revelation balanced in such a manner that one tendency does not totally submerge the other. In *Oedipus Rex*, as we have seen, the audience shares with Oedipus both his blindness and the gradual expansion of his awareness through the formal device of exposing him to knowledge that eventually proves overwhelmingly convincing. The work is a compromise between the limited consciousness of the protagonist and the increasing power of the revelations he must face (Wolheim, 1970).

Developmental Considerations in the Aesthetic Response

In his discussion of the comic, Freud (1905b) already glimpsed the importance of early childhood experiences as genetic sources of pleasure in art. These experiences include the child's manipulation of language, the shift from awkwardness to skill in motoric activity, the pleasure in mastery, the delight in play for its own sake – in nonsense, punning, clang associations, and rhyming. Word play in which meaning or thought is of little or no significance remains a source for potential pleasure in the adult, recoverable even when symbolization predominates. In the comic, the adult enjoys a sense of a mastery over a skill that at one time, in early childhood, was painstakingly acquired. There is the pleasure in recapturing the early experience and the sense of satisfaction in having surmounted the earlier difficulties. Freud commented about Charlie Chaplin:

> He is undoubtedly a great artist – although he always plays one and the same part, the weak, poor, helpless, clumsy boy for whom life turns out all right in the end. Now do you think he has to forget his own self in order to play this part? On the contrary, he invariably plays only himself as he was in his grim youth. He cannot get away from these impressions and even today he tries to compensate himself for the humiliation and deprivation of that time [Letter of March 26, 1931, in 1873–1939a, p. 405].

Yet aesthetic pleasure goes beyond a simple evocation of the childhood situation. The very experience of transformation from childhood into adulthood, the process of developing itself, contributes to the pleasure in artistic form, for the work of art, like a person, has evolved through phases of development.

The development of the personality, in the earliest stages, necessitates a move away from an initial primary narcissistic state, a state of undifferentiation, toward delineation of self and others and the development of a sense of inner and outer reality. In the process of individuation, ego boundaries are formed, and a sense of organic unity and self-cohesion develops. As the self forms in the earliest phases of ego differentiation, there is still a tendency to return to an undifferentiated state. Transitional objects aid in the gradual emergence from the symbiotic or primary narcissistic state (Winnicott, 1953). In these intermediate stages, self-objects, which bridge the developmental gap, serve as carriers for the security of the more primitive periods. One may say that the earliest expression of interest in form is the activity of giving form to the creation of the self. The first created structure is the structure of the ego.

Yet, as just stated, even after the establishment of a self, a longing for unity with the lost mother of infancy continues. Rose (1980) has referred to the tendency to reclaim the earlier state of mother-infant unity as an "irredentist impulse," and he suggests that the work of art, insofar as it substitutes for the state of narcissistic perfection, reflects aspects of the reclaimed earlier self. These wishes for reunion are often expressed in hermaphroditic terms since, as Freud similarly claimed, "only a combination of male and female elements can give a worthy representation of divine perfection" (1910b, p. 94). Not only do such early developmental states make their contribution to the psychology of the creative process, but they also affect the response to art, particularly as the response is to the work as a formed unity, which harmonizes diverse, even opposing elements.

It has been traditional to recognize the close tie between our corporeality and the theory of proportions in art. Our experience of our bodies and the cyclic nature of somatic processes is accountable for the feeling of rhythm; through our own motoric activity we gain a sense of movement and stasis, change and constancy. The early experience of establishing a dynamic equilibrium between soma and psyche, inner self and external reality, symbiosis and individuation, is reflected in the equilibrium and balance of a work. Just as a sense of narcissistic homeostasis counterbalances threats of fragmentation when the self is stressed, so the sense of organic unity of the successful art work compensates for any seeming overemphasis on one formal element over another. Rose (1980, p. 200) has pointed out that Aristotle's conception of the work or art as an imitation of an action can be understood as an imitation of the mind in action; in this sense, the art work resonates with ego activities operating harmoniously.

From a developmental perspective, aesthetic form has its source in early attempts at reconciliation of opposing trends. The experience of satisfying inner needs and testing reality, the shift from symbiosis to individuation, imply a relation between self and other which is continuous and multifaceted. In the earliest stages of the individuation process, transitional objects, which maintain the security of primary narcissism and freedom from tension, yield to more sophisticated presentations of objects, which represent both self and external reality. The art object is an externalization of the formal structure laid down by the developing self.

Yet such a conception of the aesthetic response in terms of early developmental stages, although not patently in error, is incomplete and requires further elaboration. The kinds of psychological states referred to appear too all-encompassing and too nonspecific to serve as convincing antecedents. A wide range of later experiences, many of which have nothing to do with aesthetic response (such as marked psychopathological states), can also be traced back to early narcissistic states, fusion and separation experiences, and needs to demarcate the boundaries of self and other. Somewhat more precision is offered by the suggestion that it is the mother's manner of transforming the internal and external realities for her infant that constitutes the *anlage* for the first human aesthetic experience. Bollas (1978) proposes that "the maternal aesthetic will be as idiomatic as the style of mother. The first human aesthetic, characterized by deep rapport of subject and object, underlies all aesthetic experiences where the subject feels captured in a reverential moment with an aesthetic object" (p. 394). The attraction of such a conception lies in the possibility that the roots of aesthetic response may have an empirical basis in modes of mothering. An adult may experience a reversal of the response the mother initially directed toward him as the treasured child. The valued art object becomes a focus for idealized contemplation, reverential awe, or joyous rapture—responses originally directed toward the perfectable self by the admiring parent or wished for by the child (in forms only suggested by the partially gratifying parent).

The aesthetic response must, however, also be understood within a context of communication. The artist who creates a work offers something of his own for the appreciation and enlightenment of others. The respondent who resonates with the work repeats within himself something of the process of creation the artist originally followed. The art work "resides" in an intermediate space, a transitional area that provides a matrix for creator and audience; it is a bridge in the communicative process.

Admittedly, despite the varied attempts to deal psychoanalytically with the nature of aesthetic response, a definitive or fully satisfactory view seems lacking. The multifaceted forms of art contribute to the difficulty. Even if we restrict our field to "high art," we note a wide range of forms. Are we justified in grouping together responses to Mozart's *Jupiter* Symphony, Shakespeare's *King Lear*, Tolstoi's *Anna Karenina*, the Parthenon frieze, Byron's *Don Juan*, and Leonardo's *Mona Lisa?* Is it possible that each of the major arts — music, literature, the visual arts — evokes specific responses, which differ more than they resemble one another? In literature, the ideational content may be more important, whereas in music the formal quality may predominate. What is the link between connoisseurship and the particular manner of considering a work of art that the psychoanalyst can offer? And what of the experiential nature of the aesthetic response itself? How precise is this response, and is it significantly different from other perceptual-affective experiences? A return to Freud's own aesthetic responses may contribute to clarifying the problem.

The Meaning of Freud's Aesthetic Responses

When Ernest Jones (1957) came to write the chapter in his biography dealing with Freud's aesthetic appreciation, both Ernst Kris and Freud's son Ernst urged him not to write it. They claimed that Freud lacked aesthetic appreciation, and thus Jones would have little to say that was of any value. The deficiency they referred to was an insensitivity to the visual arts and music. Freud's ability to appreciate imaginative literature — novels, drama, and poetry — was not in question. His view that John Milton was an "even greater poet" than Goethe is enough, for some, to authenticate the fine discrimination of his aesthetic judgment (Letter of August 28, 1883, in 1873–1939a, p. 48; Jones, 1957, p. 427).

As we have seen, Freud himself acknowledged that he was deaf to music (1914c, p. 211).[1] With the visual arts it is another matter. I have already referred to his visit to the Zwinger Museum in Dresden and his response to the paintings he saw there. Although he found a "magical beauty" in Raphael's *Sistine Madonna*, the picture that entranced him was Titian's *Tribute Money*. He wrote to Martha that he was deeply moved by the painting; he would have liked to have taken it with him, but there were too many people around (Letter of December 20, 1883, in 1873–1939a, p. 82). Several years later, on a visit to the Louvre, he was unmoved by the Venus de Milo, but attracted by the busts of the Roman emperors (Letter of October 19, 1885, p. 171). Anticipating the interest he would later show in Michelangelo's Moses statute, he responded to heads and human features that expressed psychological content.

Even after Freud was urged by Fliess to consider the formal features of art, he maintained a primary interest in content. He himself confessed, "I have often observed that the subject matter of works of art has a stronger attraction for me than their formal and technical qualities" (1914c, p. 211). To him, the reaction of persons moved by art resembled a "narcosis," granted that those so affected "cannot set too high a value on [art] as a source of pleasure." As Freud described it, "the enjoyment of beauty has a peculiar, mildly intoxicating quality of feeling. . . . All that seems certain is its derivation from the field of sexual feeling" (1930a, pp. 82–83).

Freud made a distinction between aesthetic response and aesthetic judgment. In his own case, he distinguished between a judgment he could make on the basis of quality of a work, even when he personally did not react in an "intoxicated manner." In order for the emotional impact of a work to affect him, he had to understand something of its meaning. This is quite apparent in his response to Michelangelo's Moses:

---

[1]It is likely that Freud's inability to appreciate music was linked to his aversion to abstraction in the visual arts. In both, language and verbalization, which were so important to Freud, are not essential for aesthetic enjoyment.

Works of art do exercise a powerful effect on me, especially those of literature and sculpture, less often of painting. This has occasioned me, when I have been contemplating such things, to spend a long time before them trying to apprehend them in my own way, i.e., to explain to myself what their effect is due to. Whenever I cannot do this, as for instance with music, I am almost incapable of obtaining any pleasure. Some rationalistic, or perhaps analytic, turn of mind in me rebels against being moved by a thing without knowing why I am thus affected and what it is that affects me [1914c, p. 211].

What Freud is referring to is a two-step procedure. He was initially drawn to a work because of the powerful effect it had on him, although the basis for this effect was not experienced consciously. He then derived a secondary satisfaction, the result of subjecting the work to an analysis in terms of latent psychic content. This analysis might be compared to that of a connoisseur who inspects a work in terms of purely formal values. Freud appreciates "psychoanalytically," i.e., the work enables him to empathize with the unconscious intent of the creator; the formal devices allow the intent to find expression. The connoisseur responds in a similar fashion in discovering the success or failure of the artist's solution to an artistic problem. Both derive an "after-pleasure," which is secondary to the initial impact a work may have (Ehrenzweig, 1965). To respond "psychoanalytically," then, is to recognize that the creator has expressed in the work something of his or her own life, using formal and stylistic means suited to such expression. The analytic respondent derives additional pleasure from this purview.

One may argue that, Freud's statement to the contrary, such a response on the analyst's part is not an aesthetic phenomenon. The psychoanalyst is using nonaesthetic categories to increase psychological understanding, not aesthetic pleasure. Eissler (1971a) has pointed out that "it has not been proven empirically that what the analyst finds in a literary work by his special technique actually plays a role in aesthetic experience" (p. 14). But it seems to me that such a disclaimer is relevant only as long as the analytic contribution confines itself to the clarification of the content of unconscious conflict in a work. With the recognition that both the content and the form of a work contribute to aesthetic appreciation, a further dimension comes into play. An analysis of the formal devices that modulate specific reader responses can reveal this mutual interdependence (see Chapter 9).

In sum, in surveying psychoanalytic contributions to the study of aesthetic response, we find that the meaning of the audience's reactions was first elucidated through the investigation of jokes. Initially, the explanation was couched in terms of drive economy and the topographic model (which is still a most useful route to understanding aesthetic response). With the developing interest in ego formation, an acknowledgment of the value of the formal devices in the art work led to a fuller understanding of aesthetic response. The aesthetic object is conceived as an externalized form of evolving self- and object representations. Thus, aesthetic pleasure has roots in the satisfaction derived from mastery, synthesis, and integration, as well as drive discharge. Psychoanalytic understanding itself, which aims at clarifying the impact of artistic means, can be considered a form of connoisseurship, an after-pleasure that adds a further dimension to the aesthetic response.

8

Comparative Views of Leonardo da Vinci and Psychoanalytic Biography

The application of psychoanalysis to the arts would seem to be most suitable to biographies of creative artists. Indeed, it has been claimed that since psychoanalysis concerns itself with the study of lives, it is a form of biography (Martin, 1983). The analyst and biographer share an interest in development and the influence of the past upon the present. Both gather data that enable them to form meaningful constructions, and both must guard against the unconscious intrusions of their own personalities which may affect their judgments of the subjects. For the analyst and the biographer, the approach is essentially interpretative – in contrast to that of the empirical scientist who forms and tests inferences based on replicable observations, or the poet or novelist who constructs primarily from the imagination, not bound by rules of evidence or considerations of veridical truth.

Freud's study of Leonardo da Vinci (1910b), his first full-length biographical work, provides an introduction to the distinctive genre of psychoanalytic biography. Freud himself had varying feelings about the book. It was one of his favorite works – "the only pretty thing" he had written (Jones, 1955, p. 347). At the same time he dismissed it as "partly fiction," certainly not a work by which the trustworthiness of his other discoveries was to be judged (Letter of November 7, 1914, in 1873–1939a, p. 306).

Giorgio Vasari (1568b) tells us that Leonardo da Vinci was invited by King Frances I to spend the last years of his life in France. The king was fond of the aging master, visited him often, and enjoyed the stimulation of his conversation. One day, as the end drew near, Leonardo was seized by a paroxysm. The king rose from his chair and, wishing to comfort the failing artist, took him in his arms. Leonardo, claims Vasari, knowing that he could have no greater honor, died in the arms of the king.

Three hundred years later, when the French painter Ingres depicted this moving scene (Illustration 8.1), he showed the king cradling Leonardo's head and grasping the dying man as if he were laying claim to a priceless possession. The exaggerated proprietary embrace of Francis in Ingres' painting admirably portrays the eagerness of the centuries to get close to the man Leonardo and to discern the complexity of his personality.

Much of the interest is accounted for by the fact that Leonardo is widely accepted as a universal genius, one of the greatest men of all time; he is treasured for the exceptional quality of his mind and his work.[1] But it is not for this reason alone that Leonardo has been a source of curiosity through the ages. What was known of him did not permit easy understanding. He presented a puzzle, a challenge calling for solution. Freud said that even in Leonardo's own time "he had already begun to seem an engima, just as he does to us today" (1910b, p. 63). Walter Pater also referred to "something enigmatical beyond the usual measure of great men" (1893, p. 77). Heydenreich (1954) wrote of the "mystery" of Leonardo, and Eissler (1961) subtitled his book on Leonardo "Psychoanalytic Notes on the Enigma."

The psychoanalyst, responsive to this challenge, is also interested in the psychological antecedents to Leonardo's creativity. Although it is generally believed that creativity of such high order is a "gift," a natural endowment, the link to personality attributes cannot be overlooked. A psychoanalytic approach reveals how the raw mate-

---

[1]There are few who dispute this general opinion, although Bernard Berenson thought "Leonardo was only the greatest of cranks" (1916, p.t/34).

Illustration 8.1 Jean Auguste Dominique Ingres, *The Death of Leonardo da Vinci*, 1818 (Paris: Musée du Petit Palais).

150

rial offered by experience may be incorporated into creative work and how motive forces may arouse or interfere with creativity (Freud, 1933b, p. 254).[2]

Vasari's Leonardo

Giorgio Vasari, Leonardo's early biographer, was firmly convinced that the zenith of art had been reached with the mature Michelangelo, Leonardo's arch-rival. Nevertheless, he wrote:

> The heavens often rain down the richest gifts on human beings naturally, but sometimes with lavish abundance bestow upon a single individual beauty, grace, and ability, so that, whatever he does every action is so divine that he distances all other men and clearly displays how his genius is the gift of God and not an acquirement of human art. Men saw this in Leonardo da Vinci, whose personal beauty could not be exaggerated, whose every movement was grace itself, and whose abilities were so extraordinary that he could solve every difficulty. He possessed great personal strength, combined with dexterity, and spirit and courage invariably royal and magnanimous, and the fame of his name so spread abroad that, not only was he valued in his own day, but his renown has greatly increased since his death.

> This marvelous and divine Leonardo. . .was capricious and fickle, for he began to learn many things and then gave them up. . . . He felt that his hand would be unable to realize the perfect creations of his imagination, as his mind formed such difficult, subtle and marvelous conceptions that his hands, skillful as they were, could never have expressed them [1568b, pp. 5, 7].

---

[2]Even though Freud stated that psychoanalysis is prepared to deal with the motive forces that awaken genius, he maintained that such investigations are not intended to "explain" genius (1933b, p. 254). Still, an analysis of motive is certainly a step in the direction of explanation. Clearly biographical studies intend to shed light on factors that contribute to creative achievement. The implications for creativity will be explored in Chapter 10.

Vasari tells us that the young Leonardo was placed in the work-
shop of Andrea del Verrocchio, and while there he painted one of
the angels in Verrocchio's *Baptism of Christ* (Illustration 8.2).
Mortified that a child should be more skillful than he, Verrocchio
never painted again. Once Leonardo frightened his father when Ser
Piero asked Leonardo to paint something on a round piece of wood

Illustration 8.2 Andrea del Verrocchio, *Baptism of Christ*, c. 1472 (Florence:
Uffizi).

for one of his peasants. Leonardo constructed a frightening Medusa composed of dead lizards, maggots, snakes, locusts, and bats, and showed it to his father in a dim light. As his father beat a hasty retreat, Leonardo said, "This work has served its purpose" (Vasari, 1568b, p. 7).

Vasari described Leonardo's fascination with Mona Lisa, the wife of Francesco del Giocondo. Leonardo worked on the painting for four years, carrying it with him on his travels. But then he left it unfinished, a further puzzlement to the diligent Renaissance biographer.

For Vasari, Leonardo was important because he gave a new dignity to the position of artist. Leonardo believed that the artist was not a mere craftsman or artisan as had been true in the Middle Ages. The artist was a creator, and in this sense, according to Vasari, he approached the divine; he could produce exact copies of nature, and he was sufficiently respected to die in the arms of a king.[3]

Yet Vasari was also troubled by Leonardo's procrastination, his tendency toward distraction, his inability to finish his works, and his remorse in not fulfilling his artistic destiny. Although Leonardo's fame will never be extinguished, Vasari regretted that "he talked much more about his works than he achieved" (1568a, p. 13). Vasari thus set the tone for our image of a great man for whom all was possible but little accomplished.

Pater's Leonardo

From the many accounts of Leonardo between Vasari and Freud, I have selected one of the most influential: Walter Pater's essay on Leonardo, written in 1869. Kenneth Clark (1973) states that Pater's

---

[3]Vasari, whose reliability is not always dependable when he has an opportunity to idealize the role of the artist, was carried away by his account of Leonardo's death. The king was, in fact, not present on the day of Leonardo's death (Goldscheider, 1948, p. 13, n. 53).

description of the *Mona Lisa* was memorized by his generation; it was regarded as a pinnacle of art criticism.[4] Pater himself was highly regarded as an essayist and critic in the last years of the nineteenth century; although for a period of several decades his reputation waned, it is currently undergoing a revival. Within the last few years, an insightful biography (Levey, 1978) and an annotated edition of his important book *The Renaissance* (1893) have contributed to the growing interest in his personality and his work.

Walter Pater (1839–1894) was a leading figure in the development of the Aesthetic Movement in England. He believed that art was to be appreciated for its own sake, not for its moral, educational, or socially meliorative function. Because he opposed the cult of beauty to the religious interests of the late Victorian era, he was criticized for unchristian and hedonistic beliefs. Like Ruskin, he claimed that the aim of all true criticism was "to see the object as, in itself, it really is." Yet he added:

> . . . the first step towards seeing [the] object as it really is, is to know one's own impression as it really is. . . . What is this song or picture, this engaging personality presented in life or in a book, to me? What effect does it really produce on me? Does it give me pleasure? and if so, what sort or degree of pleasure? How is my nature modified by its presence, and under its influence? The answers to these questions are the original facts with which the aesthetic critic has to do [1893, pp. xix–xx].

Pater thus gave prominence to subjectivity and the inner experience of the individual. In his introspective stance, he can be considered a forerunner of Freud. For Pater:

> Not the fruit of experience, but experience itself, is the end. A counted number of pulses only is given to us of a variegated, dramatic life. How may we see in them all that is to be seen in them by the finest senses? . . . To burn always with [a] hard, gem-like flame, to maintain . . . ecstasy, is success in life [1893, pp. 188–189].

---

[4]Levey (1978) similarly describes Pater's remarks on *Mona Lisa* as "the most famous piece of writing about any picture in the world" (p. 125).

When Pater came to write of Leonardo, he portrayed, not surprisingly, a Leonardo who would have felt at home within the Aesthetic Movement; Leonardo was seen as a genius who had filled his life to the brim with exquisite sensations. "His type of beauty is so exotic that it fascinates a larger number than it delights," declared Pater (1893, p. 77). "For years he seemed to those about him as one listening to a voice, silent for other men" (p. 81). Pater underlined Leonardo's "love of the impossible" (p. 82); he resembled a "sorcerer or . . . magician, possessed of curious secrets and a hidden knowledge, living in a world of which he alone possessed the key" (p. 84). In his restless investigation of Nature's secrets, Leonardo "preferred always the more to the less remote" (p. 86). "Through Leonardo's strange veil of sight things reach him . . . in no ordinary night or day, but as in faint light of eclipse, or in some brief interval of falling rain at daybreak or through deep water" (p. 87).

Like Vasari, Pater saw Leonardo as the forerunner of a new type of personality—one who no longer responded to the authority of established religion, able to follow his own instincts and satisfy his curiosity, capable of discovering the hidden secrets of Nature and exploring her mysteries for sensual delight.

With the *Mona Lisa* (Illustration 8.3), Pater pointed to "the unfathomable smile . . . with a touch of something sinister in it, which plays over all of Leonardo's work. . . . From childhood we see this image defining itself on the fabric of his dreams; and but for express historical testimony [that the painting was a portrait], we might fancy that this was his ideal lady embodied and beheld at last" (pp. 97–98). Pater asked the question that forty years later was to engage Freud: "What was the relationship of a living Florentine to this creature of his thought?" (p. 98) In answer, Pater continued:

> . . . the presence that rose thus so strangely beside the waters, is expressive of what in the ways of a thousand years men had come to desire. Hers is the head upon which all "the ends of the world are come," and the eyelids are a little weary. It is a beauty wrought out from within upon the flesh, the deposit, little cell by cell, of strange thoughts and fantastic reveries and exquisite passions. Set it for a moment beside one of those white Greek goddesses or beautiful

Illustration 8.3 Leonardo da Vinci, *Mona Lisa*, c. 1503–1507 (Paris: Louvre).

women of antiquity, and how would they be troubled by this beauty, into which the soul with all its maladies has passed. . . . She is older than the rocks among which she sits; like the vampire, she has been dead many times, and learned the secrets of the grave; and has been a diver in deep seas, . . . and trafficked for strange webs with Eastern merchants; and, as Leda, was the mother of Helen of Troy, and, as Saint Anne, the mother of Mary; and all this has been to her but as the sound of lyres and flutes, and lives only in the delicacy with which it has moulded the changing lineaments and tinged the eyelids and the hands [pp. 98–99].

Such rhapsodic sentences suggest a more than casual interest in the painting and the artist. Pater could readily find grounds for an identification with Leonardo. Pater's father had died when he was two and a half, his mother when he was fourteen – an abandonment in early life he shared with Leonardo. Initially, in choosing a career Pater was torn between the ministry and the arts; when his faith wavered, he substituted for the life of a cleric an intense interest in cultivating his sensations in response to aesthetic phenomena. Like Leonardo, he did not establish a heterosexual life; although homosexually oriented, he avoided close attachments with his own sex as well.[5] He saw his art criticism as the expression of "a passion of which the outlets are sealed" (Levey, 1978, p. 96).

Freud's Leonardo

When Freud turned to the study of Leonardo in October 1909, shortly after his return from America, he was considering the expansion of psychoanalytic knowledge to fields as yet unconquered. "We must take hold of biography," he wrote Jung. "I have had an inspiration since my return. The riddle of Leonardo da Vinci's character has suddenly become clear to me. That would be a first step in the realm of biography" (Freud and Jung, 1906–1914, p. 158).

---

[5]As in Leonardo's case, Pater's life continues to be a mystery because of his natural reticence and the pains his two sisters took to conceal his homosexuality (steps taken in response to the notoriety of Oscar Wilde's trials).

Clearly Freud was responding to the "engimatic" quality with which Leonardo had become historically imbued. For Freud, the part of Leonardo which was dedicated to the investigation of nature interfered with the artistic side. Following Vasari, Freud depicted a Leonardo who departed this life reproaching himself for neglecting his art. But what appeared enigmatic to contemporaries, for Freud was an expression of the scientific curiosity of a Renaissance man. Leonardo's interest in observing natural phenomena displaced his interest in painting. His predilection for experimentation, as in using inappropriate pigments for *The Last Supper,* interfered with the preservation of work, even within his own lifetime.

Freud delineated further contradictions in Leonardo's personality. Although seemingly peaceable and gentle, he took delight in sketching condemned criminals and he devised cruel weapons of war. Although handsome and well-favored by nature, he shunned sexuality. Freud repudiated the certainty of idealizing biographers who denied overt homosexuality in Leonardo; he accepted a homosexual disposition, but pointed to the low level of overall sexual activity. "It is doubtful whether Leonardo ever embraced a woman in passion," wrote Freud (1910b, p. 71).

Nevertheless, contended Freud, "Leonardo was not devoid of passion; he did not lack the divine spark which is directly or indirectly the driving force — *il primo motore* — behind all human activity. He had merely converted his passion into thirst for knowledge" (1910b, p. 74). According to Freud, this craving for knowledge must have been present early in Leonardo's life, and it was reinforced by sexual drives. In Leonardo's case, the childhood interest in sexual exploration did not become totally inhibited or repressed, nor did an instinctualization of thinking occur, as in the obsessional personality. Leonardo sublimated his libido into curiosity about the external world and research into natural events.

Thus far Freud, in accounting for Leonardo's personality, does not markedly strain the psychoanalytically innocent reader's credulity. It is only when Freud selects Leonardo's early memory as the crucial piece of data that the specifically psychoanalytic nature of his investigation becomes clear. Before elaborating on this finding, however, Freud presents the "objective" biographical data on Leonardo's life.

Leonardo was born in 1452 in a small town near Florence, the illegitimate son of Ser Piero, a notary, and Caterina, a peasant girl. In the year of Leonardo's birth, his father married another woman, Donna Albiera, and this marriage proved childless. A Florentine land-register document dated five years later mentions Leonardo living in his father's household. This was the extent of the objective information about his early life available to Freud in 1910.

There is, however, another reference to Leonardo's childhood, an early memory recorded by Leonardo himself. Freud quotes from Leonardo:

> 'It seems that I was always destined to be so deeply concerned with vultures, for I recall as one of my very earliest memories that while I was in my cradle a vulture came down to me, and opened my mouth with its tail, and struck me many times with its tail against my lips' [1910b, p. 82].

Although Freud quotes the original Italian from the Codex Atlanticus, his German text comes from Herzfeld (1906), and thus Freud perpetuated the error of translating the name of the bird (*nibbio* in Italian) as *Geier* or "vulture" rather than "kite."[6]

As Freud pointed out, such an early memory—in the cradle—was probably a fantasy, based on an observation or story told to Leonardo by his mother. Here Freud indicated the bipolar nature of early memories: they screen childhood experiences, and they attain a viable status because they are signifiers of later personality trends. To the psychoanalyst familiar with representation in dreams, Leonardo's memory refers back to the experience of nursing at the mother's breast and a later fellatio fantasy.[7] The fantasy would be

---

[6]This error, first noted by Maclagan in 1923, is the subject of further discussion by Wohl and Trosman (1955).

[7]It is doubtless this reading of the memory that prompts Kenneth Clark to remark that Freud's "conclusions have been rejected with horror by the majority of Leonardo scholars" (1958, p. 20).

compatible with a passive homosexual attitude on Leonardo's part, and calls to mind charges of homosexuality brought against him in his adolescence.

Freud goes on to discuss the mythological meaning of the vulture, the symbol of the Egyptian goddess Mut. Freud's purpose was to substantiate Leonardo's close tie with his mother, due to the absence of his father in his earliest years. Leonardo spent his critical first year "with his poor, forsaken real mother," emphasized Freud (1910b, p. 91). He was not taken into his father's and grandfather's household until about the age of five, when it became clear that Ser Piero's wife was not going to conceive.

Leonardo, inferred Freud, having spent the first few years alone with his mother, brooded on where babies came from and himself became a researcher. His curiosity about the flight of birds was derived from the sexual researches of his childhood. Moreover, in the absence of a male parent, Leonardo was particularly likely to endow his mother with phallic attributes. His castration anxiety, probably intense because of the eroticized nature of his tie with his mother, would also contribute toward his belief that his mother had been endowed with a penis.

Drawing on clinical work with homosexual patients, Freud saw Leonardo's homosexuality as the result of maternal seductiveness, paternal neglect, and domination by a phallic maternal figure. The boy repressed his love for his mother, identified with her, and chose objects of love modeled on his own person. As evidence for Leonardo's sexual inclination, Freud pointed to Leonardo's tendency to choose handsome boys of little ability as pupils. He nursed them when they were ill and recorded their delinquencies in his notebooks. Moreover, just as he listed all the sums he spent on his pupils, he compulsively listed the funeral expenses for his mother.

In exploring further meanings in the central kite fantasy, Freud pointed out that a sexual act is referred to by the expression: "and struck me many times with its tail against my lips." The fantasy also expresses the wish to be suckled and kissed by his mother. To highlight how this childhood fantasy remained with Leonardo in his adult life, Freud turned to the "Leonardesque" smile found in his works.

Freud was aware (as he stated in the 1919 edition) that the art connoisseur would have difficulty accepting that the enigmatic smile of the *Mona Lisa* was an original contribution, for a similar smile can be found in archaic Greek sculpture and in the figures of Verrocchio. Nevertheless, there is evidence for the importance the *Mona Lisa* had in Leonardo's emotional life: he painted this portrait for a period of four years (probably from 1503 to 1507), kept the portrait with him when he left Florence, and still had it in his possession at the time of his death in France. Since the picture was a portrait, Freud argued, it was likely that something in the sitter herself was evoked for Leonardo the memory of his mother's smile.

Something of this smile is also found in Leonardo's later *Madonna and Child with St. Anne* (Illustration 8.4). But in this picture, the smile is no longer mysterious; it is quiet and blissful. After studying this painting, Freud commented, "it suddenly dawns on us that only Leonardo could have painted it" (1910b, p. 112). Freud pointed to the presence of two maternal figures, close in age, both of whom appear to melt into and arise from a single body. Leonardo had two mothers: the mother who bore him and from whom he was "torn away," and his "young and tender" stepmother who then raised him, his father's wife, Donna Albiera. By condensing them, according to Freud, he gave compositional form to the *Maddona and Child with St. Anne*. St. Anne represents his mother Caterina; the Virgin stands for Donna Albiera. The peaceful and serene smile of St. Anne conceals the envy and rage his mother felt in having to give him up, just as she had previously had to give up Leonardo's father.[8]

Returning once more to biographical data, Freud pointed out that in his notebooks Leonardo recorded the death of his father in the following manner: " 'On July 9, 1504, Wednesday at 7 o'clock died Ser Piero da Vinci, notary at the palace of the Podestà, my father, at 7 o'clock. He was eighty years old, and left ten sons and two daughters' " (Freud, 1910b, p. 119, n. 1). Our attention is directed to

---

[8]In the 1919 edition, Freud added that Oskar Pfister had succeeded in discovering the outline of a vulture in the cloth surrounding the hips of the Madonna, with the tail pointing to the mouth of the Child! Eissler remarks that such imaginative flights induce one to be "overcautious" (1961, p. 51).

Illustration 8.4 Leonardo da Vinci, *Madonna and Child with St. Anne*, c. 1508–1510 (Paris: Louvre).

the perseveration of "7 o'clock" (although there are inaccuracies in the passage as well).[9]

Leonardo's slip, Freud suggested, was indicative of the suppression of intense affect, which found distorted expression in this pedantic and irrelevant comment on the hour of death. In his identification with his father, Leonardo treated his paintings just as his father had initially treated him: having created them, he cared no more about them. This sense of neglect extended into Leonardo's attitude toward father-surrogates as well. When his patron, Ludovico Sforza, the Duke of Milan, was taken prisoner in a war with the French, Leonardo wrote: "The duke lost his dukedom and his property and his liberty, and none of the works that he undertook was completed" (Freud, 1910b, p. 122). He thus reproached the duke with the same accusation others directed toward him.

In Freud's view, Leonardo's rebellious attitude toward his father resulted in an anti-authoritarian stance, a repudiation of religion, for which he substituted faith in his own observation of nature. Although Leonardo continued to delight in games and practical jokes, and he devised grandiose engineering schemes such as redirecting the Arno and designing impractical machines, his playful instincts were also transformed into research interests – interests that evaded the repression to which his erotic life was subject. His fascination with flying was but one example of the sublimation of his infantile sexual urges. In time, Freud observed, his scientific interests threatened to overwhelm and extinguish the expression of his artistic gifts. Then, in his fifties, after Leonardo had moved far from his art, a transformation occurred. He met La Gioconda, who awakened the memories of his mother's loving and enigmatic smile, and thus he conquered his inhibitions as an artist.

Freud was fully aware of the limitations of his study. He knew that his conclusions about Leonardo's childhood situation were based on only a small number of homosexual patients. With this in

---

[9]Ser Piero was 78, not 80, when he died. He died on a Tuesday, not on Wednesday. It is true, however, that Leonardo had eleven siblings. Incidentally, Ser Piero had four wives; his first two wives died childless. He did not have his first legitimate offspring until Leonardo was twenty-four (Eissler, 1961, p. 324).

mind, he cautioned, "If one considers the profound transformations through which an impression in an artist's life has to pass before it is allowed to make its contribution to a work of art, one will be bound to keep any claim to certainty in one's demonstration within very modest limits" (1910b, p. 107).

The Art Historians' Response to Freud

Although widely read, Freud's essay hardly met with universal approval among art historians. Not many art historians today have the prestige and scholarly reputation of Meyer Schapiro, and he offers a critical appraisal of Freud's essay on Leonardo.[10] Taking up the infantile memory, on which Freud placed so much emphasis, Schapiro (1956) examines the textual context in which Leonardo writes about the kite, noting that the kite uses its tail like a ship's rudder. As Leonardo was concerned with the relation between movement and air currents, Schapiro concludes that he was interested in the kite from a scientific point of view. (Pliny, whom Leonardo had read, had already commented on the kite and rudder connection.) In discussing the impact of the infantile memory, Schapiro points to a tradition going back to antiquity, when similar childhood experiences were assumed to be prophetic and indicators of future events. Thus he questions whether the memory tells us anything unique about Leonardo.

Schapiro also questions Freud's belief that Leonardo's mother, Caterina, was abandoned and thus lavished her passionate love upon the child. She might just as well have grown up in a supportive family, or she may have been hostile toward Leonardo (in which case Leonardo would have been glad to leave her and turn to his

---

[10]Historical criticism, of course, is as partial as psychobiography. Schapiro's art historical approach has been generally acknowledged to be "Marxist" in that he views style as responsive to historical change and art as an expression of the conflicting ideology of the times. It may be relevant that his turn to Freud's Leonardo took place in 1955, a good time for Marxist criticism to examine alternative approaches. For a discussion of Schapiro's Marxist views, see Kuspit (1978).

true father). In fact, a document discovered after Freud wrote his essay—a record of Leonardo's birth and baptism by his paternal grandfather—suggests that Leonardo was in the paternal home from birth (Möller, 1939). Moreover, as evidence of maternal hostility, there is a fable about the kite that Leonardo himself reported: " 'of the kite we read that when it sees that its children are too fat, it pecks their sides out of envy and keeps them without food' " (MacCurdy, 1956, p. 1074).

Turning next to the painting of the *Madonna and Child with St. Anne,* Schapiro points out that the image of the two mothers was not a unique and original contribution of Leonardo's. There was considerable interest in St. Anne in the latter part of the fifteenth century; earlier artists had depicted St. Anne and the Virgin together in the same painting and had shown them as also being of nearly equal age. The smiles of the women are also found in the works of others, and thus are not in themselves particularly Leonardesque. What is distinctive in Leonardo's work is not the smile per se but the mysterious passage of light and dark and the careful modeling around the mouth and chin. This style of painting, which induces a sense of reverie in the observer, is unique to Leonardo.

Having thus cast doubt on the importance Freud attached to the mother's smile, Schapiro surprisingly ventures on a psychoanalytic interpretation of his own. He examines a factor not considered by Freud. In the St. Anne painting, Leonardo introduced a truly original feature in that the traditional infant John is replaced by a lamb, which the Christ Child is mounting while his mother restrains him. A lamb is a symbol for both Christ and John the Baptist, as well as an expression of self-sacrifice. But on a deeper level, Schapiro asks, is not Leonardo exposing a homosexual wish directed to a narcissistic object?

Although Schapiro is disinclined to accept that the pyramidal form of the figures is an invention of Leonardo's, he points out that the interaction of the figures and the articulation of the parts of the body into a coherent unity are decidedly Leonardesque. Leonardo's work is distinguished by its subtle modeling, sense of atmosphere,

and the poetic mood of its extended landscape, which offsets the figures of the foreground. Leonardo was also the first to create dynam-
ically balanced compositions (as in *The Last Supper*, done while he
was still in Milan between 1495 and 1497, before he returned to
Florence and met La Gioconda). The great achievement in the St.
Anne painting, Schapiro believes, is in the balanced contrast of the
movements of the individual figures, permitting spontaneous and
conflicting gestures while still retaining a sense of attachment and
family relatedness.

Lastly, Schapiro points out that any attempt to understand the
personality of an artist must consider all of his work. Freud ignored
Leonardo's *Battle of Anghiari* (which we know through studies and
copies), his plans for the equestrian statues, his drawings of cata-
clysms and scenes of world destruction. These highlight the aggressive and violent nature of his personality, just as his *St. Jerome* reveals a masculine asceticism, and the copies of his *Leda and the Swan*
suggest his erotic side. Schapiro grants that Freud's partial success
rests in his ability to empathize with the tragic and problematic in
Leonardo's personality; his failure lies in explaining complex phenomena by single facts without accounting for historical and social
situations. But for all the faults, Schapiro concludes that with regard to the personality of Leonardo "no better answers than Freud's
have yet been given" (1956, p. 177).

In response to Schapiro's point about Leonardo's childhood
memory, one might ask whether the fact that the reporting of such
incidents from childhood is "an established literary pattern" is sufficient. What about the question of psychological motive? The historian sees Leonardo as a medium for a historical process, but ignores
the relevance of the adoption of the pattern in terms of Leonardo's
personality. Why would Leonardo choose to report such a memory?
Is it simply imitation or assimilation? This seems unlikely. Clinical
findings indicate that a screen memory must be understood in terms
of derivatives of unconscious content. Even if the memory surfaced
in the context of studying the scientific problems of flight, these
concerns served only as a precipitant for the recollection; they do
not explain its significance. Seen strictly from a historical point of

view, man appears as a passive receptacle, who simply incorporates a continuing social process. No room is permitted for man as agent, as subject to internal psychic conflict and motivated by unconscious drives (see Eissler, 1961).

A Unified Approach

In the face of such diverse views, an attempt at an integrative approach to biographical studies on Leonardo may be overoptimistic, however desirable (Farrell, 1963). Starting with the perplexing and manifestly inexplicable, the psychoanalytic biographer attempts to offer a coherent explanation of behavior and motivation, one that encompasses seeming inconsistencies, follows laws of evidence, and accords with psychological probability as currently understood. In the case of Leonardo, the puzzling nature of his personality and his work has been well documented. How can one understand his difficulty finishing his work, the inhibition of his sexual life, the remoteness and unemotional nature of his relations with others, the universal and grandiose range of his interest, the mysterious nature of the paintings themselves? A psychological explanation must consider the complexity of Leonardo's personality, without falling into the traps of superficiality and overgeneralization.

The psychoanalyst here may borrow from literary criticism. T. S. Eliot proposed that "the only way of expressing emotion in the form of art is by finding an 'objective correlative,' in other words, a set of objects, a situation, a chain of events which shall be the formula of that *particular* emotion" (1932, p. 145). When we come upon Lady Macbeth walking in her sleep, for instance, we experience her turmoil with a sense of inevitability. We have been prepared by her role in the murder of Duncan. The emotions are correlative to the set of events and experiences that precede them. In a similar way, for psychoanalytic explanation to ring true in the clinical situation, there must be a correspondence in terms of psychic intensity between two sets of events. Usually the correlative is an experience in the present that approaches a perceptual, ideational, and emotional identity with one from the past.

The limitations of a strictly historical account, one that leaves out psychological factors, can be noted in the sources Schapiro (1956) cites for the kite fantasy, such as the ancient tradition of prophetic early memories or the writings of Pliny. To the historian, the artist is a vehicle, sustaining and transmitting aspects of the past; psychology is merely problem-solving ego activity. It is as if the artist, confronted by a task, simply searched his past to find a solution. Such a view of creation is all secondary process; it omits the psychological meaning of the task, as well as unconscious factors in the aesthetic response of viewer or reader.

For the psychoanalyst, what seems disparate can be understood as unified. If we take Leonardo's early memory, the information on Leonardo's sexual life, works such as the *Madonna and Child with St. Anne* and the *Mona Lisa*, as well as additional material from the notebooks about kites and their envy, we can correlate all this with the view of his early childhood proposed by Freud, if it is amended to include the hostile component and fears of a phallic mother. The biographical information is compatible with clinical knowledge about early experience; indeed, it would be difficult to support an alternative formulation of Leonardo's early life. We still do not know why an interest in flying became a displacement from sexual curiosity, but this is a problem of the sublimation of instinct in a more general sense. It often appears that, subsequent to conflict resolution and working through, a latent adaptive or creative tendency, previously untapped, becomes available.

Inevitably, there is a variable relationship between creative activity and the underlying personality factors. Occasionally the activity may be a derivative of conflict, with the impulse or repressive tendency expressed in the work. Or sufficient ego autonomy may develop so that little of conflict or developmental arrest remains. The creative activity becomes psychologically independent of conflict and is a true emergent activity, related primarily to a historical development of a style. In Leonardo's case, the evidence suggests that the *Mona Lisa* is a work closely tied to personal experience; on the other hand, it is likely that the conception of *The Last Supper* (if not the execution) is a work commensurate with the development of the High Renaissance style and thus historically determined. Here the historian and critic can help to clarify what the tradition has made available and how the requirements of the artist's tasks are fulfilled. In any case, a loosening of the tie to symptomatic means of conflict resolution would be necessary in order for an artistic task to be successfully carried out. Failure in creativity is more likely to result from active conflict; success implies absence or surmounting of conflict. With Leonardo, his difficulty in finishing the work and experiments with pigments that would not stand up under the pressures of time tell us about his conflicted interests; his success in developing harmonious and balanced compositions is more likely an expression of ego autonomy or conflict resolution.

The Nature of Psychoanalytic Biography

Some forms of psychoanalytic biography are a separate genre, a distinctive type of discourse that serves the function of hypothesis building or hypothesis testing within the psychoanalytic field. Kohut (1960) has pointed out that Freud's paper on Schreber, a true pathography, falls into this category. He has even suggested that Freud's monograph on Leonardo "was not primarily a contribution to the comprehension of Leonardo's personality and the vicissitudes of his creativity: it was a medium for the presentation of a particular form of homosexuality" (p. 572).

Certainly when one examines the data in psychoanalytic biography, one finds an idiosyncratic aspect. It was no minor consideration that motivated Freud to include Leonardo's screen memory in the title of his book. Screen memories are the analyst's stock in trade, but in previous studies of Leonardo, the screen memory was not even a subject of mild interest. Biographers, innocent of psychoanalysis, have continued to repudiate any connection between such seemingly trivial concerns and the nature of the Leonardo's work.[11]

---

[11]See p. 159, footnote 7. In a later article on the *Mona Lisa*, Kenneth Clark writes more favorably about psychoanalytic views: "Only in the last ten years have we been made publicly aware that the theories of sexual psychologists [i.e., psychoanalysts] were not fantasies" (1973, p. 149). Clark refers here to the influence of Leonardo's homosexual orientation on his work.

An exploration of the link between the kite fantasy, homosexual tendencies, a preoccupation with flying, and the Mona Lisa's smile is more of interest to an analyst, who looks for a unifying principle correlating such seemingly disparate elements.

Leonardo's notebooks also hold a special appeal for the psychoanalyst – not only as a source for parapraxes, but also as a form of free association. That they are written in reverse from right to left and presented in disorganized fashion, combining trivial thoughts, original observations, and sketches, suggests an amalgam of spontaneity and restraint that resembles free association. From a psychoanalytic perspective, one would look for connections between seemingly disparate items on one page, or between recto and verso, as well as unconscious links between drawings and ideas expressed in verbal forms (see Eissler's [1961] attempt at such a correlation).

Lastly, the analyst is in a position to understand something about the relationship between the choice of biographical subject and the personality of the biographer. The psychoanalyst's interest in a literary hero may be an aspect of his self-analysis (Gedo, 1970a). Similarly, a work of psychobiography may be an attempt to continue the unfinished analysis of the biographer. This line of thought has been developed in terms of Freud's interest in Leonardo and the nature of the identification he established with him. Jones (1955) points out their shared passion for knowledge. Lichtenberg (1978) suggests that Freud, in explaining Leonardo's conflict between art and science and Leonardo's turn to research as a defiant response to paternal authority, was also writing of himself. Surely Freud's idealization of the deep attachment between Leonardo and his mother reflects his own fantasy of his earliest years.

Freud wrote the Leonardo study at about the same age that Leonardo painted the *Mona Lisa*. Leonardo was, in Freud's words, "at the summit of his life when . . . a further energetic advance – a new transformation came over him" (1910b, p. 134). In this light, Lichtenberg (1978) believes that the book was a response to what Freud felt were threats to his continuing creativity. Although there is no evidence to suggest that Freud was so threatened, the vicissitudes of the early psychoanalytic movement, the difficulties with his colleagues, and the inappropriate choice of Jung as his Crown Prince must have given him pause. In all probability Freud had become increasingly aware of the homosexual implications of his own relationship with Fliess, Jung, and young Viennese colleagues chosen, like Leonardo's students, not for their ability but for narcissistic purposes. Indeed, narcissism as a field for psychoanalytic inquiry is mentioned for the first time a few months before the publication of the book on Leonardo (Freud, 1910b, p. 100, n. 1).[12] Unquestionably factors in Freud's own personality resonated with Leonardo's and served as stimuli for his investigation.

L'Envoi

Leonardo da Vinci, the universal genius, enigmatic even in his own time, has been a perpetual source of fascination to biographers. From the vast number of accounts of his life that predate Freud's study, I have chosen two of the most important, those of Vasari and Pater, in order to compare varying emphases a biographer may give to the subject. Vasari, intent on elevating the status of the artist, presented a Leonardo with great gifts but flawed by the vastness of his interests. To Pater, Leonardo was a forerunner of the Aesthetic Movement—introspective, self-preoccupied, fascinated by mystery and sensation.

With the advent of psychoanalysis, new techniques could be brought to biographical study to account for seemingly inexplicable discrepancies. Leonardo's work, character, and sexuality were interrelated by Freud, using an infantile screen memory as an organizer for apparent disparities. In his enthusiasm for his undertaking, Freud admittedly did not always carefully check his data, thus marring the quality of his work. When the errors were corrected by such scholars as Schapiro, however, the reformulation sidestepped psychology in favor of a conventional historical account of sources.

---

[12]The first mention of the solution to the Leonardo problem occurs in a letter to Jung (Freud and Jung, 1906–1914).

In the seventy-five years since the appearance of Freud's book, psychoanalytic biography as a genre has acquired an acceptable position. As the findings of psychoanalysis became increasingly understood, even biographies by nonpsychoanalysts reveal an understanding of the psychoanalytic viewpoint. Edel's (1953–1972) work on Henry James and Bate's (1977) biography of Samuel Johnson give evidence of this new sensitivity. It may be assumed that as psychoanalysis continues to accumulate a storehouse of clinical wisdom, this knowledge will be applied in the biographical field. Pari passu, as in Freud's study, psychobiography may prefigure further advances in psychoanalytic science.

But what, in the end, of Leonardo himself? For a man who guarded himself with a cool reserve against the inroads of eager intruders, the curiosity of the ages—were he to know of it—would be an unwelcome intrusion. Following the invasive kite and the possessive Francis I, posterity too has been trying to get inside Leonardo.

9

Psychoanalysis and Literary Criticism: Hamlet *as Prototype*

In addition to contributing to biography, psychoanalysis has contributed to the understanding of the artistic work itself. A novel, short story, poem, or drama may be subjected to an analysis similar to that used with a neurotic symptom, a joke, or a parapraxis. The fabric of the work can be unraveled, as associations derived from primary process products of unconscious fantasy. Occasionally biographical information about the author, if available, may be used to illuminate obscurities in a text. In addition, clinical material from the psychoanalytic situation has been used to add understanding to psychological processes in fictional characters.

Just as Freud chose to write about Leonardo because of his enigmatic personality, so too was he attracted to Hamlet. The character of the prince was a "problem." Why did he seem to vacillate and delay in killing Claudius? Critics for centuries had debated the mystery of Hamlet's character, without solving the eternal riddle.

In fact, the psychoanalytic approach to *Hamlet* owes something to the perplexity of the prince himself. In Act IV, Scene iv, Hamlet, who is to be sent to England by Claudius, sees Fortinbras about to risk all in an attack on a little patch of Polish ground. Contrasting the decisiveness of Fortinbras with his own desultory behavior, he honestly states:

> . . . I do not know
> Why yet I live to say, "This thing's to do."
> Sith I have cause, and will, and strength, and means
> To do't [IV. iv. 43–46].

For a man so introspective and sensitive, this confession of helpless ignorance is remarkable in itself. Were Hamlet not alone, we might recognize the statement as a cry for help or, at the least, a request for an interpretation.

We know that Freud, confronted by such frank perplexity, enjoyed the challenge. Had Freud been present, he might have responded as he did to a young man who, in the midst of a conversation, suddenly found himself struggling to recall a forgotten quotation. He could not remember the line from Virgil's *Aeneid* in which Dido curses Aeneas, who has abandoned her. The young man, who thought Freud was looking scornful and gloating over his embarrassment, demanded, "Why not help me?" Freud agreeably rose to the real-life situation and said, "I'll help you with pleasure" (1901, p. 9).

Although Freud could do nothing to help the fictional character, he made several suggestions to critics and other readers, who were also puzzled by Hamlet's character. Freud's first efforts to contribute to literary criticism — as well as his last — are attempts to deal with the character of Hamlet (1900, pp. 269–276; 1940, p. 192).

Before turning to the psychoanalytic view of *Hamlet*, however, caution must be voiced. Psychoanalytic literary criticism has tended to isolate characters in a literary work and treat them as if they belonged in the real world, not in an imaginary one. This has led to a neglect of what Freud called the laws of poetic economy. Analysts have an important contribution to make to literature if they respond to a work as a totality and recognize that character must be studied in a context. Although deep unconscious conflicts may be present in a literary work, on their own they do not account for aesthetic impact. The effect of the work is always mediated through the literary means at the author's disposal. In the case of *Hamlet*, Shakespeare succeeds in creating in the mind of the audience a conflictual state that resonates with the world of the play. It is a measure of Shakespeare's skill that his unconscious themes continue to affect us with constantly renewed freshness.

Hamlet's Character

It has been pointed out that *Hamlet* was Freud's favorite play (Holland, 1964). He quoted more often from it than from any other literary work except Goethe's *Faust*, and he identified readily with Hamlet, whose thoughts often resonated with his own feelings. I have already noted his use of Hamlet's remark about being in readiness as he sought to resolve his disappointment over the seduction hypothesis, as well as the possibility that the play *Hamlet* was instrumental in providing insight into his own oedipal conflicts during his self-analysis (Freud, 1887–1902b, p. 217, p. 224). Freud stated that he could only analyze himself with insights he gained from observing others. Among such others, fictional characters were not exempt.

In *The Interpretation of Dreams* (1900a), Freud presents his analysis of Hamlet's character in the context of a discussion of typical dreams. In typical dreams, unacceptable motives, such as the wish to have sexual intercourse with the mother and to kill the father, appear in the manifest content of the dream. Thus the myth of Oedipus and the play fashioned from the myth resemble the typical dream. The action attains perceptual reality; it is not just experienced in the realm of unconscious fantasy. In *Hamlet*, however, we encounter a more inhibited and thus more psychologically complex situation. According to Freud, this play is a reflection of a different epoch of civilization, a result of "the secular advance of repression in the emotional life of mankind" (p. 264).

Freud's focus of interest is on Hamlet's procrastination, his inability to carry out the specific task assigned to him by the Ghost.[1] In spite of Hamlet's intense wish to revenge his father's death, he can-

---

[1]Jones (1949) elaborated on Freud's thesis, and in the *Hamlet* literature the proposition has been designated the Freud-Jones hypothesis.

not do so. Freud proposes an interpretation: Claudius, in marrying Hamlet's mother and murdering Hamlet's father, has acted out the unconscious wishes of Hamlet himself. Murdering Claudius represents something other than revenge of the father's death; it becomes tantamount to suicide. Hamlet's loathing of Claudius is explained as a reaction to the surfacing of Hamlet's own oedipal wishes. Just as Hamlet compares Claudius to his father, he must perforce compare Claudius to himself. His self-reproaches are understood as an unconscious recognition of the incestuous impulses he shares with Claudius. His repudiation of sexuality and his turning away from Ophelia are further evidence of his fixation on his mother. Freud and Jones correctly point out that, although Hamlet takes no action against Claudius, he is by no means passive. He engineers the deaths of Rosencrantz and Guildenstern, and he kills Polonius on impulse. His inhibition is specific—against the task that has the closest link with his conflict.

Although the Freud-Jones hypothesis concerning Hamlet's delay is a central psychoanalytic contribution,[2] it by no means exhausts the variety of psychoanalytic writings on the play and Hamlet's character. Even if we concern ourselves only with psychoanalytic contributions that attempt an understanding of Hamlet's character, we find an extensive elaboration of views of Hamlet's unconscious motives. Jones (1948), for instance, extended the original view with an interpretation of Hamlet's negative Oedipus complex, pointing out that Hamlet has formed a feminine attitude toward his father, and thus his repressed hatred of his father is buttressed by a homosexual inclination. This view is supported by the choice of murder through poison in the ear, which suggests a symbolic form of sexual assault.

It has also been argued that Hamlet is preoccupied with matricidal impulses.[3] Gertrude has betrayed him as well as his father by

---

[2] According to Holland, "The Freud-Jones view of Hamlet is . . . probably this century's most distinctive contribution to Shakespearean criticism" (1964, p. 165).

[3] Holland (1964) has reviewed the psychoanalytic presentation of this theme as well as the large number of other psychoanalytic contributions to the *Hamlet* literature. Their range can readily be appreciated in his encyclopedic account (pp. 163–206).

marrying Claudius, and the hostility he feels toward her aids in masking the sexual feelings directed toward her. As he starts for her chamber after the play scene, he cautions himself:

> . . . let not ever
> the soul of Nero enter this firm bosom [III. ii. 401–402].

He repudiates an identification with the Roman emperor, who was believed to have murdered his mother.

Other analytic contributions have approached the prince in terms of preodipal libidinal conflicts, pointing to Hamlet's oral impatience and anal disgust (Sharpe, 1929, 1947). Displacement of feelings toward his father permits Hamlet to express the repressed murderous intent toward his substitute, Polonius. Hamlet's procrastination is recognized as a regressive anal-withholding defense. A variety of other mechanisms of defense are invoked as well: Hamlet projects his incestuous sexual interests onto Claudius. His depressive guilt is the result of internalization of hostile impulses originally directed toward his father. The desire to revenge his father rather than acknowledge his deep-seated wish to kill him is an example of a reaction formation.

Further psychoanalytic studies examine Hamlet in a developmental context. The most comprehensive attempt to analyze Hamlet's character from the ego developmental perspective is that by Eissler (1971a). Erikson (1968) sees Hamlet as a delayed adolescent, looking for a view of reality toward which he can be faithful; in this view, Hamlet seeks to surmount his tendency toward "identity diffusion." Kohut (1971) depicts Hamlet in terms of his search for a cohesive self: Hamlet, an idealist, must come to grips with a world filled with disillusionment. As the play progresses, then, his naive idealism gives way to a more realistic view of reality.

Psychoanalytic Explanations of Fictional Characters

Is the psychoanalyst justified in treating a fictional character with the same interpretative approach with which one treats a patient in analysis? Jones (1948) answers this question by pointing out that a theater audience certainly treats a character in a play as if he were real; after the play, motives are discussed and argued about as if it had all "really" happened. Members of the audience speculate about the character's formative experiences, before the events of a play, and reflect on how they might affect the action. Since the audience reacts as if a character were a living person, "to that extent," claims Jones, "must he have had a life before the action of the play began" (1949, pp. 18–19). Jones adds that, to many members of the audience, fictional characters like Hamlet seem more alive than people in real life. For him, the qualities of "seeming alive" and "being real" are justifications for the analytic approach.

Eissler (1971a) delineates the psychoanalytic approach as one seeking to equate fictional "characters with living human beings in an attempt thereby to unearth the unconscious motivations of the former" (p. 7).[4] In his view, "analysis along the lines of psychological content can produce its best results when it treats Shakespeare's plays as if they were full-fledged human reality" (p. 11). That at times the characters seem "more human than living people" (p. 14), he suggests, is because they are "ideal-types," intensifications of nature and a sign of the superiority of art to life.

The psychoanalytic emphasis on the character of Hamlet as the main concern of the play has not fared well, however, among literary critics. In spite of Dover Wilson's admiration for Jones's book, he contended that "to abstract one figure from an elaborate dramatic composition and study it as a case in a psychoanalytic clinic is to attempt something wrong in method and futile in aim" (1951, p. vii). Even in psychoanalytic circles there has been criticism of this attempt to equate aesthetic illusion with external reality. Gedo (1972b) argues that to take literary characters as real people fails to distinguish the literary realm from observational data. The dramatist has added or subtracted from the level of realistic perception

---

[4]Eissler does, however, add a dampening footnote: "Whether or not this can be done satisfactorily from the psychoanalytic viewpoint is not here the question" (p. 7, n. 2). He then refers the reader to Kohut's paper on the methodology of applied psychoanalysis (1960).

and has thus changed a real context into one which is more generalizable and abstract.

Even Freud was aware of the problems in forgetting the distinction between illusion and reality. In discussing Jensen's *Gradiva*, he pointed out that, unlike real people, the characters are the product of the author's mind, which is more a refractive or obscuring medium than an absolutely transparent one (1907b, p. 41). Freud accepted that Rebecca West, in *Rosmersholm*, is a creation of Ibsen's imagination, not a living person. As a result, the "laws of poetic economy" governed the presentation of her situation (Freud, 1916a, p. 329). Even when an imaginative writer appears in the guise of a psychologist, he is likely to simplify and abstract, and thus distort the complications of psychological reality (Freud, 1905a, p. 60).[5]

A further criticism of psychoanalytic approaches to character refutes the point Jones and Eissler found so convincing—the sense of "living reality" a literary figure may communicate. Skura (1981) protests that the sense of the character's reality stems from the character's fit into the world created by the author. To understand Hamlet's world, we do well to recall that Hamlet lives in a Denmark that is not only "rotten" but is also a world in which a *real* ghost appears to assign him the task of revenge. Within a month of his father's death, his mother has married his uncle—a relationship at best ambiguous if not clearly incestuous. Not only has Hamlet's stepfather murdered his father, but he plots to murder Hamlet as well. Hamlet is continuously spied upon, and he is in constant danger. The woman he loved is warned not to have anything to do with him. His former schoolfriends are enlisted to transport him to his death. And he is still mourning the death of his father when he is beset by all these aditional troubles.

How, in such a world, can one say that the Oedipus complex predominates in Hamlet's concerns? Indeed, Hamlet's sense of reality is

---

[5]As we have seen, however, this awareness did not prevent Freud from offering the view that Hamlet was in the throes of the Oedipus complex and even countering when the literary world did not accept this "obvious" solution to the riddle of Hamlet, that such recalcitrance was understandable as a readiness in "the mass of mankind to hold fast to its infantile repressions" (1940a, p. 192).

sharpened for us by how he adapts in this world, measuring out deceit for deceit, antic disposition for the antics to which he is exposed. With this emphasis on the contextual link between character and the world of the play, it becomes an act of surgical excision to isolate an unconscious conflict as the explanation for the riddle of Hamlet's personality.[6]

The Case for Character Analysis

Is there still room for a psychoanalytic approach to Hamlet's character? I believe so, particularly if we narrow our sights to explanations that remain within the context of the play itself. Even Dover Wilson, who cannot accept an explanation of Hamlet's delay in terms of the Oedipus complex, by no means dismisses the study of "Hamlet's makeup." He himself discusses Hamlet in terms of unconscious personality components and recognizes the presence of dynamic conflict, drive and defense. In describing Hamlet's state as he approaches Gertrude following the play scene, Dover Wilson writes, "murderous impulses must be kept in leash" (1951, p. 244). Although he does not offer an explanation of Hamlet's behavior (as Freud and Jones attempted), his comments are compatible with a psychoanalytic view of structural conflict.

The "living" quality continues to call forth a tendency to respond as if psychological laws should apply.[7] As noted in the case of Hamlet, the interest in motive is in part abetted by the prince's own puzzlement about why he acts or fails to. And other characters in the play are similarly preoccupied; Polonius, Claudius, Gertrude, and

---

[6]Tom Stoppard, who creates another (although related) world in *Rosencrantz and Guildenstern Are Dead* (1967), manages to deaden Hamlet's "liveliness," even when using Shakespeare's lines, in order to brighten the reality of his two protagonists.

[7]A return to an interest in character and the ambivalence this involves emerges in Honigmann's statement: "Whilst no self-respecting critic will henceforth wish to place Shakespeare's stage-persons on a psychiatrist's couch, to fish in imagined minds for a past that never was, a psychological or natural bias still remains appropriate when we discuss a play's life-like characters" (1976, p. 4).

Ophelia are all troubled by the prince's motives and speculate accordingly. We, as they, are encouraged to theorize about what Hamlet is up to; we even form opinions about the correctness of his self-observation. Is he only fooling himself, for instance, when he does not kill the king in the prayer scene; does he really want to kill the king while he is sinning so he will go to Hell?

Again, an understanding of Hamlet's personality, or that of any literary character, can only be valid if it makes sense within the context of the literary work, i.e., if the content of the work provides the psychological explanation. Certainly, in *Hamlet*, we are meant to be puzzled by his personality, and this ambiguity is essential to the depth of the play. In Freud's view, a work of art, such as Jensen's *Gradiva*, in which the motives of the hero are easy to interpret, can justifiably be dismissed as formulaic and thus a minor work. From this perspective, Freud's impatience with a readership that would not accept the Oedipus complex as *the* solution to the Hamlet riddle seems more a reaction to the resistance to psychoanalysis than an expression of a conviction about a final resolution.[8]

If we adhere to a textual theory of unconscious motivation, we may not arrive at the deepest layer that Freud aimed for, but we may actually remain closer to the method of the clinician. Three examples may clarify what I have in mind here. When the Ghost first informs Hamlet that the story given out about his death is false, that in fact he was murdered by his brother, Hamlet's initial response is: "O my prophetic soul" (I.V.40). The psychoanalyst is familiar with similar responses to a well-timed interpretation. The twentieth-century analysand may say, "I knew you were going to say that"—an indication that the analysand already harbored such a thought preconsciously, because of the surfacing of an unconscious derivative, barely recognized by the eye of consciousness. Hamlet is presented in the first throes of an awareness of the world in which he is actually living, and we are left with the dimly perceptible feel-

---

[8]It is of interest in this regard that, immediately following his claim that he had "solved" the Hamlet problem in *An Outline of Psycho-Analysis* (1940a), Freud added his doubts about Shakespeare's identity—as if he had to substitute one enigma for another, and thus perhaps betraying his lack of conviction about the initial claim.

ing that the murder of his father was a thought he had already considered. The question of whether Hamlet was harboring murderous feelings toward his father is thus brought to our attention as a percept, much as an analyst would sense such a percept while listening to a patient.

Another example. In the soliloquy following the arrival of the players, Hamlet reproaches himself for his shortcomings. The chief player, in describing the grief of Hecuba at the death of Priam, had been so overcome by emotion that his color changed and he began to weep. In his soliloquy, Hamlet chastizes himself—but not for a failure to act. He contrasts himself to the player who can summon up so much feeling—

> But in a fiction, in a dream of passion
> . . . his whole function suiting
> With forms to his conceit [II.ii.562–567].

Turning inward, Hamlet continues:

> Yet I, a dull and muddy-mettled rascal, peak
> Like John-a-dreams, unpregnant of my cause,
> And can say nothing [II.ii.560–564].

Here Hamlet compares himself to a pregnant woman who has not yet experienced the quickening of the fetus; his deficiency is in felt conviction that adds form to speech or action. Unlike the player, Hamlet cannot feel the emotion appropriate to his assigned task of revenge. He has not yet accepted the command of the Ghost as a responsibility that derives from his own sense of values and goals. His course is unclear. In reality the uncontrolled emotionality of the player, might carry him away (as indeed, he is carried away in this soliloquy). How can he find a form of expression commensurate with his own beliefs? What he chooses, at this point in the play, is to express indirectly, through the play-within-the-play, the truth he knows. In a deceitful world he adapts by practicing deceit.

My last example of how a psychoanalytic perspective may enhance our understanding of Hamlet's character involves the graveyard scene. The Ghost, Hamlet Senior, Old Fortinbras, Claudius, and Polonius may all be considered as types of father figures. But not until the last act does Hamlet encounter a mortal and psychologically significant father figure who leads to resolution. In the graveyard scene we learn that the loving father, the father who in a psychological sense "raised" him, was Yorick, the king's jester. Old Hamlet, we are informed, was absent at the time of his son's birth, fighting a duel; it was Yorick who bore Hamlet "on his back a thousand times." As Morton Millman (personal communication) suggests, Hamlet's propensity for jest and puns, his readiness to turn to humor and banter, seems based on an identification with Yorick.

Holding Yorick's skull, Hamlet recalls, "Here hung those lips that I have kissed I know not how oft" (V.i.189–190). In accepting the death of his psychological father, Hamlet is then able to face the inevitability of his own death: "The readiness is all. Since no man of aught he leaves knows, what is't to leave betimes? Let be" (V.ii.223–225). Subsequently, there is no further mention of the Ghost or the former king. Hamlet, in trusting to inexorable fate, makes himself a participant to Claudius' plot, and in this way carries out his task.

In emphasizing Hamlet's Oedipus complex, Freud was expressing his own need to universalize and authenticate the importance of his discoveries. It is striking that although, as noted in Chapter 8, he tended to be tentative about his views regarding Leonardo da Vinci's personality, referring to his book on Leonardo as "partly fiction" (1873–1939a, p. 306), when it came to an actual fictional character, he expressed no such caution. Partly this certainty was lodged in his identification with Hamlet and the importance of the play as an instrument in his self-analysis. His conviction also owed something to his views on fantasy and the connection he saw between *Hamlet* and *Oedipus Rex* in terms of the "secular advance of repression." But, whatever the reason, Freud can be faulted for giving his explanation of a fictional character as much if not more credence than interpretations about the personality of a real person.[9]

---

[9]Lewin (1946) has remarked that such psychoanalytic studies become a parlor game for analysts, a means for discharging clinical frustrations or unresolved conflict by working with patients who cannot talk back, who are more like the "ideal" cadaver-patients of the anatomy laboratory, for whom doctors in their regressive moments long.

To reiterate: a more limited approach to character study in literature, an approach based on direct evidence in the literary work itself, is likely to be more productive. From this view we can maintain
our perspective on the imaginative world and the aesthetic intent of
a work. Interestingly, Freud himself pointed to the limitations of
treating single characters apart from the play, as if they were to be
understood as real people. In discussing Lady Macbeth, he remarks
on the difficulties in comprehending her motives if she is considered
as a single character, and here Freud leads us back to the text, the
context of events, and her relationship with Macbeth. It is Macbeth, not his wife, who after the murder hears the cry, "Sleep no
more! Macbeth does murder sleep . . . Macbeth shall sleep no
more." But it is Lady Macbeth who then becomes psychotic and
whose sleep is disturbed. It is Macbeth who stands helpless with
bloody hands, but it is Lady Macbeth who later cannot rid the stain
from her hands (Freud, 1916a, pp. 323–324). We, as an audience, are
affected by a total context in which both their reactions have to be
placed. Indeed, the complexity of the context, the divisability of
motive, contributes to the power of the play.

An Integrated Psychoanalytic Contribution to Literature

An approach that carefully attends to the interrelationships
among deeper layers of experience given surface expression, the
modes of representation of unconscious fantasy, and the nature of
audience response offers an opportunity for the integration of a psychoanalytic approach with literary criticism.[10] The minds of the creator and the audience share a storehouse of fantasy, which serves as
a common ground for creation and response. The contents of the
storehouse, both as universal primitive fantasies and in their transformations into related daydreams, energize a literary work. The
more primitive and thus potentially chaotic the underlying fantasy,

---

[10]Skura's thoughtful book (1981) maps out the territory in which such an
exploration can occur.

the more likely a preconscious daydream will offer a structure or defensive organization in order to avoid the possibility of trauma.

The task for the psychoanalytic critic is to establish the connections between surface and depth without becoming formulaic and thus minimizing the complexity of the literary work. The work of integration may be aided by the nature of fantasy itself. Even though some fantasies are more primitive than others—the wish for symbiotic union or merging with mother's body, for instance, is more primitive than a boy's oedipal fantasy of displacing his father in order to impregnate his mother—there is a tendency toward overlap in fantasy: an earlier stage of fantasy can affect the emergence of a later stage or, regressively, a later stage can change the representation of what preceded it. With the addition of symbolization, the shift from levels of experience which are purely physical and concrete to the abstract and transcendent, comes a wide range of expression for a variety of experiences.

As an example, in *Hamlet* we may choose among multiple meanings attached to the image of speaking, hearing,' and penetration through the ear. The primal scene and oedipal fantasy are suggested when we learn that Claudius killed the king by pouring poison in his ear, and in the dumb show we observe a nephew pour poison into his uncle's ear. When Hamlet harangues Gertrude, his words "like daggers enter her ears." Yet the ear is also an organ for communication. One character reaches out to another in order to clarify, understand, and find meaning. Already in the first scene, Barnardo, to convince the skeptical Horatio of the Ghost, says, "he will assail your ears" (I.i.33). The Ghost feels his estrangement from humanity so accutely he cannot tell the secrets of his prison-house to "ears of flesh and blood." He further refers to the whole state of Denmark as an ear, which "is by a forged process of my death/ rankly abused" (I.v.36–38). Indeed, Ewbank (1977) remarks that the words "ear" and "ears" occur twenty-four times in *Hamlet*, more frequently than in any other play by Shakespeare.

Here, then, the primitive fantasy finds a sublimated form of expression, resonating with multiple chords of meaning. It is not enough, however, to establish that meanings expressive of social or philosophical concerns are referrable to primitive layers of fantasy. The primitive fantasy is followed through a variety of changes, all of which affect the nature of our response. Indeed, in part, the impact stems from the very transformations in the nature of fantasy. Just as an infantile fantasy is not the same as an adult fantasy, so the literary work shifts the archaic amalgam of emotions and ideas into more complex forms. Works of art clearly vary in the distance they maintain from primitive fantasy; we may well be repelled by works in which there is insufficient distance.[11]

In abandoning the position that a literary character can be analyzed in the same way as a person in real life, I am not implying that a literary work as a whole does not include forms of unconscious fantasy. To the contrary, the locus of fantasy is simply shifted from the characer to the work as an entity. Not only are such fantasies present, but they are deployed through a wide variety of literary "defense mechanisms," which modulate states of tension and anxiety in the responding psyche. One might say that these fantasies are expressed through representational means analogous to the forms of thinking present in the dream work; they thus follow the laws of primary process ideation. The dream work, although partially in the service of censorship and disguise, performs an expressive and representational function. The mechanisms of displacement and substitution, in particular, serve toward this end. The quality of pictorial and perceptual reality, the organizing work of secondary revision, and the latent capacity for interpretability demonstrate that there is more to the dream than the emergence of a disguised wish. If we consider Freud's statement that "dreams are nothing other than a particular *form* of thinking" (1900a, p. 506, n. 2), we can see a connection between dreams and literary texts in terms of the evoked associational links that derive from latent fantasy. The matrix of associational ideas and sense, stirred by both dreams and literary works,

---

[11]Kris (1952) offers an example of the intrusion of an unmodulated narcissistic fantasy in the autobiographical novel of Baron Corvo, which repels the reader and permits little aesthetic distance.

are as much a part of their structure as the underlying fantasies to which they are connected.

The psychoanalytic situation can serve as a model for the relation between the reader of a literary work and the literary text. There is a rhetorical function to the way in which a speaker tries to move an audience. Similar rhetorical devices are invoked by analysands to move the analyst. If we consider the social context appropriate to early stages of development, we may place the origins of literary work in the "transitional space" of the first shared symbols in exchanges between mother and child (Winnicott, 1953). The literary work thus has important transference implications. Genetically it belongs in the "playground" area of the mind, an "as if" area in which alternative views of self and other can be proposed (Freud, 1914e, p. 154). Freud's description of the transference as "a piece of real experience . . . of a provisional nature" in the "intermediate region between illness and real life" (1914e, p. 154) may serve to underscore the intermediate quality of reality associated with literature.

A further contribution to understanding comes from the analyst's mode of listening to clinical material. The analyst's attitude of evenly hovering attention, the exploration of transference, and the utilization of nascent countertransference attitudes for understanding touch on Coleridge's "willing suspension of disbelief" in order to welcome the shadows as they appear from the imagination (1817, Chapt. 14). Just as the analyst resonates with and responds empathically to the productions of the analysand in an analytic hour, segments of a literary work can be examined for their evocative nature. Literary or dramatic devices are used for concealment and revelation, for clarity and obfuscation, in order to advance or retard a narrative. As analysis permits the overcoming of resistance, so a literary work moves toward the deployment of revelation.

In both literature and analysis, conditions for revelation are established, and these conditions become as much the subject for investigation as the content of the revelations themselves. Indeed, much of literature moves us because of the way material is presented. From this perspective, our understanding of *Hamlet* may

benefit from a view of the work in terms of the processes that underlie an analytic session.

Let us examine the first scene of *Hamlet* in some detail. I shall assume that what analysts have found in the play, if not in the character of Hamlet, is indeed there. The play presents a variety of oedipal
constellations in the context of a world in which incest, patricide,
libidinized sadism, deceit, fear of retaliation, guilt, and attempts at
regressive and adaptive resolution are manifest. In addition, the
play reveals ego developmental progressions, with examples of sons
who take varying steps at reconciling themselves to and freeing
themselves from paternal demands (Eissler, 1971a). But these
"deeper" layers of psychological concern must be developed by dramatic devices, which are reacted to by an audience on a perceptual
and immediate level; it is these dramatic devices that carry the impact of the play.

In the first scene of *Hamlet*, the audience is deliberately kept in a
state of ambiguous tension, lacking clarity regarding the meaning of
the events as they occur.[12] One finds oneself in a state of conflict,
with a sense of partial disorganization and expectation, continually
wondering about the meaning of the events portrayed. In the midst
of this ambiguity, one is subjected to a series of stimuli that dimly reflect the deeper psychological levels of the play's structure.

Although the play opens with sentinels standing watch, at the
point of changing guard, it is paradoxically the replacement who
first asks: "Who's there?," as if demanding the password. The password itself ("Long live the King") implants in our minds as early as
the third line that the issues of the play involve life and death matters concerning kings. When Francisco, the relieved guard, tells us
that he is "sick at heart," we have the sense of trouble brewing, but
we have no sense of why, and our attention is quickly directed elsewhere. If we speculate at all about the source of the trouble, because
of the guards, we are likely to imagine a military threat to the realm.

---

[12]Booth (1969), although he does not approach the play from an acknowledged
psychoanalytic perspective, has admirably described the first scene in terms of shifting tension states and their effect on an audience.

But no, we soon find out, the threat is supernatural. With the entrance of the skeptical Horatio, as we are again returned to the military imagery, our "fortified" ears are assailed (I.i.31-32) by Barnardo's explanation. Like an attentive audience in the theater, the characters onstage are urged to sit down to hear what is going on. Then suddenly, before Barnardo can even get to the verb of his first sentence, the Ghost appears. Yet the Ghost is speechless, and again our expectations are frustrated; the action of the play takes the place of an explanation. We are like Horatio and the sentries, who watch and wait but don't understand.

Again, we are told that the danger is probably to the state, and having been well frightened, we and the actors are once more urged to sit down to hear an explanation for the present strict watch. Each time we are told only enough to partially relieve our tension; the explanation seems peripheral to the immediate situation, and we are left frustrated. What Horatio offers us is a view of the political situation on the outside, although we are prodded to think of the death of a king (Old Fortinbras) and a son (Young Fortinbras) who is resolved to right the wrongs done to a dead father. We are then reminded of the supernatural events on the night that Julius Caesar was assassinated, and once more the Ghost suddenly appears as an omen. Again, the Ghost does not speak, for all Horatio's urging him to explain himself. When the Ghost disappears at the crow of a cock, we are again given seemingly irrelevant information, this time about the behavior of ghosts in response to the crowing of cocks, irrelevant to our interests. Then, without much sense of resolution or understanding, we are urged to welcome a less upsetting intruder, "the morn in russet mantle clad" (I.i.166). And now, at the end of the scene, we are offered the promise that young Hamlet (mentioned for the first time) will be introduced to throw light on the problem.

In the first scene, then, we are buffeted about by pulls toward chaos, offered only sops of partial understanding. We start in the dark, and we end with a dawning. The surface appears incoherent, but there is an underlying order and repetitiveness to the events, which suggests a proper sequence. The next scene, opening on the color, light, and splash of the regal procession, brings us into the light of day, but it does not take long before we once more become perplexed by a disparity in the events. We soon hear that this imposing king has married his sister-in-law, and he talks strangely of "defeated joy," with "mirth in funeral" and "dirge in marriage" (II.ii.10–12). Now death is linked to sexuality and marriage to disaster. What seems like order in the play comes apart, and we are all prepared to side with Hamlet, the threat to this specious order, with the first words he speaks—words addressed primarily to us, the audience.

Booth comments that we are directed "to the brink of intellectual terror" (1969, p. 151). In the midst of seeming orderliness and secondary process ideation, we are moved by ambiguous and contradictory events, which stir displaceable and freely mobile cathexes within us. Although the audience starts by watching a revenge play, it is soon thrown into conflict in trying to decide whether the barriers to revenge are external or internal.

Or is this a play about choosing to live? We are presented with a wide variety of views concerning suicide. Is suicide a heroic act or an act of cowardice? Does it lead to a resting peace or eternal damnation? At any given moment we may believe one view, and shortly thereafter find the opposing view attaining credibility. The audience initially is told that Hamlet will pretend to be mad, but then he acts mad or at least mad enough to make his state ambiguous. The play offers a continuous reminder that there are more things in heaven and earth than are dreamt of in our philosophy.

Shakespeare mediates conflict by throwing each member of the audience into conflict. He uses a repeated series of actions that stimulate and partially resolve, only to stimulate once more. Each time a derivative conflict state is stirred by the author, there is sufficient tension resolution to permit progression to another level. But the conflict is never resolved without encouraging us to take one step further. Even with the mass slaughter at the end of the play and the reappearance of the original funeral theme, we are left with a beginning, the new reign of Fortinbras. Like the ending of a good analysis, or more specifically the resolution of the transference, anything can still happen.

It seems to me that a psychoanalytic approach to literature has much to offer through a detailed examination of the text in the fashion I have suggested. Each segment of a narrative fulfills a function through a direct impact on the audience. Insofar as a literary work is evocative of underlying fantasies, the form of the work can be examined in order to determine how the effect takes place. We may find that nonspecific forms of conflict formation and resolution have more to do with aesthetic response than the evocation of universal fantasies per se. In the case of *Hamlet*, we respond to a wide variety of literary effects, and the success of the play is only distantly related to a primary psychological constellation.

10

Psychoanalytic Views of Creativity

From a psychoanalytic approach to an artistic work, we are led to an examination of the creative process itself. Here we return to an area that is clearly of psychological interest and central to clinical concerns. Often clinicians finds themselves working with patients whose conflicts and inhibitions concern their creativity, and a successful psychoanalysis may lead to heightened creativity. In this light it is surprising that although Freud wrote extensively about artistic creativity, he tended to minimize the worth of the psychoanalytic contribution. "We must," he owned, "admit that the nature of the artistic function is . . . inaccessible to us along psychoanalytic lines" (1910b, p. 136), and he conceded that "before the problem of the creative artist analysis must, alas, lay down its arms" (1928, p. 177). But these disclaimers were also qualified. In his preface to Marie Bonaparte's *The Life and Works of Edgar Allan Poe: A Psychoanalytic Interpretation*, he stated that "investigations of this kind are not intended to explain an author's genius, but they show what motive forces aroused it and what material was offered by destiny" (1933b, p. 254). A consideration of the "motive forces" that arouse creativity is certainly a substantial contribution, not to be dismissed lightly.[1]

---

[1]I believe with Ricoeur (1976) that Freud's disclaimers were in part rhetorical flourishes meant to minimize resistance on the part of the reader. Freud may also have been displaying, as a result of an identification with the creative artist, the customary reluctance of highly creative people to examine the roots of their own creativity.

Nevertheless, there are many difficulties in studying the psychology of creativity. It is highly improbable that such a complicated psychological process can be explained by a single formulation. There are many modes of creativity, so any explanation must deal with a range of types. In addition, creativity by its very nature implies an emergent phenomenon, and thus is not subsumed under or easily reducible to prior deteminants. Some individuals who dismiss the psychological contribution consider creativity primarily an "innate gift," a God-given talent to write, paint, carve, perform, or compose, and they disavow any "motive forces" behind the tendency. Freud himself frequently referred to artistic creativity as a "gift"—a gift both "miraculous" (1930b, p. 211), and "unanalyzable" (1928, p. 179). Yet, whatever the role of talent, I believe that a concern with the creative process may add to our understanding of the work of art. Just as the work of the creative artist is a statement about creativity and its antecedents, so the study of the creative process illuminates the nature of the work itself.

Freud and the Moses of Michelangelo

Freud's paper on the Moses statue (1914a) is of interest for several reasons. It was initially published anonymously, and he did not "legitimize" it until much later (see Letter of April 12, 1933, in 1873–1939a, p. 416). Of all his mature works, this essay is one of the least psychoanalytic, if not in method, then certainly in terms of depth of understanding. In contrast to the intensity with which literary scholars have reacted to his views on *Hamlet*, the paper on Moses has been disregarded or treated as largely irrelevant by art historians. Janson (1968), one of the few prominent art historians who has confronted Freud's interpretation of the statue, believes Freud erred in seeing the statue as representing a specific moment in Moses' life. What has been generally overlooked is that Freud's paper may be considered a contribution to the psychology of creativity.

Freud wrote "The Moses of Michelangelo" in 1913, after spending many hours in San Pietro in Vincoli, the church in Rome where the statue stands (see Illustration 10.1). In his words:

Illustration 10.1 Michelangelo, *Tomb of Pope Julius II*, detail of Moses, c. 1513–1515 (Rome: S. Pietro in Vincoli).

No piece of statuary has ever made a stronger impression on me than this. How often have I mounted the steep steps from the unlovely Corso Cavour to the lonely piazza where the deserted church stands, and have essayed to support the angry scorn of the hero's glance! Sometimes I have crept cautiously out of the half-gloom of the interior as though I myself belonged to the mob upon whom his eye is turned – the mob which can hold fast no conviction, which has neither faith nor patience and which rejoices when it has regained its illusory idols [1914c, p. 213].

Freud reacted to the contrast between the outward calm and the inward emotion of the work, and his attention was drawn to two particular features of the work: the position of the right hand and the two Tables of the Law. Freud surmised that Michelangelo was depicting a moment at which Moses, having descended from Mt. Sinai with the Tables of the Law, has seated himself. Suddenly he hears the clamor of the people worshipping the Golden Calf. The statue, in Freud's view, depicts the final result of a series of movements and emotional reactions of Moses to the backsliding apostasy. Freud noted that the long, flowing beard is pulled to Moses' right by his right hand, and some strands from the left side of the beard are caught by the right index finger. In addition, the Tables of the Law are tilted and held to the side by the right arm while Moses looks to his left.

Freud surmised that these gestures were not merely formal devices but meaningful, with psychological significance. As Moses sees the people dancing around the Golden Calf, his immediate reaction is to jump to his feet in a fury. His right hand reaches for his beard, half-discharging the violence of his rage on his own being. The spontaneous gesture, however, frees the Tables, which almost fall and shatter. In an instant Moses senses the threatened destruction and grasps the Tables, steadying them against his side and the rock upon which he sits. We still see some of the strands of the beard entwined in the hand, before their release in the protective gesture that preserves God's Commandments.

Freud even illustrated the movement he assumed took place in order to account for the appearance of the statue (Illustration 10.2).

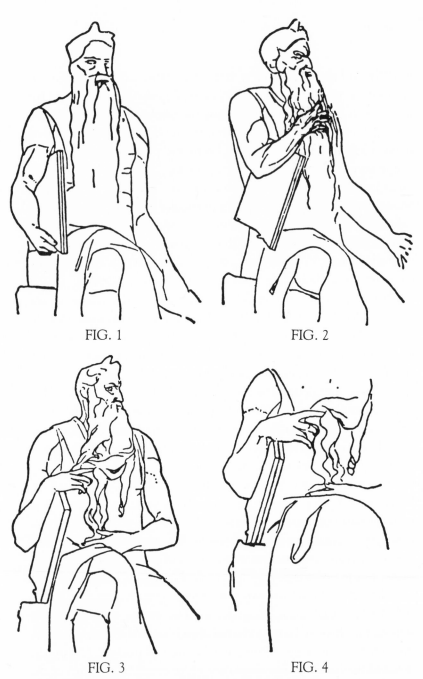

FIG. 1   FIG. 2

FIG. 3   FIG. 4

Illustration 10.2 Sigmund Freud, Drawings after Michelangelo's *Moses* (1914c). Reprinted by permission from *The Standard Edition of the Complete Psychological Works of Sigmund Freud*, Vol. 13, ed. James Strachey (London: Hogarth Press, 1955), pp. 226–227.

Initially, in Figure 1, Moses is presented sitting calmly; in Figure 2, enraged, he is about to jump to his feet; Figures 3 and 4 display the statute as it actually exists, following the inhibition of the outburst. Moses, according to Freud, is tempted to take vengeance, but he overcomes the temptation and keeps his passion in check. The statue reveals the calming effort in the face, the suppressed movement in the hand and torso, and the urge to rise in the left foot. Moses is not merely depicted at a particular moment in his life; recall Freud's claim that he "becomes a concrete expression of the highest mental achievement that is possible in a man, that of struggling successfully against an inward passion for the sake of a cause to which he had devoted himself" (1914c, p. 233).

Characteristically Freud related his view of the statue to the events in Michelangelo's life. The Moses statue was intended for the tomb of Pope Julius II, Michelangelo's patron. The pope and Michelangelo were both men with violent tempers, given to outbursts of sudden anger, and both were doomed to failure given the difficulty of completing the Herculean tasks they undertook (Julius in his attempts to unite Italy under papal domination; Michelangelo in his superhuman artistic projects). The statue, then, was both a reproach against the dead pope and a self-criticism of Michelangelo's own violent and passionate nature.

The creative man of action and the creative artist, Freud believed, must both struggle with the problem of taming instincts and transformation through sublimation.[2] In other words, a psychoanalytic view of creativity must address itself to the fate of the instincts and their transformation in the process of psychological development. An intermediate step in the developmental sequence is the withdrawal of libido from external objects onto the ego so that partial deinstinctualization may occur. The statue itself, in representing rage diverted from external objects onto the body of Moses, presents a visual image of this partial taming of instinct. Outwardly directed instinctual investments are represented by the turn of the

---

[2]Although Freud initially viewed sublimation as a diversion of sexual instincts toward a new, nonsexual aim and object, he also recognized a similar transformation in aggressive instincts (Jones, 1957, p. 464).

head and the gaze of the eyes. The reversal and turning of instinct upon the self, with the attenuation of aim, is depicted in the play of the hand in the beard, pulling the beard toward the right and back, balancing the gaze toward the left and forward. In this way the form of the statue itself expresses an aspect of the drive transformation underlying the development of creativity.

Once again we note Freud turning to a work of art to express a conceptual advance as well as a personal concern. As I stated in Chapter 5, Freud's view of the Moses statue was directly related to his own life experience and the structure of his personality. Freud responded to a view of Moses struggling with inner rage in the face of idolatry. He established an identification with a foresaken leader whose teachings would be repudiated because of the longing of the mob for easy solutions and illusions. Freud saw himself as one whose discoveries would be ignored during his lifetime. In the early years of discovery, he thought he was doomed to live out his days in isolation like Robinson Crusoe on his desert island (Freud, 1914b). After recognition did come, he then had to reconcile himself to the apostasy of Jung, Adler, Stekel, and others who turned away from the harsh truths he discovered. It was during the midst of the struggle with Jung in 1912 over the central position of the libido theory that he arrived at his interpretation of the Moses statue. He saw in the psychoanalytic dissidents the recalcitrant neo-pagans who returned to worship the Golden Calf.

From this perspective, it is likely that Freud's venture into psychoanalytic art criticism served as a means for self-analysis. If his introspective capacity aided him in his analysis of the intent of Michelangelo, his analysis of the Moses statue may have helped him in the resolution of his own turmoil and rage at the dissidents. I have already cited his awareness of his identification with Moses revealed in his letter to Ferenczi after the separation from Stekel: "At the moment the situation in Vienna makes me feel more like the historical Moses than the Michelangelo one" (Letter of October 17, 1912, in Jones, 1955, p. 367). His immediate reaction was that of the Moses who broke the Tables in anger rather than that of the Moses who preserved them.

For Freud, Michelangelo's Moses was not only the creative leader who led his people out of bondage. He also viewed the statue as an awesome and scornful father who made him all too conscious of his own faults and shortcomings—a figure whose intense eyes he invested with the authority of Brücke, whose gaze had long before made him feel guilty and condemned (Fuller, 1980).[3] It was Brücke, the scientist with rigorous standards, committed to the pursuit of truth, whom he saw as a superego representative and as an ideal.[4] And it was the memory of Brücke's eyes that "would throughout his life appear at any moment when he might be tempted to any remissness in duty or to any imperfection in executing it scrupulously" (Jones, 1953, p. 39). Yet Freud himself was one of the apostates who turned away from the hard science of Brücke.

In Freud's interpretation of the Moses statue, then, we note several factors in the psychoanalytic contribution to creativity. An analyst may enlarge the understanding of a creative work by bringing into awareness the determinants of his or her own subjective reactions in resonating with the work.[5] The use of analytic subjectivity here is of course open to the criticism that the interpreter may put more of himself in the work than the creator intended. Freud considered this problem in his Moses study, and he delayed making his conclusions public for this reason. But in the end he consented to publish, pointing out that in the case of Michelangelo—"an artist in whose work there is so much thought striving for expression"—it

---

[3]As noted on page 195, in describing the statue, he wrote of "the angry scorn of the hero's glance," and he crept out of the half-gloom of the church "as though I myself belonged to the mob upon whom his eye is turned" (1914c, p. 213). In regard to Brücke, who chastised him for coming late when he was a demonstrator at the Physiological Institute, he wrote, "what overwhelmed me were the terrible blue eyes with which he looked at me and by which I was reduced to nothing" (1900a, p. 422).

[4]As Lowenfeld (1956) has remarked, "Identification with great men of the past seems to be an aspect of the growth of greatness in men, one of the conditions which make it possible" (p. 685).

[5]We are close here to the early understanding of the term "empathy" (*Einfühlung*) as used by Worringer (1908) and to the productive use of countertransference reactions in the clinical setting (Racker, 1957).

was justifiable to give him the credit for complexity. Freud added that the creative work itself may be only an incomplete outward expression of the artist's mind, striving toward some "utmost limit" (1914c, p. 236). It is then left to the mind of the viewer to complete the artist's task.

We are reminded that Freud embarked on his extensive analysis of the Moses statue in order to understand why the figure had such a powerful effect upon him. He started with the sense that the statue was an awesome reminder of his deficiencies. However, his final analysis of the statue had less to do with the sense of being intimidated and more with Moses as a representative of heroic self-control. The Moses who moved him most deeply was a symbol of paternal forbearance and restraint. As I noted in Chapter 5, the father whom he, as a boy, found lacking in combativeness was now an ideal prototype for generativity—for the man willing to deny the indulgence of his own passions for the sake of a cause to which he was totally committed, the fathering of psychoanalysis.

The Psychoanalytic Contribution to Creativity

Clearly, such a complex psychological process as creativity is not to be understood solely in terms of drive components and reactions against them. In many ways we are dealing with a phenomenon on the opposite end of a continuum which extends all the way from a parapraxis or a simple neurotic symptom. If we take as an example a slip of the tongue Freud was fond of using, we can note the difference required in explanatory power between simple, uncomplicated psychic acts and more complex ones. Quoting from a newspaper account of 1900, Freud described how "the President of the Lower House of the Austrian Parliament *opened* the sitting a short while ago: 'Gentlemen [the President stated]: I take notice that a full quorum of members is present and herewith declare the sitting *closed!*' In this particular case, the explanation was that the President secretly *wished* he was already in a position to close the sitting from which little good was to be expected" (1901, p. 59).

The explanation rests on an appreciation of the social circumstances of the time, the conflictual state of Austrian political life, and the close affiliation between words of opposite meaning— "closed" and "open." Here we favor an explanation that reveals to us the unconscious intent of the speaker. But when we come to creativity, there are no such unequivocally clear intrusions into the designs of the ego. Indeed, should such symptomatic and untimely interferences occur, they are likely to be seen as failures or deficiencies in creativity.

What, then, is an ego definition of artistic creativity? Creativity can be seen as the expression of an adaptive ego whose function is to produce an object that is imaginatively new, communicable, and socially valued. The artist's creative process is then the result of the synthesis of relatively autonomous ego functions, organized to carry out a solution to aesthetic problems (Corbin, 1974; Rothenberg, 1979). The emphasis in such a limited definition is totally on the ego and the adaptive mechanisms at its disposal in problem solving. Although the definition is wide-ranging enough to cover all cases, it lacks an individualized and experiential base. Specifically, no allowance is made for conflict as a potential instigator.

Analysts have noted a connection between psychological dysfunction and creative activity in individuals, and have puzzled over this connection. As early as 1897, as noted in Chapter 4, Freud was prepared to accept that "the mechanism of creative writing is the same as that of hysterical phantasies" and that Shakespeare was right in juxtaposing poetry and madness (the fine frenzy) (1887– 1902b, p. 208). Freud, however, also considered creativity as an end result in the resolution of psychological conflict.

A definition of creativity in terms of the ego capacity for problem solving is meant to rebut the argument of the negative case. Not all creative people are in turmoil, and one undisturbed artist may be enough to dethrone Freud's early claim. Surely there have been many creative artists who have been, as Freud said of himself, "approximately normal" (1900a, p. 105). Presumption of pathology is not necessary and need not apply. Nevertheless, the creative artist, like the rest of humankind, has an unconscious, with unacceptable wishes, anxieties and defenses, a capacity for regression, desublimation, and transference, and ego functions in varying autonomous states.

Freud (1914d), going beyond his initial 1897 formulation, found a further connection between creativity and illness. He saw the need to create—to make something beyond oneself—as a reaction to an exclusive narcissistic preoccupation (an illness). Freud quoted with favor God's words as imagined by Heine in his poem "Schöpfungslieder VII":

> Krankheit ist wohl der letzte Grund
> Des ganzen Schopferdrangs gewesen;
> Erschaffend konnte ich genesen,
> Erschaffend wurde ich gesund.[6]

Illness here is defined as archaic narcissistic immersion; creation evolves from a need to dissipate excessive inner energy.

A few years later, in 1917, adding a passage to the book on slips, Freud put the link more modestly when he commented on Strindberg's uncanny ability to understand the secret nature of parapraxes. His "genius in recognizing such things was, it is true, *assisted* by grave mental abnormality" (1901, p. 212; my italics). Pathology may be facilitating.

But more important is Freud's view on the connection between repression and creativity. Throughout his work Freud presumed a link between what is deeply repressed, yet in a potentially activated state, and the need to find substitutes for repressed content in some form of human activity. This need is in evidence in the dream and in the tendency to use displacement. This search for substitutes is described by Freud as a factor in the origin of myths and tragic drama (1913). We noted, in Chapter 4, that Freud suggested that Goethe protected himself against suicide by displacing his internal conflicts onto Werther. Kohut (1957) in his analysis of Thomas Mann's *Death in Venice* notes how the author safeguards his artistic creativ-

---

[6]"Illness was no doubt the final cause of the whole urge to create. By creating, I could recover; by creating I became healthy" (1914d, p. 85, n. 3).

ity by displacing his conflicts onto the protagonist of the story. It may be the case that the number and wealth of substitutes for repressed content are related to the extent of the repressive forces as well as the opportunities for finding derivatives.[7]

Such an approach to creativity places the emphasis on propensities for transformation, on the tendency of the ego to rework mechanisms originally used for purposes of defense and protection against anxiety and fears of dissolution and fragmentation. This emphasis on the ego's role balances the earlier interest in instinct as the important factor.

It is also possible to consider the creative artist in terms of idiosyncratic ego attributes that make creative solutions possible. Much of academic psychology and experimental research on creativity has looked to these ego factors.[8] Among psychoanalysts, Greenacre (1957, 1958, 1963) has made substantial contributions to this area in delineating the creative person's greater sensitivity to sensory stimulation, greater awareness of relations between disparate forms, and wider responsiveness to body states and inanimate objects. Greenacre even questions the usefulness of sublimation or neutralization as an essential concept in creativity. Often, she contends, the gifted personality at work appears to be propelled by unmodified libidinal and aggressive drives, truly "in a fine frenzy rolling," totally caught up in the creative activity. Frenzy here is not pathology but intensity.

Having considered a limited descriptive view of the creative process in terms of the ego functions, I turn to a more extensive view,

---

[7]Freud quotes in this context Ariel's words from *The Tempest:*

> Full fathom five thy father lies;
>   Of his bones are coral made;
> Those are pearls that were his eyes:
>   Nothing of him that doth fade,
> But doth suffer a sea-change
>   Into something rich and strange [1913, p. 155, n. 2].

[8]Rothenberg and Hausman (1976) have collected a book of readings on creativity, which includes forty-five selections by philosophers, psychologists, psychoanalysts, educators, literary artists, and scientists. Less than ten of the selections are by psychoanalysts.

keeping in mind the distinction Freud made between "motive forces" that arouse creativity and "material offered by destiny." It should be clear that the development of any aspect of creativity may be affected by a quality of innate disposition, talent, or "giftedness." But a level of explanation that turns to constitutional factors to find a way out of a conceptual impasse seems particularly unsatisfactory. We would be better to simply admit that there are factors we do not yet understand than to opt for such closure in the interests of filling explanatory gaps.

As I noted in discussing the Moses statue, artistic creativity starts with the vicissitudes of the instincts, with the taming of drives for purposes other than direct satisfaction. Not only does the act of creation have a quality of "driveness" about it, but crucial aspects of the creative activity maintain a clear link with sexuality. Further, Freud stated that when sexual curiosity is diverted or sublimated toward art, because of "concealments" of the sexual object induced by civilization, sexual excitation becomes directed toward "beauty" as an abstraction (1905c, p. 156).[9] Aggressive drives are subjected to similar shifts in development and are also coordinated in the activities of construction and composition. Insofar as inventiveness and originality necessitate a break with and destruction of previous ways of relating to reality, derivatives of aggressive energies are used in effecting the break.

Patterns of identification with parental creativity—whether maternal and gestational or paternal, procreative, and under phallic influence—affect the modality of creative expression. In Freud's case, we have been informed of the great impression made upon him by his mother's seemingly magical ability to re-create for him, by rubbing her hands together, the blackish scales of earth from which life springs (see Freud, 1900a). His identification with his father was another matter. Freud wrote that the child is motivated by the wish to be quits with his father, to be relieved of the burden of gratitude for the "gift of life." In giving life to his own children, as his fa-

---

[9]Although in our own artistic era beauty has become an ambiguous quality, the reference remains apt in that the artistic object is still characterized as unified, coherent, or harmoniously formed, qualities implying an idealized standard.

ther did to him, a man becomes "his own father" (Freud, 1910c, p. 173). Creativity is also stirred by attitudes of rebelliousness and defiance against the father as authority, generalized as the dead past or stale tradition requiring revitalization. The frequent references to the created work as the artist's "baby," comparisons with incubation, pregnancy, and labor, highlight the significance of the creative work within the oedipal constellation.

Nor can restitutive creativity, regeneration as a reaction to loss, be underestimated. Here we deal with a variety of views of what constitutes loss. There may be actual abandonment by a parent in early life, by death or desertion, or deficiencies in empathic parenting or an emotional separation; the child may then turn away from objects to seek satisfaction in narcissistic activities. The loss may be experienced as an act of fate or an omnipotent result of inner rage. In the latter case, a sense of guilt and a need to make restitution become paramount. Normal mourning in the young child is apt to be interfered with, and the awe, power, and idealization associated with the parent in early life becomes transferred to the artistic activity and its product. The creative process may thus become an attempt to work through aborted grief reactions. Even when secondary autonomy develops, remnants of the old loss are evident.[10] The sense of union the creative artist experiences with the work may be an attempt to reestablish a bond with the lost object of childhood.

Closely related to object loss and attempts at subsequent restitution is the factor of early traumatization from a variety of other sources. Here we deal with inadequate modes of dealing with infantile stimulation, inappropriate modes of gratification, fixation, archaic forms of psychosexual discharge, and traumatization due to physical illness and deformity affecting body image. The perfect form corrects the imperfect body (Niederland, 1976).

At this point the skeptical reader may cry out: How characteristic that conflict and deficiency tend to be emphasized in a psychoanalytic explanation of the creative process! Certainly conflict and defi-

---

[10]"The creation of a musical composition (such as a requiem) is the mourning for the loss and transition of the composer's self as well as the creative end-product of the mourning process," writes Pollock (1975, p. 435).

ciency are the raw material of the clinical analytic situation, the factors that bring a patient to treatment. "It is not the absence of conflict but rather an optimal distance from conflict that determines the future development of autonomous ego functions," comments Szekely (1981, p. 424). Thus, an inquiry into the nature of the creative process must consider the transition across the distance and propose bridging concepts to account for the occurrence of creative activity rather than inhibition, symptom, or character defect. So far, investigators have concentrated on opposite poles in their studies. On the one hand, they have explored the instinctual and conflictual underpinnings, as Freud did in his book on Leonardo or as the Kleinians do when they emphasize the need to restore the destroyed love object (Segal, 1952). On the other hand, investigators have turned their attention to the ego processes invoked in carrying out a creative task. Rothenberg (1979), for instance, stresses that the creative person can actively conceive of two or more antithetical ideas or images at the same time (Janusian thinking), and can actively conceive two or more discrete entities occupying the same space, thus leading to new identities (homospatial thinking). Arieti (1976) also highlights the cognitive ego, adding to the primary and secondary processes a tertiary process—a new synthesis of the two.

Among intermediate processes that bridge the conceptual gap, displacement appears indispensable in understanding those cases where conflict and deficiency are clearly determining elements. Although the creative solution is fed by associative links that promote optimal distancing, it may still retain a hold in an original conflictual matrix. This is not to deny the presence of artistic giftedness. Even artistic talent, however, can be considered as functionally related to attempts at conflict resolution or compensation for developmental deficiencies. Noy (1972) comes close to this view when he suggests that the preferred medium of artistic expression gains its importance from a significant emotional experience. Here, as in considering aesthetic response (Chapter 6), we look for an early experience in which artistic modes of expression and communication are chosen to fulfill drive needs. On the other hand, displacements may find subjective expression in the form of fantasies about being influenced and emotional attachment to idealized figures. Often these fantasies are unconscious and repudiated in order to preserve an artistic talent believed vulnerable and subject to potential destruction (Chapter 3).

As an example of the type of displacement I have in mind, consider an event in the early life of one of our modern poets. When Sylvia Plath was two and a half, in an attempt to hold her mother's attention following the birth of her brother, she would "read" the newspapers and spell out letters in the presence of her nursing mother. This attempt to divert her mother was later reinforced by the mother's wishes for the child to fulfill her own unfulfilled literary ambitions. For the young child, letters and words, their arrangement on a page, became a rhythmic equivalent for the nursing experience, a passionate form of expressing her own needs—although it was only later, as she relived the experience when nursing her own second child, that she became aware of its impact (see Weisblatt, 1977).

At this point one might note, as a further attempt to clarify nonconflictual elements in creativity, that the art work is often a statement about the creative process. Embedded in the structure of the work may be the steps leading to its formation. The work reflects the artist's self, is spurred by narcissistic longing and idealized as the projected perfected state. Contemporary analytic interest in Michelangelo lies in his depiction of the link between process and result, in his need to demonstrate the work of his hand through the lack of finish, chisel marks, and remnants of uncarved block (Liebert, 1983).

The psychoanalytic study of creativity is an attempt to study the vicissitudes of creativity, its variability and function as well as its unconscious meanings. Creative artistic expression may appear in both the absence and presence of psychological turmoil (Gedo, 1970b). The analyst is interested in the emotional intensity with which an artist pursues the task, as well as the passion and enthusiasm with which an audience experiences the work. Esman contends "that the artistic gift and its exercise in the creation of formal structures is an innate capacity probably determined by genetic constitution and that it operates autonomously" (1979, p. 309). Yet even if one highlights the formal aspects of an artist's concerns, one cannot disregard that creative ability is rooted in the personality and linked to maturational tasks. When we are confronted with the presence of psychological understanding in great works of art, understanding the psychoanalyst arrives at only through the laborious method of the clinical situation, we assume that the artist's innate creativity is nurtured by significant psychological experience, which is then communicated through the work. Thus, although there is little to quarrel with in the position that the capacity for creativity is "an innate gift," there is much to recommend a position that the developmental vicissitudes to which the gift is exposed belongs in the purview of the psychoanalytic approach.[11]

A creative person must come to terms with an innate capacity if it is to flourish. The potentially creative person is likely to be regarded as different, bizarre, and strange by early caretakers, who do not understand a unique vision; the budding artist may have to learn to live with the feeling of being "a cuckoo in a nest of sparrows" (Gedo, 1972b, 1979). He or she has the problem of having to live with an idiosyncratic, potentially alienating view of reality (Eissler, 1967). It is only later in the life of the creative adolescent or early adult, when a figure capable of appreciating the person's potential originality appears, that the creativity can flower. The creative urge needs an accepting ambience and validation.

In sum, a psychoanalytic view of creativity starts with the conception of the taming of drive. Even if we assume the presence of some constitutionally given talent, such talent must be trained and molded by experience and tradition before it can be put to use. The drives are enlisted in the service of talent whether in the conception or execution of a work. In the case of Michelangelo, not only do we

---

[11]As mentioned (p. 193), Freud repeatedly referred to artistic ability as a "gift," thus suggesting the link with the "gift of life,' which comes from the father (1910c, p. 173). The gift of creating passes from mother to child, and in turn the oedipal boy wishes to return the gift to his mother in the form of a child like him. Because of this oedipal meaning, the assumption of innate giftedness carries a burden of responsibility or guilt for the artist.

encounter aggressive content but we are also informed of the aggressive vigor with which he attacked a block of stone, how even in old age he could chip away more marble than other sculptors.

With regard to the question of the relative weight to attach to autonomous ego factors as opposed to conflict, psychopathology, and deficiencies in personality development, we are dealing with a complementary series, which varies from individual to individual. Native talent can serve the personality as a means for expressing and thus discharging conflict. Motive forces born of conflict, pain, and attempts at resolution can arouse latent creative ability. They are the materials offered by destiny.

Conclusion

In viewing Freud's relation to the imaginative world, I do not thereby oppose that world to another that is real, scientific, or the world in which we live. My wish has been to stress that humanist culture and art have provided an access to psychological reality, which is the primary concern of psychoanalysis. Freud grew up in the matrix of this culture, was deeply affected by it, turned to it when the narrow scientific view was inadequate to his purposes, and then in turn enriched the arts through psychoanalytic findings. Psychoanalysis in its way has become a part of the humanist tradition, a new liberal art continuing to add depth and insights to criticism and further understanding of the human condition.

In spite of the depth of Freud's interest in the arts, he was distressed by the allegation that his method was essentially "artistic." He believed that such a designation was meant to denigrate psychoanalysis as a science. Yet he had to reconcile his own intense artistic leanings, as well as his awareness of the influence of artistic work on the development of psychoanalysis. I have noted his tendency to dismiss the fact that his case histories read like short stories as unrelated to any personal preference but simply the result of the nature of the subject matter he was studying. Jones suggested that the artistic longings became submerged; he wrote of a "demon," a "fantastic self," which Freud had to keep ruthlessly in check (Jones, 1955, p. 431.) To some extent this aspect of Freud's self found a home in his sense of Jewish identity. Once he came to accept that he could not avoid the resistances mobilized by the new science and that Jung was not necessary in order to remove the taint of ethnic insularity, he openly embraced his Jewishness. Freud could even turn to the matter of influence and discover how the ideas which seemed to him so revolutionary had been suggested to him by others, secondarily reinforced by empirical findings, and incorporated in an organized body of knowledge.

At this point it was possible to turn in earnest to the arts and demonstrate what the new science could add to their understanding. In doing so Freud found an entirely new group of adherents as well as critics. Not only did creative artists and critics respond to psychoanalytic contributions, but psychoanalytic practitioners — those whose predominant activities were clinical — found a route for the satisfaction of their own imaginative aspirations. With time, interests initally labeled "applied psychoanalysis" have become a meeting ground for the meeting of science and art. When Freud wrote that the triumph of his life was that he could return through psychoanalysis to the primary human concerns to which the arts address themselves, he was presenting himself as a modern-day Everyman. He opened the path for future generations of psychoanalysts to work toward a cultural integration. With the psychoanalytic study of the aesthetic response, the lives of great men, literary and artistic works and the processes of creativity, the methods of depth psychology became a potential horn of plenty. The contribution of psychoanalysis to the understanding of that part of human nature which is expressed in our highest cultural achievements may be as incisive as the contribution to the treatment of psychological disorders.

References

Abend, S. M. (1974), Problems of identity. *Psychoanal. Q.*, 43:606–637.

Abraham, K. (1922), Father-murder and father-rescue in the fantasies of neurotics. In *The Psychoanalytic Reader*, ed. R. Fliess. New York: International Universities Press, 1948, pp. 334–342.

Abrams, M. H. (1953), *The Mirror and the Lamp*. New York: Oxford University Press.

_____ (1971), *A Glossary of Literary Terms*. New York: Holt, Rinehart & Winston.

Amacher, P. (1965), *Freud's Neurological Education and Its Influence on Psychoanalytic Theory* [*Psychological Issues*, Monogr. 16]. New York: International Universities Press.

Anderson, G. K. (1965), *The Legend of the Wandering Jew*. Providence: Brown University Press.

Andersson, O. (1962), *Studies in the Prehistory of Psychoanalysis*. Norstedts: Svenska Bokförlaget.

Angel, E. (1975), The taming of Freud's passions. *Council News* (Council of Psychoanalytic Psychotherapists), March, pp. 22–23.

Arieti, S. (1976), *Creativity: The Magic Synthesis*. New York: Basic Books.

Bakan, D. (1965), *Sigmund Freud and the Jewish Mystical Tradition*. New York: Schocken Books.

Barclay, J. R. (1959a), Franz Brentano and Sigmund Freud: A comparative study in the evolution of psychological thought. Unpublished doctoral dissertation, University of Michigan, Ann Arbor.

_____ (1959b), Themes of Brentano's psychological thought and philosophical overtones. *New Scholastism*, 33:300–318.

Barea, I. (1966), *Vienna*. New York: Knopf.

Basch, M. F. (1976), Theory formation in Chapter VII: A critique. *J. Amer. Psychoanal. Assn.*, 24:61–100.

Bate, W. J. (1977), *Samuel Johnson*. New York: Harcourt, Brace.

Berenson, B. (1916), *Study and Criticism of Italian Art*, 3rd Series. London: Bell.

Beres, D. (1965), Psychoanalysis, science and romanticism. In *Drives, Affects, Be-*

havior, Vol. 2, ed. M. Schur. New York: International Universities Press.

Berkower, L. (1969), The enduring effect of the Jewish tradition upon Freud. *Amer. J. Psychiatry*, 125:103–109.

Bernays, A. F. (1940), My brother, Sigmund Freud. *Amer. Mercury*, 51:335–342.

Bernfeld, S. (1944), Freud's earliest theories and the school of Helmholtz. *Psychoanal. Q.*, 13:341–362.

———— (1947), An unknown autobiographical fragment by Freud. *Amer. Imago*, 4:3–19.

———— (1949a), Freud's scientific beginnings. *Amer. Imago*, 6:163–196.

———— (1949b), Sigmund Freud, M.D., 1882–1885. *Int. J. Psychoanal.*, 32:204–214.

———— (1951), Freud and archaeology. *Amer. Imago*, 8:107–128.

Bettleheim, B. (1983), *Freud and Man's Soul*. New York: Knopf.

Binswanger, L. (1956), *Erinnerungen an Sigmund Freud*. Bern: Francke.

Bloom, H. (1973), *The Anxiety of Influence*. New York: Oxford University Press.

———— (1975), *A Map of Misreading*. New York: Oxford University Press.

Bollas, C. (1978), The aesthetic moment and the search for transformation. *The Annual of Psychoanalysis*, 6:385–394. New York: International Universities Press.

Booth, S. (1969), On the value of *Hamlet*: In *Reinterpretation of Elizabethan Drama: Selected Papers from the English Institute*, ed. N. Rabkin. New York: Columbia University Press.

Breuer, J., & Freud, S. (1893–1895a), Studien über Hysterie. *Gesammelte Werke*, 1. London: Imago.

————, ———— (1893–1895b), Studies on hysteria. *Standard Edition*, 2. London: Hogarth Press, 1955.

Brücke, E. T. (1928), *Ernst Brücke*. Wien: Springer.

Burnham, J. C. (1967), *Psychoanalysis and American Medicine, 1894–1918 [Psychological Issues*, Monogr. 20]. New York: International Universities Press.

Bush, M. (1967), The problem of form in the psychoanalytic theory of art. *Psychoanal. Rev.*, 54:5–35.

Butler, E. M. (1935), *The Tyranny of Greece over Germany*. New York: Macmillan.

Clark, K. (1958), *Leonardo da Vinci: An Account of His Development as an Artist*, Rev. Ed. Baltimore: Penguin, 1967.

———— (1973), Mona Lisa. *Burlington Mag.* 115:144–150.

Clark, R. W. (1980), *Freud: The Man and the Cause*. New York: Random House.

Coleridge, S. T. (1817), *Biographia Literaria*. London: Oxford University Press, 1965.

Corbin, E. J. (1974), The autonomous ego functions in creativity. *J. Amer. Psychoanal. Assn.*, 22:568–587.

Cranefield, P. F. (1957), The organic physics of 1874 and the biophysics of today. *J. Hist. Med.*, 12:407–423.

———— (1966), Freud and the "School of Helmholtz." *Gesnerus*, 23:35–39.

Cuddihy, J. M. (1974), *The Ordeal of Civility*. New York: Basic Books.

Deri, F., & Brunswick, D. (1964), Freud's letters to Ernst Simmel. *J. Amer. Psychoanal. Assn.*, 12:93–109.

Derrida, J. (1978), Coming into one's own. In *Psychoanalysis and the Question of Text*, ed. G. H. Hartman. Baltimore: Johns Hopkins University Press.

Deutsch, H. (1942), Some forms of emotional disturbance and their relationship to schizophrenia. *Psychoanal. Q.,* 11:301–321.

Dorer, M. (1932), *Historische Grundlagen der Psychoanalyse* Leipzig: Meiner.

Dover Wilson, J. (1951), *What Happens in Hamlet.* Cambridge: Cambridge University Press.

Edel, L. (1953–1972), *Henry James,* Vols. 1–5. Philadelphia: Lippincott.

Edelson, J. T. (1983), Freud's use of metaphor. *The Psychoanalytic Study of the Child,* 38:17–59. New Haven: Yale University Press.

Ehrenzweig, A. (1965), *The Psychoanalysis of Artistic Vision and Hearing.* New York: Braziller.

_____ (1967), *The Hidden Order of Art.* Berkeley: University of California Press.

Eissler, K. R. (1961), *Leonardo da Vinci: Psychoanalytic Notes on the Enigma.* New York: International Universities Press.

_____ (1965), *Medical Orthodoxy and the Future of Psychoanalysis.* New York: International Universities Press.

_____ (1966), *Sigmund Freud und die Wiener Universität.* Bern: Huber.

_____ (1967), Psychopathology and creativity. *Amer. Imago,* 24:35–81.

_____ (1969), Irreverent remarks about the present and future of psychoanalysis. *Int. J. Psychoanal.,* 50:461–471.

_____ (1971a), *Discourse on Hamlet and Hamlet.* New York: International Universities Press.

_____ (1971b), *Talent and Genius.* New York: Quadrangle Books.

_____ (1978), Creativity and adolescence. *The Psychoanalytic Study of the Child,* 33:461–517. New Haven: Yale University Press.

Eliot, T. S. (1932), *Selected Essays.* London: Faber & Faber.

Ellenberger, H. (1965), Charcot and the Salpêtrière school. *Amer. J. Psychother.,* 19:253–267.

_____ (1970a), *The Discovery of the Unconscious.* New York: Basic Books.

_____ (1970b), Methodology in writing the history of dynamic psychiatry. In *Psychiatry and Its History,* ed. G. Mora & J. L. Brand. Springfield, Ill.: Thomas, pp. 26–40.

Erikson, E. H. (1955), Freud's "The Origins of Psychoanalysis." *Int. J. Psychoanal.,* 36:1–15.

_____ (1956), Problems of identity. *J. Amer. Psychoanal. Assn.,* 4:56–121.

_____ (1958), *Young Man Luther.* New York: Norton.

_____ (1968), *Identity: Youth and Culture.* New York: Norton.

Esman, A. (1979), The nature of the artistic gift. *Amer. Imago,* 36:305–311.

Ewbank, I. (1977), Hamlet and the power of words. In *Aspects of Hamlet,* ed. K. Muir & S. Wells. Cambridge, Eng.: Cambridge University Press, 1979.

Fancher, R. (1977), Brentano's psychology from an empirical standpoint and Freud's early metapsychology. *J. Hist. Behav. Sci.,* 13:207–227.

Farrell, B. (1963), On Freud's study of Leonardo. In *Leonardo da Vinci: Aspects of the Renaissance Genius,* ed. M. Philipson. New York: Braziller.

Freud, M. (1957), *Sigmund Freud: Man and Father.* London: Angus & Robertson.

Freud, S. (1873–1939a), *Letters of Sigmund Freud,* ed. E. L. Freud. New York: Basic Books, 1960.

_____ (1873-1939b), Sigmund Freud: Briefe, ed. E. L. Freud. Frankfurt am Main: Fischer, 1968.

_____ (1884), Ein Fall von Hirnblutung mit indirekten basalen Herd symptomen bei Scorbut. Wein. med. Wschr., 34 (9):244; (10):276.

_____ (1885), Ein Fall von Muskelatrophie mit ausgebreiteten Sensibilitäts-störungen (Syringomyelie). Wien. med. Wschr., 35 (13):389; (14):425.

_____ (1886a), Akute multiple Neuritis der spinalen und Hirnnerven. Wien. med. Wschr., 36 (6):168.

_____ (1886b), Observations of a severe case of hemi-anaesthesia in a hysterical male. Standard Edition, 1:23-31. London: Hogarth Press.*

_____ (1887-1902a), Aus den Anfängen der Psychoanalyse: Briefe an Wilhelm Fliess, Abhandlungen und Notizen. London: Imago, 1950.

_____ (1887-1902b), The Origins of Psychoanalysis: Letters to Wilhelm Fliess, Drafts and Notes, ed. M. Bonaparte, A. Freud, & E. Kris. New York: Basic Books, 1954.

_____ (1888a), Hysteria. S.E.,, 1:41-57.

_____ (1888b), Preface to the translation of Bernheim's Suggestion. S.E., 1:75-85.

_____ (1889), Review of August Forel's Hypnotism. S.E., 1:91-102.

_____ (1891), On Aphasia. New York: International Universities Press, 1953.

_____ (1892-1893), A case of successful treatment by hypnotism. S.E., 1:117-128.

_____ (1892-1894), Preface and footnotes to the translation of Charcot's Tuesday Lectures. S.E., 1:133-136.

_____ (1893a), Charcot. S. E., 3:11-23.

_____ (1898), Sexuality in the aetiology of the neuroses. S.E., 3:263-285.

_____ (1899), Screen memories. S.E., 3:303-322.

_____ (1900a), The interpretation of dreams. S.E., 4 & 5.

_____ (1900b), Die Traumdeutung. Gesammelte Werke, 2 & 3. London: Imago.

_____ (1901), The psychopathology of everyday life. S.E., 6.

_____ (1903-1904), Contributions to the Neue Freie Presse, III: Obituary of Profes-sor S. Hammerschlag. S.E., 9:225-256.

_____ (1905a), Fragment of an analysis of a case of hysteria. S.E., 7:7-122.

_____ (1905b), Jokes and their relation to the unconscious. S.E., 8.

_____ (1905c), Three essays on a theory of sexuality. S.E., 7:130-243.

_____ (1907a), Contribution to a questionnaire on reading. S.E., 9:245-247.

_____ (1907b), Delusions and dreams in Jensen's Gradiva. S.E., 9:7-95.

_____ (1908), Creative writers and day-dreaming. S.E., 9:143-153.

_____ (1909), Notes upon a case of obsessional neurosis. S.E., 10:155-318.

_____ (1910a), Five lectures on psycho-analysis. S.E., 11:7-55.

_____ (1910b). Leonardo da Vinci and a memory of his childhood. S.E., 11:63-137.

_____ (1910c). A special type of choice of object made by men (Contributions to the psychology of love, I). S.E., 11:165-175.

_____ (1911), Formulations on the two principles of mental functioning. S.E., 12:218-226.

_____

*Hereafter all references to the Standard Edition (published by Hogarth Press, London) are abbreviated S.E.

———— (1913), Totem and taboo. S.E., 13:1–162.

———— (1914a), Zur Geschichte der psychoanalytischen Bewegung. *Gesammelte Werke*, 10. London: Fischer.

———— (1914b), On the history of the psycho-analytic movement. S.E., 14:7–66.

———— (1914c), The Moses of Michelangelo. S.E., 13:211–236.

———— (1914d), On narcissism: An introduction. S.E., 14:73–102.

———— (1914e), Remembering, repeating and working through. S.E., 12:147–156.

———— (1914f), Some reflections on schoolboy psychology. S.E., 13:241–244.

———— (1915), Our attitudes towards death. S.E., 14:289–300.

———— (1916a), Some character-types met with in psycho-analytic work. S.E., 14:311:-333.

———— (1916b), On transience. S.E., 14:305–307.

———— (1916–1917), Introductory lectures on psycho-analysis. S.E., 15 & 16.

———— (1917a), A metapsychological supplement to the theory of dreams. S.E., 14:220–235.

———— (1917b), Mourning and melancholia. S.E., 14:243–258.

———— (1918a), From the history of an infantile neurosis. S.E., 17:7–122.

———— (1918b), The taboo of virginity. S.E., 11:193–208.

———— (1919), The 'uncanny.' S.E., 17:219–256.

———— (1920a), Beyond the pleasure principle. S.E., 18:7–64.

———— (1920b), A note on the prehistory of the technique of analysis. S.E., 18:263–265.

———— (1921), Group psychology and the analysis of the ego. S.E., 18:69–143.

———— (1923), Joseph Popper-Lynkeus and the theory of dreams. S.E., 19:261–263.

———— (1924), A short account of psycho-analysis. S.E., 19:191–209.

———— (1925a), An autobiographical study. S.E., 20:7–70.

———— (1925b), Letter to the editor of the Jewish Press Centre in Zürich. S.E., 19:291.

———— (1925c), The resistances to psycho-analysis. S.E., 19:213–222.

———— (1925d), Selbstdarstellung. *Gesammelte Werke* 14:33–96. London: Imago.

———— (1926a), Address to the Society of B'nai B'rith. S.E., 20:273–274.

———— (1926b), Ansprache an die Mitglieder des Vereins B'nai B'rith. *Gesammelte Werke*, 17:51–53. London: Imago.

———— (1926c), Inhibitions, symptoms and anxiety. S.E., 20:87–174.

———— (1926d), The question of lay analysis. S.E., 20:183–258.

———— (1927), The future of an illusion. S.E., 21:5–56.

———— (1928), Dostoevsky and parricide. S.E., 21:177–194.

———— (1930a), Civilization and its discontents. S.E., 21:59–151.

———— (1930b), The Goethe prize. S.E., 21:206–212.

———— (1930c), Preface to the Hebrew translation of *Totem and Taboo*. S.E., 13:xv.

———— (1930d), Das Unbehagen in der Kultur. *Gesammelte Werke*, 14:421–506. London: Imago.

———— (1933a), New introductory lectures on psychoanalysis. S.E., 22:5–182.

———— (1933b), Preface to Marie Bonaparte's *The Life and Works of Edgar Allan Poe: A Psychoanalytic Interpretation*. S.E., 22:254.

———— (1936), A disturbance of memory on the Acropolis. S.E., 22:239–248.

_____ (1937), Analysis terminable and interminable. S.E., 23:216–253.

_____ (1938), A comment on anti-Semitism. S.E., 23:291–293.

_____ (1939a), Der Mann Moses un die Monatheistische Religion. Gesammelte Werke, 16:101–246. London: Imago.

_____ (1939b), Moses and monotheism. S.E., 23:7–137.

_____ (1940a), An outline of psycho-analysis. S.E., 23:144–207.

_____ (1940b), Some elementary lessons in psycho-analysis. S.E., 23:279–286.

_____ (1969), Some early unpublished letters of Freud. Int. J. Psychoanal., 50:419–427.

_____ & Abraham, K. (1907–1926), A Psychoanalytic Dialogue: The Letters of Sigmund Freud and Karl Abraham, ed. H. C. Abraham & E. L. Freud. New York: Basic Books, 1965.

_____ & Jung, C. G. (1906–1914), The Freud/Jung Letters, ed. W. McGuire. Princeton, N.J.: Princeton University Press, 1974.

Frey, A. (1900), Conrad Ferdinand Meyer: Sein Leben und Seine Werke. Stuttgart: Cotta.

Fry, R. (1924), The Artist and Psychoanalysis. London: Hogarth Press.

Fuller, P. (1980), Art and Psychoanalysis. London: Writers & Readers Publishing Cooperative.

Gay, P. (1978), Freud, Jews, and Other Germans. New York: Oxford University Press.

Gedo, J. E. (1968), Freud's self-analysis and his scientific ideas. Amer. Imago, 25:99–118.

_____ (1970a), The psychoanalyst and the literary hero: An interpretation. Compr. Psychiat., 11:174–181.

_____ (1970b), Thoughts on art in the age of Freud. J. Amer. Psychoanal. Assn., 18:219–245.

_____ (1972a), Caviare to the general. Amer. Imago, 29:293–317.

_____ (1972b), On the psychology of genius. Int. J. Psychoanal., 53:199–203.

_____ (1979), The psychology of genius revisited. The Annual of Psychoanalysis, 7:269–283. New York: International Universities Press.

_____ & Pollock, G. H., Eds. (1976), Freud: The Fusion of Science and Humanism [Psychological Issues, Monogr. 34/35]. International Universities Press.

_____ & Wolf, E. S. (1970), The "Ich" letters. In Freud: The Fusion of Science and Humanism, ed. J. E. Gedo & G. H. Pollock. New York: International Universities Press, pp. 71–86.

_____ & _____ (1973), Freud's novelas ejemplares. The Annual of Psychoanalysis, 1:229–317. New York: Macmillan.

Gicklhorn, J., & Gicklhorn, R. (1960), Sigmund Freuds akademische Laufbahn im Lichte der Dokumente. Vienna: Urban an Schwarzenberg.

Gicklhorn, R. (1969), The Freiberg period of the Freud family. J. Hist. Med., 24:37–43.

Goethe, J. W. von (1782), Essay on nature. In Maxims and Reflections of Goethe, trans. T. B. Saunders. New York: Macmillan, 1893, pp. 207–213.

_____ (1811–1822), Poetry and Truth, Vol. 2. London: Bell & Sons, 1913.

Goldscheider, L., Ed. (1948), Leonardo da Vinci. London: Phaidon.

Gombrich, E. H. (1966), Freud's aesthetics. *Encounter*, 26:30–40.

Greenacre, P. (1957), The childhood of the artist: Libidinal phase development and giftedness. *The Psychoanalytic Study of the Child*, 12:47–72. New York: International Universities Press.

——— (1958), The family romance of the artist. *The Psychoanalytic Study of the Child*, 13:9–36. New York: International Universities Press.

——— (1963), *The Quest for the Father*. New York: International Universities Press.

Griggs, K. A. (1973), "All roads lead to Rome": The role of the nursemaid in Freud's dreams. *J. Amer. Psychoanal. Assn.*, 21:108–126.

Grinberg, L., & Rodriguez, J. F. (1983), The influence of Cervantes on the future creator of psychoanalysis. Paper presented at the 33rd International Congress of Psychoanalysis, Madrid.

Grollman, E. (1965), *Judaism in Sigmund Freud's World*. New York: Block.

Guillian, G. (1959), *J. M. Charcot 1825–1893: His Life, His Work*. New York: Hoeber.

Handlin, O. (1967), Jews in the culture of Middle Europe: In *Studies of the Leo Baeck Institute*, ed. M. Kreutzberger. New York: Unger.

Helmholtz, H. von (1882), *Wissenschaftliche Abhandlungen*, Vols. 1 & 2. Leipzig: Barth.

Herder, J. G. von (1768), Fragmente über die neuere Deutsche Litteratur. In *Sämmtliche Werke*, ed. B. Suphan. Berlin: Weidmannsche Buchhandlung.

Herzfeld, M. (1906), *Leonardo da Vinci: Der Denker, Forsche und Poet. Nach den veröffentlichen Handschrifften*, 2nd ed. Jena: Diederichs.

Heydenrich, L. H. (1954), *Leonardo da Vinci*, Vols. 1 & 2. New York: Macmillan.

Holland, N. N. (1964), *Psychoanalysis and Shakespeare*. New York: McGraw-Hill.

Holmes, K. R. (1983), Freud, evolution and the tragedy of man. *J. Amer. Psychoanal. Assn.*, 31:187–210.

Holt, R. R. (1965), Freud's cognitive style. *Amer. Imago*, 22:163–179.

Honigmann, E. A. J. (1976), *Shakespeare: Seven Tragedies*. New York: Barnes & Noble.

Hyman, S. E. (1962), *The Tangled Bank*. New York: Atheneum.

Janson, H. W. (1968), The right arm of Michelangelo's "Moses." In *Festschrift für Ulrich Middledorf*, ed. A. Kosegarten & P. Tigler. Berlin: de Gruyter.

Johnston, W. M. (1972), *The Austrian Mind*. Berkeley: University of California Press.

Jones, E. (1948), The death of Hamlet's father. In *Essays in Applied Psychoanalysis*, Vol. 1. London: Hogarth Press, pp. 9–15.

——— (1949), *Hamlet and Oedipus*. New York: Norton.

——— (1953), *The Life and Work of Sigmund Freud*. Vol. 1. New York: Basic Books.

——— (1955), *The Life and Work of Sigmund Freud*. Vol. 2. New York: Basic Books.

——— (1957), *The Life and Work of Sigmund Freud*. Vol. 3. New York: Basic Books.

Jung, C. G. (1961), *Memories, Dreams, Reflections* New York: Pantheon.

Kahler, E. (1967), The Jews and the Germans. In *Studies of the Leo Baeck Institute*, ed. M. Kreutzberger. New York: Unger.

Kanzer, M. (1957), Contemporary psychoanalytic views of aesthetics. *J. Amer. Psychoanal. Assn.*, 5:514–524.

Kaufmann, W. (1980), *Discovering the Mind, Vol. 3: Freud versus Adler and Jung.* New York: McGraw-Hill.

Klein, D. B. (1981), *Jewish Origins of the Psychoanalytic Movement.* New York: Praeger.

Knoepfmacher, H. (1979), Sigmund Freud in high school. *Amer. Imago,* 36:287–300.

Kohut, H. (1957), *Death in Venice* by Thomas Mann: A story about the disintegration of artistic sublimation. *Psychoanal. Q.,* 26:206–228.

⎯⎯⎯ (1960), Beyond the bounds of the basic rule. *J. Amer. Psychoanal. Assn.,* 8:567–586.

⎯⎯⎯ (1966), Forms and transformations of narcissism. *J. Amer. Psychoanal. Assn.,* 14:243–272.

⎯⎯⎯ (1971), *The Analysis of the Self.* New York: International Universities Press.

Kris, E. (1952), *Psychoanalytic Explorations in Art.* New York: International Universities Press.

Kuspit, D. B. (1978), Meyer Schapiro's Marxism. *Arts Magazine,* 53:142–144.

Lehmann, H. (1966), Two dreams and a memory of Freud. *J. Amer. Psychoanal. Assn.,* 14:388–405.

Lesky, E. (1965), *Die Wiener medizinische Schule im 19. Jahrhundert.* Graz/Kolm: Herman Böhlaus Nachf.

Levey, M. (1978), *The Case of Walter Pater.* London: Thames & Hudson.

Lewin, B. (1946), Counter-transference in the technique of medical practice. *Psychosom. Med.,* 8:195–199.

⎯⎯⎯ (1970), The train ride. *Psychoanal. Q.,* 39:71–89.

Lichtenberg, J. D. (1978), Freud's Leonardo: Psychobiography and autobiography of genius. *J. Amer. Psychoanal. Assn.,* 26:863–880.

Liebert, R. S. (1979), Michelangelo's early works: A psychoanalytic study in iconography. *The Psychoanalytic Study of the Child,* 34:463–525. New Haven: Yale University Press.

⎯⎯⎯ (1983), *Michelangelo.* New Haven: Yale University Press.

Lovejoy, A. O. (1923), On the discrimination of romanticism. In *Essays in the History of Ideas.* Baltimore: Johns Hopkins University Press, 1948.

Lowenfeld, H. (1956), Sigmund Freud. *J. Amer. Psychoanal. Assn.,* 4:682–691.

MacCurdy, E., Ed. (1956), *The Notebooks of Leonardo da Vinci,* Vols. 1 & 2. New York: Braziller.

Mahony, P. (1982), *Freud as a Writer.* New York: International Universities Press.

Malcolm, J. (1981), *Psychoanalysis: The Impossible Profession.* New York: Knopf.

Marcus, S. (1974), Freud and Dora: Story, history, case history. *Partisan Rev.,* 41:12–23, 89–108.

Martin, J. (1983), William Faulkner: Construction and reconstruction in biography and psychoanalysis. *Psychoanal. Inquiry,* 3:295–340.

Marx, O. M. (1967), Freud and aphasia: An historical analysis. *Amer. J. Psychiat.,* 124:815–825.

Masson, J. M. (1983), Review of *Freud, Biologist of the Mind: Beyond the Psychoanalytic Legend* by Frank J. Sulloway. *J. Amer. Psychoanal. Assn.,* 31:739–747.

McGrath, W. J. (1967), Student radicalism in Vienna. *J. Contemp. Hist.,* 2:183–201.

_____ (1974), Freud as Hannibal: The politics of the brother band. *Central European Hist.*, 7:31–57.

Merlan, P. (1945), Brentano and Freud. *J. Hist. Ideas*, 6:375–377.

_____ (1949), Brentano and Freud: A sequel. *J. Hist. Ideas*, 10:451.

Meyer, B. (1903), Conrad Ferdinand Meyer. In *Der Erinnerung seiner Schester.* Berlin: von Gebruder Paetel.

Meynert, T. (1885), *Psychiatry*, trans. B. Sachs. New York: Putnam & Sons.

Miller, J. A.; Sabshin, M.; Gedo, J. E.; Pollock, G. H.; Sadow, L.; & Schlessinger, N. (1969), Some aspects of Charcot's influence on Freud. *J. Amer. Psychoanal. Assn.*, 17:608–623.

Milton, J. (1667), *Paradise Lost.* New York: Odyssey Press, 1935.

Möller, E. (1939), Der Geburtstag des Lionardo da Vinci. *Jahrbuch der preussichen Kuntsammlungen*, 60:71–85.

Mora, G., & Brand, J. L., Eds. (1970), *Psychiatry and Its History.* Springfield, Ill.: Thomas.

Muschg, W. (1930), Freud also Schriftsteller. *Die Psychoanalytische Bewegung*, 2:467–511.

Niederland, W. G. (1960), The first application of psychoanalysis to a literary work. *Psychoanal. Q.*, 29:228–235.

_____ (1976), Psychoanalytic approaches to artistic creativity. *Psychoanal. Q.*, 44:185–212.

Noy, P. (1972), About art and artistic talent. *Int. J. Psychoanal.*, 53:243–250.

_____ (1979), Form creation in art: An ego-psychological approach to creativity. *Psychoanal. Q.*, 48:229–256.

Ornston, D. (1982), Strachey's influence: A preliminary report. *Int. J. Psychoanal.*, 63:409–426.

Pater, W. (1893), *The Renaissance,*, ed. D. L. Hill. Berkeley: University of California Press, 1980.

Pollock, G. H. (1975), Mourning and memorialization through music. *The Annual of Psychoanalysis*, 3:423–436. New York: International Universities Press.

Priest, P. N. (1970), The influence of Freud's teachers and self-analysis on the evolution of psychoanalytic theory: A re-evaluation. *Brit. J. Psychol.*, 43:19–29.

Racker, H. (1957), The meanings and uses of countertransference. *Psychoanal. Q.*, 26:303–357.

Rancurello, A. C. (1968), *A Study of Franz Brentano.* New York: Academic Press.

Reik, T. (1968), *The Search Within.* New York: Funk & Wagnalls.

Ricoeur, P. (1976), Psychoanalysis and the work of art. In *Psychiatry and the Humanities*, Vol. 1, ed. J. Smith. New Haven: Yale University Press, pp. 1–33.

Riese, W. (1958), Freudian concepts of brain function and brain disease. *J. Nerv. Ment. Dis.*, 127::287–307.

Ritvo, L. B. (1970), Panel report: The ideological wellsprings of psychoanalysis. *J. Amer. Psychoanal. Assn.*, 18:195–208.

Roazen, P. (1969), *Brother Animal.* New York: Knopf.

Robert, M. (1976), *From Oedipus to Moses.* Garden City, N.Y.: Doubleday/Anchor Press.

Rogawski, A. (1970), Young Freud as a poet. In *A Celebration of Laughter*, ed. W.

M. Mendel. Los Angeles: Mara Books.

Rose, G. J. (1980), *The Power of Form* [*Psychological Issues*, Monogr. 49]. New York: International Universities Press.

Rosen, V. H. (1961), The relevance of "style" to certain aspects of defence and the synthetic function of the ego. *Int. J. Psychoanal.*, 42:447–457.

Ross, D. (1969), The "zeitgeist" and American psychology. *J. Hist. Behav. Sci.*, 5:256–262.

Rothenberg, A. (1979), *The Emerging Goddess: The Creative Process in Art, Science and Other Fields*. Chicago: University of Chicago Press.

———— & Hausman, C. R. (1976), *The Creativity Question*. Durham, N.C.: Duke University Press.

Rothman, S., & Isenberg, P. (1974a), Freud and Jewish marginality. *Encounter*, December, pp. 46–54.

————, ———— (1974b), Sigmund Freud and the politics of marginality. *Central European Hist.*, 7:58–78.

Rubinfine, D. (1958), Panel report: Problems of identity. *J. Amer. Psychoanal. Assn.*, 6:131–142.

Sachs, H. (1944), *Freud, Master and Friend*. Cambridge, Mass.: Harvard University Press.

Schafer, R. (1973), The concepts of self and identity and the experience of separation-individuation in adolescence. *Psychoanal. Q.*, 42:42–59.

Schapiro, M. (1953), Style. In *Aesthetics Today*, ed. M. Philipson. Cleveland: Meridian Books/World, 1961.

———— (1956), Leonardo and Freud: An art-historical study. *J. Hist. Ideas*, 17:147–178.

Schick, A. (1968–1969), The Vienna of Sigmund Freud. *Psychoanal. Rev.*, 55:529–551.

Schlessinger, N.; Gedo, J. E.; et al. (1967), The scientific style of Breuer and Freud in the origins of psychoanalysis. *J. Amer. Psychoanal. Assn.*, 15:404–422.

Schönau, W. (1968), *Sigmund Freuds Prosa: Literarische Elemente seines Stils*. Stuttgart: Metzlersche.

Schorske, C. E. (1961), Politics and the psyche in *fin de siècle* Vienna: Schnitzler and Hofmannsthal. *Amer. Hist. Rev.*, 60:930–946.

———— (1967), Politics in a new key: An Austrian triptych. *J. Mod. Hist.*, 39:343–386.

———— (1975), Politics and patricide in Freud's *Interpretation of Dreams*. *The Annual of Psychoanalysis*, 2:40–60. New York: International Universities Press.

Schwaber, P. (1976), Scientific art: The interpretation of dreams. *The Psychoanalytic Study of the Child*, 31:515–533. New Haven: Yale University Press.

Segal, H. (1952), A psycho-analytic approach to aesthetics. *Int. J. Psychoanal.*, 33:196–207.

Shakespeare, W. (1600–1601), *Hamlet*, ed. E. Hubler. New York: New American Library. Signet, 1963.

Shakow, D., & Rapaport, D. (1964), *The Influence of Freud on American Psychology* [*Psychological Issues*, Monogr. 13]. New York: International Universities Press.

Sharpe, E. F. (1929), The impatience of Hamlet. In *Collected Papers on Psychoanalysis*, ed. M. Brierley. London: Hogarth Press.

_____ (1947), An unfinished paper on Hamlet. In *Collected Papers on Psychoanalysis*, ed. M. Brierley. London: Hogarth Press.

Shengold, L. (1966), The metaphor of the journey in "The Interpretation of Dreams." *Amer. Imago*, 23:316–331.

Simon, E. (1957), Sigmund Freud, the Jew. In *Publications of the Leo Baeck Institute, Year Book 2*. London: East West Library, pp. 220–305.

Skinner, Q. (1969), Meaning and understanding in the history of ideas. *Hist. & Theory*, 8:3–53.

Skura, M. A. (1981), *The Literary Use of the Psychoanalytic Process*. New Haven: Yale University Press.

Stanescu, H. (1971), Young Freud's letter to his Rumanian friend Silberstein. *The Israel Annals of Psychiatry and Related Disciplines*, 9:195–207.

Stengel, E. (1954), A re-evaluation of Freud's book "On Aphasia." *Int. J. Psychoanal.*, 35:85–89.

Sterba, R. F. (1969), The psychoanalyst in a world of change. *Psychoanal. Q.*, 38:432–454.

Strachey, J. (1966), General preface. In S. Freud, *Standard Edition 1*. London: Hogarth Press, pp. xiii–xxii.

Stoppard, T. (1967), *Rosencrantz and Guildenstern Are Dead*. New York: Grove Press.

Sulloway, F. J. (1979), *Freud, Biologist of the Mind: Beyond the Psychoanalytic Legend*. New York: Basic Books.

Szekely, L. (1981), Psychoanalysis: Its tragic vision of "Conditio Human" and the theological drama. *Int. Rev. Psychoanal.*, 8:423–431.

Tausk, V. (1919), On the origin of the "influencing machine" in schizophrenia. *Psychoanal. Q.*, 2:519–556, 1933.

Trilling, L. (1950), *The Liberal Imagination*. New York: Viking Press.

Trosman, H. (1965), Freud and the controversy over Shakespearean authorship. *J. Amer. Psychoanal. Assn.*, 13:475–498.

_____ (1969), The cryptomnesic fragment in the discovery of free association. *J. Amer. Psychoanal. Assn.*, 17:489–510.

_____ (1973), Freud's cultural background. *The Annual of Psychoanalysis*, 1:318–335. New York: Macmillan.

_____ & Simon, M. A. (1973), The Freud library. *J. Amer. Psychoanal. Assn.*, 21:646–687.

Vasari, G. (1568a), Life of Leonardo da Vinci, painter and sculptor of Florence, trans. A. B. Hinds In *Leonardo da Vinci*, ed. L. Goldscheider. London: Phaidon, 1948.

_____ (1568b), *Lives of the Most Eminent Painters, Sculptors, and Architects*, trans. G. duc de Vere. London: Warner, 1912.

Vitz, P. C. (1983), Sigmund Freud's attraction to Christianity: Biographical evidence. *Psychoanal. Contemp. Thought*, 6:73–183.

Waelder, R. (1965), *Psychoanalytic Avenues to Art*. New York: International Universities Press.

Weisblatt, S. (1977), The creativity of Sylvia Plath's Ariel period: Toward origins and meanings. *The Annual of Psychoanalysis*, 5:379–404. New York: International Universities Press.

Weiss, J. (1947), A psychological theory of formal beauty. *Psychoanal. Q.*, 16:391–400.

Winnicott, D. W. (1953), Transitional objects and transitional phenomena. *Int. J. Psychoanal.*, 34:89–97.

Wittels, F. (1924), *Sigmund Freud: His Personality, His Teaching, and His School.* London/New York: Allen & Unwin/Dodd, Mead.

_____ (1931), *Freud and His Time.* New York: Liveright.

Wohl, R. R., & Trosman, H. (1955), A retrospect of Freud's Leonardo. *Psychiat.*, 18:27–39.

Wolf, E. S. (1971), *Saxa Loquuntur:* Artistic aspects of Freud's "The Aetiology of Hysteria." *The Psychoanalytic Study of the Child,* 20:535–554. New York: International Universities Press.

Wolheim, A. (1970), Freud and the understanding of art. *Brit. J. Aesthetics,* 10:211–224.

Wordsworth, W. (1798), Lyrical ballads. In *The Poems of Wordsworth.* London: Oxford Standard Authors, 1950.

Worringer, W. (1908), *Abstraction and Empathy.* London: Routledge & Kegan Paul.

Wortis, J. (1954), *Fragments of an Analysis with Freud.* New York: Simon & Schuster.

Zilboorg, G., & Henry, G. W. (1941), *A History of Medical Psychology.* New York: Norton.

Zweig, S. (1943), *The World of Yesterday.* New York: Viking Press.

Index

A

Abraham, Karl, 23, 60
Adler, Alfred, 101, 118, 118n, 198
Adler, Viktor, 14, 42
Aeneas, 23, 174
Aesthetic judgment, 145
Aesthetic Movement, 154–155
Aesthetic response, 132–147, 206, 212
  after-pleasure, 146, 147
  conflict model, 137
  developmental considerations, 140–144
  drive content, 135–137
  economics of, 134–136
  to formal devices, 137
  structural approach, 136–140
Aesthetics, psychoanalytic theory of,
  133–147
Ahasuerus, 103, see also Jews, wandering
American War of Independence, 5
Andreas-Salomé, Lou, 125
Anna O., 69, 120
Anti-Semitism, 12, 21, 34, 42, 93, 94–95,
  102, 103
Ariel, 203n
Ariosto, Lodovico, 50
Aristotle, 29, 126
Art, 70–88, 129, 132–134, 141–144, 193, 198,
  211–212
Artistic gift, 133, 149, 193, 206, 208n
Artistic tradition, 130, 139, 166–167
"As if" personality, 66
Auersperg, Anton, 74
Austro-Hungarian Empire, 11–15

B

Barnardo, 189
Bate, Walter, 172
Beaumarchais, Pierre Augustin Coron, 74
Beer-Hoffmann, Richard, 16
Benedikt, Moritz, 53, 65
Berenson, Bernard, 149n
Berger, J. N., 11
Bernays, Martha, 15, 38, 48
Bernhardt, Sarah, 74
Bernheim, Hippolyte, 51
Bible, 51
Binswanger, Ludwig, 65
Biography, 87, 132, 148–171, 212
  psychoanalytic, 167–172
Bismarck, Otto von, 14
Bizet, Georges, 75
  works of
    Carmen, 75
B'nai B'rith, Society of, 102
Bonaparte, Marie, 192
  works of
    The Life and Work of Edgar Allan Poe: A
    Psychoanalytic Interpretation, 192
Börne, Ludwig, 68
Bourgeois Ministry of the 1860s, 11
Brandes, Georg, 81–82
Braun, Heinrich, 13–14, 51
Brentano, Franz, 3, 29–34, 54, 64, 126
  works of
    Psychologie vom Empirischen Standpunkt,
    32
    Neue Räthsel, 33

Breslau, 92
Breuer, Josef, 51, 53, 56–58, 64, 69
  style of, 120
Brücke, Ernst Wilhelm von, 4, 8n, 15, 28,
    29, 32–39, 42, 51, 53, 64, 199, 199n
  works of
    *Die Physiologischen Grundlagen der
      neuhochdeutschen Verskunst,* 35
    *Physiologie der Farben fur die Zwecke des
      Kunstgewerbes,* 35
Buff, Charlotte, 70–71
Buffon, Georges Louis Leclerc, Comte de,
    127, 131
Bürger, Gottfried, 74
Butler, Eliza Marian, 23
  works of
    The Tyranny of Greece over Germany, 23
Byron, George Gordon, 6
  works of
    Don Juan, 144

C

Caesar, Julius, 47, 94, 189
Capgras psychosis, 104–105
Carlyle, Thomas, 73
  works of
    Sartor Resartus, 73
Caterina, mother of Leonardo da Vinci,
    159, 160, 161, 164
Catullus, 23
Cervantes Saavedra, Miguel de, 41n, 74
  works of
    Don Quixote, 41n, 74
Cézanne, Paul, 140
Chaplin, Charlie, 141
Charcot, Jean-Martin, 15, 28, 42, 44, 47–49,
    51, 53, 56–58, 63, 69
  works of
    Leçons du mardi de la Salpêtrière, 63
Charlemagne, 84–85
Charles I of England, 75
Christ, Jesus, 76, 91
Christian Socialism, 12
Christianity, 3, 17
Chrobak, Rudolf, 56–58, 69
Cicero, 23
  works of
    Orations, 23

Clark, Kenneth, 159n, 169n
Clark University, 124
Classic style, 115n
Classicism, 21–24, 52
Claudius, 173, 176, 180, 182, 183
Claus, Carl, 37
Coleridge, Samuel Taylor, 187
Comic, 140–141
Coquelin, Alexandre, 74
Coquelin, Benoit Constant, 74
Corinth, 98
Corvo, Baron, 186n
Crane, Hart, 69
Creative writing, 70–72, 82, 87, 136
Creativity, 16, 50, 55, 59, 132, 168, 192–209,
    212
Creativity, psychoanalytic contribution to,
    200–209
  and ambience, 208
  art work as a statement about creative
    process, 207
  complementary series of factors, 209
  and conflict, 201
  defiance of father, 205
  drive, taming of, 197, 208
  early traumatization, 205
  ego definition of, 201
    role of ego, 203, 206
  identification patterns, 204–205
  motive forces, 192
  and narcissism, 202
  and parapraxis, 200–201
  repression and displacement, 202–203
  restitution, reaction to loss, 205
  reversal of instinct, 197–198
  sexuality, 204
Crusoe, Robinson, 198
Czech nationalism, 12

D

Dante, 48, 92–93
  works of
    Divine Comedy, 92–93
Darwin, Charles, 23, 51
Darius, 23
Daulia, 98–99
Delacroix, Eugène, 51
Delphi, 98–99
Delphic oracle, 98

Demosthenes, 23
Developmental aspects to aesthetic
    response, 140–144
Dickens, Charles, 74
  works of
    The Chimes, 74
    The Battle of Life, 74
Diderot, 6
  works of
    The Nephew of Rameau, 6
Dido, 23, 174
Displacement, 71–72, 85, 134, 168, 179,
    202–203
  as an intermediate process in creativity,
    206–207
Dollinger, Johann, 31
Dostoevsky, Fyodor, 133
  works of
    The Brothers Karamazov, 133
Dreams and jokes, 134–135
  mechanisms
    condensation, 134
    displacement, 134
  pleasure in, 134–135
Dream process, 67–68
  dream work, 186
  link with literary texts, 186–187
Dreams, typical, 80, 175
Dresden, 75, 94, 145
  Zwinger Museum, 145
Du Bois-Reymond, Emil, 8n, 35–36
Dumas, Alexandre, 73
  works of
    Dame aux Camelias, 73

E

Eberhart, Richard, 62
Economics of aesthetic response, 134–136,
    147
Edel, Leon, 172
Ego functions and aesthetic response,
    137–140, 147
Ego, as a problem-solving agent, 138
Ego psychology and style, 129–131
Egypt, 103
Eliot, George, 74
Eliot, Thomas Stearns, 62, 167
  objective correlative, 167
Empathy, 199

Empedocles, 69
Enlightenment, Age of, 51, 52
Eros, 9, 23
Esquirol, Jean-Etienne Dominique, 41
d'Este, Cardinal Ippolito, 50
Esther, 94
Exner, Sigmund, 51

F

Family romance fantasy, 85
Fantasy, 70–72, 84–85, 87
  hysterical, 70–72, 85
  protective function of, 71–72
  transformation of unconscious fantasy in
    literary work, 184–191
Fates, 10
Fechner, Gustav Theodor, 3
Ferenczi, Sandor, 101
Fictional characters, 177–180
  understood contextually, 181–191
Flechsig, Paul, 41
Fleischl von Marxow, Ernst von, 51
Fliess, Wilhelm, 38–39, 76, 78, 83, 84, 87,
    145, 171
Fluss, Emil, 27, 111
Fluss, Gisela, 27–28
Forel, Auguste, 39
Form, 86–88, 137–144, 191
  definition of, 139
Fortinbras, 173, 189, 190
  Old Fortinbras, 182, 189
Francis I, 149, 153n, 172
Francisco, 188
Free association, 68
Freiberg, 27, 90–92, 99, 101, 103,
    see also Příbor
French Revolution, 5
Freud, Emmanuel, 94
Freud, Ernst, 144
Freud, Jakob, 11, 18, 79, 82, 90–92, 99, 101
Freud, Martin, 95
Freud, Sigmund
  adolescent love affair, 26–28
  aesthetic responses of, 144–146
  on biography, 151n
  cases, 76–78
    August P., 77
    Dora, 19, 78, 117–118, 120–121
    Elisabeth von R., 114

Katharina, 113–114
  mother unable to nurse, 77
Classical education, 21–24
on creativity, 192–209
dreams of
  dream of botanical monograph, 68
  "Hollthurn" dream, 95
  dream of "Irma's injection," 97
on *Hamlet*, 173–177, 183, 193
  identification with Hamlet, 81–83, 183
identification with literary figures, 83
influences on, 3–23, 50–69
interest in art and literature, 70–88
interest in nature, 7–11
interest in politics, 11–15
Jewish identity of, 17, 89–107, 211–212
journeys of, 89–103
on Leonardo da Vinci, 148–151, 157–164,
    173, 183, 206
  Freud's identification with Leonardo,
    170–171
  Schapiro's criticism of Freud's view,
    164–167
library, 20, 24, 32, 33, 43
medical school, curriculum of, 29
medical training, 39–45
modes of influence on, 50–69
on Moses of Michelangelo, 193–200
  as awesome father, 195, 199
  drawings of, 195–197, Illustration 10.2
    (p. 196)
  inhibition of rage, 195–197, Illustration
    10.2
  as paternal forbearance and restraint,
    200
neurological research, 45–47
Oedipus complex of, 99
Privatdozent in neuropathology, 41–42, 44
research: anatomical, histological,
    physiological, 37–39
research in neuroanatomy and
    neuropathology, 41–47
secondary school education of, 22–24
self-analysis, 78–79
on style, 112–119
  self-criticism of his style, 115–116, 117
style of, 111–127
  use of analogies, 123
  use of aphorism and epigram, 124–125
  balance of abstract and concrete, 125

dialogue, 122–123
use of dualities, 129
essay style, 125
figures of speech, 128–129
use of metaphor, 116, 128–129
narrative, 120–122
parallelism in sentence structure, 128
rhetorical devices, 126, 128–129
word order, 128
translation of, 114–115
travel phobia, 92, 101
works of
  On Aphasia, 46
  Beyond the Pleasure Principle, 127
  *Fragment of an Analysis of a Case of
    Hysteria*, 78, 121
  The Interpretation of Dreams, 20, 23, 30,
    40, 45, 60, 78, 80–82, 86, 93, 95,
    97–98, 115–117, 115n, 119–120, 123,
    124, 175
  Introductory Lectures on Psychoanalysis,
    122, 126
  *Jokes and Their Relation to the
    Unconscious*, 133
  "Moses of Michelangelo," 193–200
  Outline of Psychoanalysis, 119, 181n
  Project for a Scientific Psychology, 43
  The Psychopathology of Everyday Life, 23
  The Question of Lay Analysis, 122, 126
  Studies on Hysteria, .77–78, 112, 120
  Three Essays on the Theory of Sexuality,
    126
  "On Transience," 125
Freud-Jones hypothesis regarding *Hamlet*,
    175–176, 175n, 176n

G

Galicia, 18, 90–91
Gellert, Christian, 74
German culture, 11–15, 20
German nationalism, 11–15
Germany, 11–15
Gertrude, 176–177, 180
Gesellschaft der Aerzte, 77
Gestalt psychology, 140
Giocondo, Francesco del, 153
Giocondo, Mona Lisa del (La Gioconda),
    153–157, 163
Goethe, Johann Wolfgang von, 4, 6, 8–9, 26,
    28, 70–73, 87, 202

works of
  Faust, 73, 175
  On Nature, 8–9, 26, 51
  The Sorrows of Young Werther, 5, 70–72,
     84, 88
Goethe Prize, 112n
Gomperz, Elise, 30
Gomperz, Theodor, 30, 34
  works of
    Greek Thinkers, 30
Gottfried von Strassburg, 73
  works of
    Tristan and Isolde, 73
Grote, George, 30
Guildenstern, 81, 176
Gymnasium, 22, 24, 54, 94, 111
  curriculum, 23

H

Haman, 94
Hamilcar, 59, 91
Hamlet, character of, 81–83, 173–191
  accepts death of psychological father, 183
  deficient conviction, 182
  Freud's identification with Hamlet, 81–83,
     183
  identity diffusion, 177
  matricidal impulses, 176–177
  mechanisms of defense, 177
  negative Oedipus complex, 176
  Oedipus complex, 175–177, 179n, 183
  oral impatience, 177
  perplexity, 173–174
  preconscious awareness, 181–182
  procrastination, 175–176
  in search of cohesive self, 177
Hammerschlag, Samuel, 89
Hannibal, 17, 23, 59, 91
Hebel, Johann Peter, 74
Hebrew, 89
Hecuba, 182
Heine, Heinrich, 74
Hell, 92–93
Helmholtz, Hermann von, 34, 36–37
Helmholtz school, 3, 32, 34–35, 37
Henry VIII, 13n
Herbart, Johann Friedrich, 3, 54
Herder, Johann Gottfried von, 6, 74, 111n
Herodotus, 23

Hoffmann, Ernst Theodor Amadeus, 6
Hofmannsthal, Hugo von, 16
Homer, 23
  works of
    Iliad, 23
    Odyssey, 23
Homosexuality, 160, 169
Horace, 23
Horatio, 189
Hugo, Victor, 74
  works of
    The Hunchback of Notre Dame, 74
Humboldt, Alexander von, 22
Humboldt, Wilhelm, 22
Hypnosis, 61

I

Ibsen, Henrik, 120
  works of
    Rosmersholm, 179
Identification, 65, 67
Identity, concept of, 90, 103–107
  developmental considerations, 105–107
  experience of continuity, 104
  separation, 105
  solidarity, 104
  uniqueness, 104
Imprinting, 66
Influence, 50–69, 154, 212
  awareness of, 53–55
  fears of, 60–64
  pathology of, 65
  psychology of, 64–69
  repressed, 65
  unconscious sources of, 53–54, 61, 65–69
Influencing machine, 65–66
Ingres, Jean-Auguste Dominique, 149
  works of
    The Death of Leonardo da Vinci,
       Illustration 8.1 (p. 150)
Itzig, 39

J

Jabneh, 103
Jackson, John Hughlings, 46
James, Henry, 172
Jacob, 103

Jensen, Wilhelm, 88
    works of
        Gradiva, 88, 179, 181
Jerusalem, 100, 103
Jerusalem, Wilhelm, 70–73
Jewish identity, 89–107
Jewish tradition, 4, 17–21, 94
    mystical, 19–20
Jews, 11, 12, 13, 16–21, 93, 102–103
    as anti-hero, 92, 103
    emancipated, 96
    marginal, 96
    militant, 94–95, 103
    "tolerated," 90
    wandering, 91n, 101–103
Jocasta, 80
Jochanan ben Zakkai, Rabbi, 103
Johnson, Samuel, 172
Jokes, 133–136, 147
Journeys, 90–103
    symbolic meaning of, 98, 102, 104, 107
Julius II, 197
Jung, Carl, 88, 101, 171, 198, 212

K

Kabbala,19–20
Kant, Immanuel, 32
    works of
        The Critique of Pure Reason, 32n
Karlsbad, 100
Kestner, Georg, 70–71
Kite, 159, 164–165, 168, 172
Kreisler, Fritz, 75
Kris, Ernst, 144

L

Laius, 98–99
Leipzig, 92, 94
Leonardo da Vinci, 9, 75, 130, 148–171
    birth of, 159, 165
    death of, 149, 161
    death of father, 161
    dynamic balance in composition,
        165–166, 169
    early memory, 159, 168, 169
    as enigma, 149, 158
    father of, 152–153, 159
    Freud's view of, 157–164
    homosexuality of, 158–160, 165, 168

Ingres' view of, 149–150, Illustration 8.1
    (p. 150)
"Leonardesque" smile, 160–161, 165
    parents of, 159
    Pater's view of, 153–157
    pyramidal style of, 130, 165
    rebellious attitude, 163
    scientific interests, 163
    sexuality of, 158
    slip of, 161–162
    Vasari's view of, 151, 153, 155
    works of
        Battle of Anghieri, 166
        Codex Atlanticus, 159
        The Last Supper, 166, 168
        Leda and the Swan, 166
        Madonna and Child with St. Anne, 161,
            Illustration 8.4 (p. 162), 165, 168
        Mona Lisa, 144, 153, 154, 154n, 155–157,
            Illustration 8.3 (p. 156), 161, 168
        notebooks, 170
        St. Jerome, 166
Leseverein der deutschen Studenten, 13–15,
    42
Lessing, Gotthold Ephraim, 74, 120
    works of
        Emilia Galotti, 71
Liberal culture, 11
Lichtenberg, Georg, 73
Lindner, Gustav Adolf, 54
    works of
        Lehrbuch der empirischen Psychologie nach
            genetischer Methode, 54
Literary criticism, 173–191
Literature, 70–88, 120–127, 131, 144,
    173–191, 212
    integrated psychoanalytic contribution to
        literature, 184–191
Lithuania, 17
Livy, 23
    works of
        History of Rome, 23
London, 103
Ludwig, Carl, 35, 38
Lueger, Karl, 12–13

M

Macbeth, 184
Macbeth, Lady, 167, 184
Mahler, Gustav, 16
Mann, Thomas, 126, 202

works of
Death in Venice, 202–203
Marburg, 95
Masséna, André, 17
Mengs, Anton Raphael, 52
Meseritsch, 93
Meyer, Betsy, 85
Meyer, Conrad Ferdinand, 84–86, 118n
works of
Die Hochzeit des Monchs, 84, 86
Huttens letzte Tage, 84
Die Richterin, 84–86, 88, 118n
Meynert, Theodor, 14, 36, 41, 42–46, 48, 77
works of
Klinische Vorlesungen über Psychiatrie, 43
Psychiatrie, 43
Michelangelo, 100–101, 151, 197, 199–200,
207, 208–209
works of
Moses, 100–101, 145, 193–200,
Illustration 10.1 (p. 194)
Mill, John Stuart, 30, 74
Milton, John, 73, 86, 144
works of
Paradise Lost, 73
Moira, 10
Molière (Paquelin, Jean Baptiste), 74
Moravia, 18, 90, 92
Morel, Bénédict-Augustin, 41
Moses, 19, 100–101, 103, 193–200
Mozart, Wolfgang Amadeus, 74, 75, 144
works of
Jupiter Symphony, 144
The Magic Flute, 74
The Marriage of Figaro, 75
Müller, Johannes, 34
Music, 74–75, 144, 145n, 146
Mut, 160

N

Napoleon I, 17, 47
Narcissus, 23
Nature, 3–11, 80, 155, 158, 163
Naturphilosophie, 7–8, 32, 36, 52
Nazi occupation of Austria, 103
Neoclassical revival, 21, 52, 115n
Nero, 177
Neue Freie Presse, 74
Neurology, 43–47
Neuroses, sexual etiology of, 55–64, 69

Nietzsche, Friedrich Wilhelm, 14, 54–55, 60,
62, 64
Nothnagel, Hermann, 40–41

O

Oedipus, 23, 79–82, 86, 98–100, 132, 175
Freud's identification with Oedipus, 82
Oedipus complex, 6, 61, 79–81, 83, 86, 99,
175–177, 179n, 205, 208n
Ophelia, 81, 181
Orvieto, 93
Ovid, 23
works of
Metamorphoses, 23

P

Painting, 75–76, 144, 145
Pan-Germanism, 12, 13
Palma, 84–85
Paris, 15, 28, 74, 75
Louvre, 145
Parthenon frieze, 144
Passover, 100
Pasteur, Louis, 48
Pater, Walter, 149, 153–157, 171
on Mona Lisa, 155–157
works of
The Renaissance, 154
Pathography, 169
Plath, Sylvia, 207
Plato, 23
works of
Apology, 23
Crito, 23
Pleasure in art
in drive satisfaction, 135–137
in form, 137–140
Pleasure in jokes, 135–136
as incentive bonus and forepleasure,
135–136
lifting of inhibition, 135
primitive mentation, 135
Pliny, 164, 168
Poetic economy, laws of, 174, 179
Politics, 5, 11–15
Polonius, 176, 177, 180, 183
Pompeii, 88
Pound, Ezra, 62
Priam, 182

Přibor (see Freiberg), 18
Psychoanalytic situation, 67, 206
  as model for relation between reader and
      literary text, 187–188
Purim, 94

R

Raphael, 75, 87
  works of
    Sistine Madonna, 75, 145
Reinhardt, Max, 16
Remarque, Erich Maria, 21
Repression, 81, 137, 138, 202–203
Repression, theory of, 54, 124
Richter, Jean Paul, 6, 73
Riesa, 94
Rilke, Rainer Maria, 125
Romanticism, 4–7, 19, 24, 51
Rome, 98, 100, 102, 115, 193
  San Pietro in Vincoli, Church of, 100
Rosencrantz, 81, 176
Ruskin, John, 154

S

Sallust, 23
Salpêtrière, 15, 47
Sardou, Victorien, 74
Schapiro, Meyer, 164–167, 171
  dynamic balance in Leonardo, 165–166
  the kite, 164–165
  on Leonardo's childhood, 164–165
  on Leonardo's infantile memory, 164
  on the Madonna and Child with St. Anne,
      165
Scheffel, Josef Victor von, 74
Schelling, Friederich Wilhelm Joseph von, 7,
      32
Schiller, Frederich von, 74
  works of
    Die Rauber, 74
Schizophrenia, 65–66
Schnitzler, Arthur, 16
Scholz, Franz, 41, 45
Schönberg, Arnold, 16
Schönerer, Georg von, 12–13
Schopenhauer, Arthur, 14, 64
Schreber, Daniel, 41, 169
Science, 25–49, 53, 77
  biological, 28, 52

Self, 66, 104, 106, 107, 141–143, 147
  self-cognizance, 104–105
  self-representations, 105–106
Self-objects, 141
Sexual bondage, 66
Sforza, Ludovico, Duke of Milan, 163
Shakespeare, Hamnet, 82
Shakespeare, William, 10, 48, 71, 72, 81–83,
      86
  works of
    Hamlet, 73, 81–83, 88, 133, 136,
        173–191, 193
      Act I, Scene 1, 188–190
    Henry IV, Part I, 10
    King Lear, 184
    The Tempest, 203n
    Twelfth Night, 73
Signorelli, Luca, 93
Silberstein, Edward, 27, 73
Smith, Adam, 52
Social Democracy, 12
Society of Psychiatry and Neurology, 78
Sophocles, 28, 72, 132
  works of
    Ajax, 23
    Antigone, 23
    Oedipus Rex, 72, 79, 81, 88, 94, 98–99,
        133, 140, 175, 183
Spitzer, Daniel, 74
Stekel, Wilhelm, 101, 198
Stemma, 84–85
Stevens, Wallace, 62
Strachey, James, 114–115
Stoppard, Tom
  works of
    Rosencrantz and Guildenstern Are Dead,
        180n
Structural approach to aesthetic response,
      136–140
Style, 111–131
  constancy of, 130
  dialogue, 122–123
  discontinuity of, 130
  dogmatic approach, 118–119
  figures of speech, 128–129
  genetic approach, 118–119
  as linguistic expression, 127–129
  narrative style, 120–122
  organizing principle, 129
    cycles, 129
    evolutionary, 129

observer response, 129
parallelism in sentence structure, 128
and the psychoanalytic situation, 130
pyramidal configuration, 130
word order, 128
Style, the psychoanalysis of, 127–131
expression of synthetic ego, 129–130
in the psychoanalytic situation, 130
regression of style, 130
Styria, 95
Sublimation, 138, 158, 163, 168, 197, 203
Superego role in aesthetic response, 136–137

T

Tacitus, 23
works of
History, 23
Tell, Wilhelm, 123
Teufelsdroeckh, Diogenes, 73
Textual theory of unconscious motivation,
181–184
Thanatos, 23
Thermopylae, 23
Titian, 76, 87
works of
Tribute Money, 76, 145
Titus, 103
Tobler, G. C., 8n
Tolstoi, Leo, 144
works of
Anna Karenina, 144
Tourette, Gilles de la, 15
Tragedy, 79–80
Transference, 67, 121, 128, 187, 191, 202
Transitional objects, 141, 143
Transitional space, 143–144, 187
Translation of Freud into English, 114–115

U

Uhland, Ludwig, 74

V

Van Dyck, Anthony, 75
Vasari, Giorgio, 149–153
on Leonardo da Vinci, 149, 151–153, 155,
171
Venus de Milo, 145
Vere, Edward de (Earl of Oxford), 82
Veronese, Paolo, 75

Verrochio, Andrea del, 152, 161
works of
Baptism of Christ, Illustration 8.2 (p. 151)
Vesuvius, Mount, 88
Vienna, 4, 13, 15–17, 31–32, 56, 92, 101, 102,
114, 198
General Hospital, 39, 40, 45
University of, 14, 28–31, 34, 39, 42, 54
Vinci, Donna Aliera da (Leonardo's
stepmother), 159, 160, 161
Vinci, Ser Piero da (Leonardo's father),
152–153, 159, 161
death of, 161
Virgil
works of
The Aeneid, 23, 28, 124, 174
Vischer, Frederich Theodor, 74
Voltaire, 52
Vulture, 159, 161

W

Waelder, Robert, 22
Wagner, Richard, 14
Weltanschauung, 52
Wertheimstein, Josephine, 30
West, Rebecca, 179
Wilde, Oscar, 61, 64, 157n
Winckelmann, Johann Joachim, 52, 115n
Wordsworth, William, 6, 7, 51
Wulf, 84–85
Wulfrin, 84–85
Wundt, Wilhelm, 32
Wurzburg, 31

X

Xenophon, 23
works of
Anabasis, 23
Cyropaedia, 23
Xerxes, 23

Y

Yom Kippur, 96
Yorick, 183

Z

Zeitgeist, 51–53
Zionism, 12
Zohar, 19